...dark times - the
... near its end - I am in a cabin
... into the side of a cave - everyone I
... ever loved is in there with me - the
window is barricaded but we notice
... just pass - the outer dark - there is
... noise of threat to the door is opened
... the Resurrected Jesus who
... - he invites my family and
... to follow him - the cave wall
... - I am alone & outside wondering
... I chose not to follow - I try to reenter the
... but the door is protected by angry dogs
... fear not my dog. - I took this dream
... and now to Tibet - It bothers me because
now it tells a truth about me I don't want
admit to.
... is notorious for the angry dogs that live
... and its temples. Many tourists tell of
... bitten - sometimes by packs of dogs.
...a Monastery there is only one old dog. As
... to draw him he moves from position to
... trying to discourage my unsolicited
... There is not an angry bone in his
...- he has penetrating golden brown eyes -
...of the qualities of a lion - he seems to want
... me "Isn't there any way a being can get
... peace they need without someone bothering
... - I thought as a dog I could withstand
... the human race more completely & get on
... what is really important. So can you
... BUG OFF! - can't you see this fur & bone
... blood is no more me than the rock you
... sitting on.
... as long as I can remember my worst
... nightmare has been about investigators finding
...dence to connect me with past murders. In the
... am the evidence builds up until I am hunted
... my accusers who are convinced of my guilt. My
...ors usually transform into wolf like dogs.
By the time they catch up with me I have
...turned to the crime scene - a Hansel and gretel
...tches house of horrors - I try to run to the room
... are my parents are sleeping - the long dark
...allway to their room has a paralysing effect
... my muscles - I fight, heart pounding
...inst invisible ...

An accuser
appears in the blood
stained cloths - the dogs
are barking and tear at
my legs - there are now
three accusers and they
no longer bear any resemblance
to dogs or humans - they are
demons grotesquely assembled
from decomposing bodies -
one has a stick with a
crescent moon shaped hook
on the end - it pokes at my
chest to gather my soul -
my fear is so extreme I force
myself to wake.

There is not the slightest
inclination in my heart to
follow a Buddhist path.
But I have had many dreams of coming to
Tibet. The strongest dream was after I met
the 14th Dalai Lama in Sydney in 1996. He allowed
me to draw him - so we were alone together for some time.
In the dream he was back in Tibet - we met in an
identical large monastery assembly hall to Depuing -
I was showing him my portrait of him but it kept
dissolving and changing as we spoke. Our conversation
was about the dissolution of the self and about how
no painting can depict what a being is - just the
temporary states of being it manifests as - the task
of a visual artist seemed hopeless if attempting to
depict true reality through visual appearances -
Well old dog? perhaps the murdered victims of all my
nightmares are former selves and the most horrifying
reality for the self is evidence of how much of itself
it has murdered.

George Gittoes AM is an artist, activist and filmmaker born in Rockdale, NSW, in 1949. After working with Andy Warhol and the Black Panthers in New York, he returned to Sydney and co-founded the Yellow House in Kings Cross with fellow artist Martin Sharp. George then spent a decade travelling all through Australia making documentaries and furthering his art. In 1986, he took his camera abroad to film the Sandinista women revolutionaries of Nicaragua. Since then, he has chronicled conflicts in Somalia, Cambodia, Western Sahara, Northern Ireland, Bosnia, Bougainville, East Timor, South Africa, Palestine, Iraq, Pakistan and Afghanistan. In between, he has won many prizes for his painting – including twice being awarded the Blake Prize for Religious Art. George's acclaimed documentaries include *Bullets of the Poets* (1986), *Soundtrack to War* (2004), *Rampage* (2006), *Miscreants of Taliwood* (2009) and *Snow Monkey* (2015). All the while he has campaigned for peace, confronting injustice where he finds it and inspiring creativity, tolerance, respect and humanism in all he has met.

George Gittoes was awarded the Sydney Peace Prize in 2015. He is a father to Harley and Naomi, and lives in Werri Beach with partner Hellen Rose. *Blood Mystic* is his first book.

Blood Mystic

George Gittoes

MACMILLAN
Pan Macmillan Australia

George Gittoes
Salem
2019

Returning the Peacocks to the Yellow House
Sept 12 2014

CONTENTS

FOREWORD

Although a lifelong disbeliever, I'm willing to accept the possibility that the Messiah has returned. Once again as a provocateur and a prophet though not as a carpenter, this time as a painter and a film-maker. Not born in Bethlehem but in Rockdale.

His adventures have taken him from the Yellow House in Kings Cross to his Yellow House in Jalalabad. While the Saviour from Sydney oft revisits a Middle East still dominated by contesting imperialisms (only the Romans seem to be missing) he no longer limits his audience to potential Christians. His wanderings are world wide – pretty much wherever there's a war.

He reaches out to everyone, from atheists to Muslims. And as with his predecessor he does so at great personal risk.

The possibility that George Gittoes is the Saviour – sharing his anger, his politics and his compassion – has been growing on me over the many years I've known him. Every time this most compelling of characters appears in my studio the spiritual and physical resemblance has grown.

George can be found in Nicaragua, the Philippines, Cambodia, Rwanda, Somalia, Bosnia or Bougainville. He brings back words and images – drawings, paintings and films – from South Africa, Palestine, Iraq and Afghanistan.

Somehow, almost miraculously, this fearless, foolish and formidable fellow survives. And everywhere he goes, as this spectacular book attests, he transforms lives. He has the gift of finding and releasing the creativity in others, often in the most difficult and dangerous of circumstances.

Not only one of the most remarkable Australians, George Gittoes is one of the most remarkable humans it's been my honour to know.

As an atheist I pray for him.

Phillip Adams AO

George Gittoes Chronology

1949

Born Rockdale, Sydney

1968

Travels to New York and works with Andy Warhol and African American artist Joseph Delaney

1970

Establishes Yellow House Potts Point with Martin Sharp; creates his Puppet Theatre

1977

Shoots *Rainbow Way* which screens at Sydney and Melbourne Film Festivals

1980

Shoots and distributes short film *Refined Fire*

1986

Shoots and releases *Bullets of the Poets* feature-length documentary about Sandinista women poets and revolutionaries in Nicaragua

1989

Travels to the Philippines for *Crows over Canefields* series of photographs and paintings

1990–1992

Creates *Heavy Industry* paintings and photographs documenting the steel industry's downturn and shift to Asia

1991

Wins Blake Prize for painting *Ancient Prayer*

1993

Travels to Somalia and Cambodia to document peace keeping with photography, drawing and painting

1994

Travels to Western Sahara, Algeria, Sinai, Israel and Southern Lebanon to continue documenting peace keeping

Documents the lead up to and triumph of the first democratic elections in South Africa

1995

Travels to Rwanda, witnesses the Kibeho massacre of thousands of innocent internal refugees

Awarded Blake Prize for the Rwanda painting *The Preacher*

1996

Travels to Bosnia and produces a series of works based on the people of Sarajevo

1997

Receives Member of the Order of Australia for 'service to art and international relations'

1998

Works at the Central Academy of Fine Arts in Beijing China and travels the Yangtze to document the Three Gorges Dam project and then Tibet

Works with Peace Monitors in Bougainville

1999–2000

Focuses on the inhumanity of landmines – travelling to Thailand, Burma, Cambodia, Pakistan and Afghanistan to collect the stories and pictures of the victims

Works in East Timor, Rwanda and Congo as well as continuing his work on Landmine Victims in Pakistan and Afghanistan

Minefields exhibition shown at Palace of the Nations (UN) Geneva and Moscow

2001

Travels to South Africa three times to attend his exhibition Lives in the Balance

Documents conflict between Palestinians and Israeli IDF in Gaza.

The attacks of 9/11 end the era of work centered on the hopes generated by peace keeping

2002

Travels with *Medecins sans Frontiers* following the US invasion of Afghanistan

2003–2004

Travels to Iraq four times to make the film *Soundtrack to War*

2006

Works in Miami to make the film *Rampage* in the ghetto of Brown Sub

2007

Shoots *Miscreants of Taliwood* in the tribal belt of the North West Frontier of Pakistan

2009–2010

Travels back to Afghanistan, Iraq and Kuwait to develop *Descendence* series of works. Relocates studio to Berlin

Miscreants of Taliwood released

Makes three Pashtun dramas in the tribal belt of Pakistan – *Moonlight, Starless Night* and *The Flood*

2011

Moves to Jalalabad in Afghanistan to continue assisting the Pashtun Film Industry and makes three dramas, *Talk Show, The Tailor's Story* and *Love City*

Establishes multi-disciplinary arts centre Yellow House Jalalabad and begins shooting documentary film *Love City*

2012–2013

Continues work at the Yellow House Jalalabad and premieres *Love City* at the Sydney Film Festival

2014

I Witness retrospective exhibition of forty-five-year career at Hazelhurst Regional Gallery New South Wales

Begins shooting the third documentary in the *What the World Needs Now* series, titled *Snow Monkey* and again based in Jalalabad

2015

Snow Monkey premiered at Melbourne International Film Festival and International Documentary Festival Amsterdam

Returns to the Yellow House Jalalabad to assist with Women's Workshops

Awarded Sydney Peace Prize

2016

Moves to Werri Beach on the south coast of New South Wales and establishes a new studio

Snow Monkey shown at Sheffield Documentary Festival and wins Contemporary Lives Award at Biografilm Festival, Bologna, Italy

Begins work on *Brown Sub* a sequel to *Rampage* which revisits the Lovett Family in Miami

Snow Monkey nominated for AACTA Best Feature Documentary

Autobiographical book *Blood Mystic* released

Climacus

MEN ONLY

The ladder to Paradise

Blood Mystic

In 1994, I followed the footsteps of Moses to the monastery of Saint Catherine in the Sinai Desert. Outside the chapel containing the (still living!) Burning Bush, I sat down on a worn stone block beside an old Greek monk. I felt spiritually dizzy, as if magnetic forces were drawing me into a cloud of unknowing and I needed to gather myself before attempting to climb the mountain which towered above.

The monk was dressed in long black robes, a high cylindrical black cap and he had a long, greying beard with a few flecks of black remaining. I didn't expect him to speak English and was surprised when he asked me to show him what was in my sketchbook.

I had become fascinated by the geometry of a tile pattern that seemed to have solved the ancient mathematical quest of squaring the circle and had made a copy. He smiled to see this and then turned to my sketch of the icon of the *Ladder to Paradise* by St John Climacus. He told me that I puzzled him and wanted to know more about my life. I described my film work in Nicaragua and showed him some reproductions of my drawings from Somalia and Cambodia. He told me that he was the custodian of the collection of icons – many of which had me enchanted beyond words. He said my drawings like *Death and the Boy* from Cambodia and *Mirow and Awliya* from Somalia were modern icons and told me that if I ever wanted to I could be a guest of the monastery and paint some works for their collection.

I confessed to him that, although I had been born in a Christian country, I couldn't honestly call myself a Christian. He interrupted me by putting one of his very large fingers over my lips and said, 'No, you are a Blood Mystic'.

I asked him what he meant and he explained that there have always been blood mystics, especially during medieval times. If there was plague, these mystics would comfort the dying. During times of war, they would not take up weapons but join the soldiers and console them when they were grieved by the loss of comrades or troubled by their actions. They would also tend to the wounded. He said blood mystics were able to do this because they had certain knowledge of the eternal and inde-structible nature of the soul. Their mystical experiences of life beyond their physical bodies took away all fear of their own death.

As I climbed the holy mountain ascended by Moses 1,400 years before Christ, the idea that I was some kind of modern-day mystic played on my mind.

When I reached the top there was a small kiosk and the Bedouin manning it seemed to recognise me. He asked if I would mind his stall until he returned. I found myself preparing Turkish coffee and selling Coca-Cola to tourists on the pilgrimage to the summit.

As I stirred sugar into coffee and passed it over the counter in paper cups – with the change for the dollar notes I'd been handed – I slowly decided *blood mystic* sounded right. However people may interpret it, that is what I am.

I decided if I could write a book I would call it *Blood Mystic*, and perhaps now it is finished I can know some peace.

George Gittoes Oct 2016

15

Australian High Commission.
Islamabad.

Subject: Serious behead ~~threat~~ threat to George Gettos

I am telling about the person in the subject George Gettos, a film maker & War Journalist, painter/artist. He made an doucomentry, in which showed Taliban as terrorists to the world. After that he made two more doucomentries and in that he again make the same mistake. In 2011-12 in Afghanistan made doucomentries against taliban and showed Taliban with bad image. The doucomentry named "The Miscreants of Taliwood". I am also linked with some organization. George is comming to Pak and Afghanistan in order to make doucomentry against Taliban. I am giving you information that if he camed to Pakistan and Afghanistan, he will be killed and beheaded, his vedio will be showed to the world.

The person who is leading and helping is Mr. Raza Shah. SPEDO, an ngo director, he will also beheaded. Consider me as ur friend and don't leak this information and stop him from comming to Pakistan and Afghanistan.

Informer
XYZ.

Back to the Heart of Darkness

I am well into my sixties. I should be planning to buy a beach house with a studio where I can paint when I'm not surfing and snorkelling. Instead I'm gazing at the rugged mountains of Afghanistan from 2,000 feet. Soon I'll be weaving down the mountain road from Kabul to Jalalabad, dodging the oil tankers that are prime targets for Taliban rockets. In my pocket will be a copy of the letter the Taliban hand-delivered to the Australian embassy declaring George Gittoes their mortal enemy and threatening to decapitate me on live TV.

Yet I feel at home because I'm back at war.

Over the last thirty years my mission has been to place myself at the cross-roads of history when war is inevitable and be there when it happens. I do this by conscious choice.

I am not alone. In the seat next to me, toasting our mission with a glass of champagne, is Hellen Rose, wild and sexy and the only person I've ever agreed to take to war with me. Hellen will strut into our future, in her high heels, as aware of the risks as I am.

This flight is taking us back to our second home, the Yellow House in Jalalabad, only a few blocks away from Osama bin Laden's bombed-out compound, where he lived in the lead-up to 9/11. The snow-capped mountains of Tora Bora where he took refuge can be seen from our back garden. Once back in Jalalabad we will be soft targets, not suited up in cams and Kevlar body armour with a tank to get around in and a fortress to retreat to at night.

An election is scheduled for 5 April, and all the news channels are already accusing the Taliban of beginning a campaign of murder and intimidation destined to lead to civil war against whatever government is elected.

The first time I flew into Kabul, long before 9/11, it was under Taliban control and I didn't have a visa, so I knew I would be arrested as soon as I stepped off the plane. More recently, I flew in knowing there was a paid contract on my life and hit men would be waiting. I'd received information that my previously trusted Pashtun driver had been paid $15,000 and given a sex holiday in Balochistan to forget loyalty and deliver me to these professional killers.

Most people would see that as a good reason not to return. But my strategy is never to back down, so I called in a favour from an old mate and when I got off the plane there was an armoured vehicle and guys with guns and body armour to protect me. I saw the jaws of my potential killers drop as we sped past. This wasn't going to be the day they killed George Gittoes.

Jalalabad is a Taliban city, close to the border with Pakistan, where art, film, music and dance and the mingling of men and women are forbidden. By teaching and encouraging all forms of creativity, the Yellow House is a red rag to a bull. But my duty is to support young Afghan artists and filmmakers as they face this threat to their future. Soldiers die for flags. There is nothing I believe in more than freedom of expression, than art.

I've spent enough time as a guest of the world's armies to know I would never want to be part of them, and they would never know how to be me. Soldiers rarely have to worry about where their next meal is coming from, where they will find a bed to sleep, how they are going to be transported, who will look after them if they're wounded or sick or how they are going to find the money to pay their electricity bills back home – all of that is provided. They are expected to gird their loins and not think about the opposite sex until their return. Their job is to follow orders and not ask questions. But when I go into harm's way, it's not a directive passed down from politicians and generals to commanding officers, it's on my own initiative.

There is no greater test in this life than to face death. Survive and you will move to another level. All religions were born from this fear and promise an afterlife. Everything fears death, even a cockroach will scuttle away from being stomped on. But there are those who rush towards what others fear and use their fear to live life to the maximum. Soldiers know something similar to this, but I think few would be comfortable calling themselves mystics. I'm an artist. I carry cameras, pencils and brushes – not guns – across the frontline.

An old Sufi once defined a mystic to me as someone who 'seeks what cannot be found'. The mystics' advantage is their certainty of what is beyond material existence.

My life has been threatened in many wars and I've seen more pain and death than anyone should. But I still describe myself as an optimist. Wherever there is war, there need to be artists willing to create in the face of it – the ultimate act of resistance to the destroyers.

This is the way of the Blood Mystic.

Rebel Without a Cause

When I was a kid growing up in Villiers Street in Rockdale in Sydney's south, I would go around on 'dump days' looking for discarded prams and then take the wheels off them to make gravity-run hot rods. Inspired by the scene in *Rebel Without a Cause* where James Dean and a young gang play chicken in stolen cars driving towards an ocean cliff, some local kids and I took our billycarts to an incline that ran down to a steep precipice. We lined up and set off, gathering speed as we neared the edge. As it got scary most kids braked, leaving myself and one other boy hurtling down the hill. But where he managed to brake right on the rim, I went over. As I flew through the air I thought, 'This isn't going to be good.' I landed hard and my bare foot connected with the jagged edge of an old gallon can. The sharp edge went through one side and out the other. My mother was used to this kind of thing and angrily told me she didn't want to look, instructing I go the bathroom and put my foot in the tub 'to stop the blood getting everywhere'.

My sister Pam got me, bleeding profusely, to casualty at St George Hospital where the doctors diagnosed me as 'one chop sort of a barbie' – that is, mentally deficient. All my life people have seen there is something missing in me – *fear*.

ʹFEAR AND KIBEHO

Uwimiana is fifteen years old and has been willing to pose in the faint light of the Zambat camp in Kibeho while I do this drawing. He's one of the crowd of displaced persons who have pushed themselves up against the razor-wire perimeter hoping nearness to the UN force will give them some protection. All here believe they are to be killed by the Rwandan Patriotic Army (RPA) soldiers tomorrow. They do not trust us when we tell them they are going to be taken out by trucks to be repatriated in their home villages. Uwimiana keeps passing his fingers across his jugular in a throat-cutting gesture. It's his way of insisting that without UN protection he will be killed by machete on the morrow. His eyes speak only of fear.

At Kibeho, the camp for internally displaced refugees in Rwanda, I found myself in the midst of the slaughter of thousands of people, mainly innocent Hutu families. They had taken sanctuary at Kibeho College, a Catholic school for girls, because pupils had seen visions of the Virgin there several years previously so they trusted the Mother of God to protect them. It was a year since the beginning of the genocidal killing that had shocked the world. These Hutu refugees knew the Tutsi army wanted to use the 'cover' of the world's guilt to get revenge.

Much of the killing happened during the night. The nights at Kibeho were like a horror movie. Groups huddled in the dark fearing imaginary supernatural monsters known as *Shetani*, believing the machete-wielding killers were possessed by them. Mothers died with their babies still clinging to them and the sound of their cries merged with bursts of automatic gunfire.

One morning I went to the deep trench covered by timber that people used as a toilet. I'd unzipped my fly and was about to piss, when I was startled by a pair of eyes looking up at me through a gap in the timber. A woman had spent the night hiding in the filth with two babies wrapped tightly to her body in a sarong and two other children hugging her hip. There was absolute terror in her eyes as she mistook me for a Tutsi soldier who had found her hiding place and come to kill her. She and her children had spent the night up to their knees in faeces and urine. I called for help and we dragged her out.

In the next trench was a man. In the dark, hearing the sounds of the massacre, he had lost his mind. He would only lie on his side and not get up. The Zambian soldiers who helped me to drag him out decided he was *Interhamwe* – Hutu paramilitary – and didn't deserve further help. I got a bucket of water and threw it over him hoping it would clean away the filth and snap him out of his stupor. When the water hit his chest a condom came partly out of his shirt pocket – white and rubbery.

The RPA soldiers were slaughtering people with both machine guns and machetes. Their commander had warned me that if he saw me taking photos he would kill me. They all knew what they were doing was a war crime and that my photos could be used as evidence.

In the embankment on the side of the road I saw the soil move and came closer to see an eye blink open. A man had dug himself into the soil in the hope of not being seen.

In this atmosphere of total fear, I came to a place misty with smoke haze and heard low singing. A preacher with a ragged Bible was reading to his flock from the New Testament. I recognised the Sermon on the Mount:

Blessed are those who mourn,

for they will be comforted.

Blessed are the meek,

for they will inherit the earth.

Blessed are those who hunger and thirst for righteousness,

for they will be filled.

Blessed are the merciful,

for they will be shown mercy.

Blessed are the pure in heart,

for they will see God.

Blessed are the peacemakers,

for they will be called children of God.

Blessed are those who are persecuted because of righteousness,

for theirs is the kingdom of heaven.

He was sitting on a sack of some kind, very exposed, but all those around him were calm. The preacher's courage and faith had given them back their dignity. I took some photos and he nodded, acknowledging my presence. I asked him if he wanted me to stay, on the chance this could make the killers wary of attacking the group. Pointing to my camera, he said, 'They are probably more interested in killing you than us', but there was something I could do for him. He'd been entrusted with three boys made orphans during the night and he asked if I could try to get them to safety. I took their hands.

To get to the UN position with refugee wards wasn't easy as the RPA had created a gauntlet. Earlier, I'd been helping two boys to safety when an RPA soldier stopped a UN officer behind me who was helping a mother and her baby. When the woman's ID card didn't pass scrutiny and the UN guy refused to hand them over, a junior RPA officer lifted his handgun and shot the woman point-blank in the head. He then allowed me to pass on with the boys.

I got the preacher's boys to relative sanctuary. On the way I passed the man with the condom hanging from his pocket. A group of RPA led by an officer, distinguished by his black beret, were heading towards him. They ignored me and shot him without even slowing their pace.

I made my way back to where the preacher and his flock had been. No-one was standing. The area was flattened and still – all were dead. I couldn't find the body of the preacher with his distinctive yellow coat but I never forgot him as a man whose faith had enabled him to overcome fear and bring comfort to those around him.

They ignored me and shot him without even slowing their pace.

Blessed are the pure in heart, for they will see God.

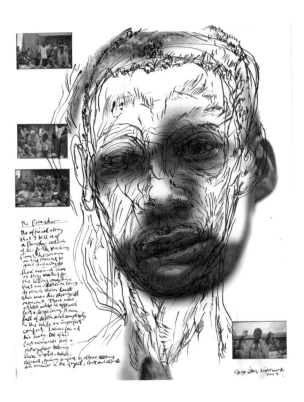

The Preacher

The official story
that I tell is of
a Tutsi-looking
of his faith reading
time. He was an
an eye moving to
give dignity to
those around him
as they waited for
the killing machine
that we remember being
to reach them but
this was his strongest
moment. There were
others while he appeared
lost & despairing. A man
full of doubt and complexity
the while an imperfect
comfort. I never found
his body. One of his
last moments was of a
photographer taking
these shots while
defiant, giving comfort to others, sobbing
an answer in the gospel, lost and alone.

Calga others Lightwork 2003

Big George with Little George on Rex

Grandfather and Nana go shopping

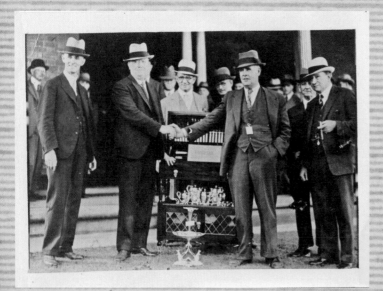

Winning 1935 City Tattersals Cup with Fairoic

With brother Alf and a Fox brother

BIG GEORGE

My grandfather, George Halpin, was born on a ship sailing to Australia. His Dublin family were Irish Protestant. The story we were told was that there was an agreement in the family that he be named George Halpin and nothing more. His excited parents, passing through Sydney Heads, decided to christen him George Sydney Halpin. For this the baby was disinherited back in Ireland.

I was named after him and this didn't make it easy for me to get the cooperation of the IRA or the broader Catholic community of Garvaghy Road. It's something no-one would think or care about back in Australia, but in Northern Ireland there's no more Protestant/ Royalist name than George.

From my earliest years Grandfather George would begin the sentence, 'Never marry a ...' and I would have to finish it with, '... a Catholic'. On our way to school, if we saw Catholic kids in their blue uniforms we were encouraged to throw stones at them and call out 'Dirty tikes!' But we never understood the reason for this hate and I ended up marrying a Catholic.

I've never known a harder man than Grandfather George. Our nana told us that when they were living poor on the northern rivers my grandfather would travel to distant country towns, arriving separately to a couple of his cronies. Grandfather would find the toughest man in the pub and provoke him into coming out the back for a bare-knuckle contest. Grandfather would take such a terrible beating onlookers would call out to end the fight. His mates would, at this point, begin to take bets on Grandfather winning. By then the odds would favour the local so when the cronies had taken all the bets they could, they signalled the real fight to begin. Grandfather would take the poor bastard apart. Sometimes cops woke up to the scam and Grandfather would be thrown into jail and given an additional beating by the coppers.

Grandfather often related the story of the time he had been drinking heavily while playing high stakes cards with a group of gangsters and racing men when he noticed one of them cheating and called him out on it. A gunfight resulted and Grandfather killed his opponent. The other players were in cahoots with the dead man to fleece Grandfather of his money. They rushed him and beat him close to death, then took him with his horse and sulky to The Gap – a high cliff in Sydney's east where many people commit suicide. They wanted to make his death look like he'd killed himself after a big gambling loss.

Many of his bones were broken in the fall but Grandfather managed to crawl back to the top. He dragged himself to his sulky and his faithful horse found the way home. Wonderful, faithful Nana got him into the bath, washed the blood away and reset the bones. A year of constant nursing got Grandfather back on his feet. The moral of the story for George Halpin? 'I never drank again.'

Grandfather had punching bags out near Nana's laundry and we kids would watch him whale away at them like George Foreman preparing to fight Muhammad Ali. Grandfather trained his boxers for the ring with the same kind of severity and discipline he used to train his horses to race.

George Halpin had five daughters, no sons. I was his only grandson, child of his favourite, most loyal daughter, Joyce. Thus it was always intended that I take over his interests. George trained me to fight from the very day I was born. I was an overdue arrival and my hands had begun to deteriorate so doctors at the maternity wing of St George Hospital wrapped my little mitts in bandages. George arrived to see my hands balled into fists and declared me a fighter.

Grandfather practised Irish street-fighting. I'm biased but I firmly believe it to be the most effective and devastating school of martial arts around. Irish street-fighters make other fighters look like ballet dancers. Their sole purpose is to put their opponents down and down fast – it doesn't matter to them how ugly it looks. After watching a judo demonstration by Korean masters at our local police boys' club, Grandfather stood up and loudly declared to the crowd, 'Aesthetics has nothing to do with fighting.'

Old George's training of 'Young George' began early. When I was six he produced a bucket of sand and showed me how to punch. My fists got hard like hammers, my fingers steely as knives. Through the years that followed I thought I'd done everything to please Grandfather until he showed me something else. On this day I was fourteen and walking up our street, past the lane that led to his stables. I was cocky because his training meant I'd never had to back down to a school bully, but two older boys came out of the shadows and started throwing punches. I tried to fight back but they were taller and stronger.

Seeing me bloodied at the brow, nose and mouth but unwilling to cut and run, one of the boys said in pity, 'Nothing personal, kid, your grandfather paid us to do it.'

Hurting all over I hobbled back to our house and told Mum that Grandfather had paid a couple of louts to beat me up. Mum showed me no sympathy. 'Grandfather must have had a good reason,' she said. She dragged me up to his house. He was having a shave and I can still see his face in the mirror. 'What has he done?' my mother asked. Grandfather just shrugged. 'Nothing. He had to learn to take a beating.'

My grandfather held a power over my mother that my father could not break. George's house and stables were at 43 Villiers Street. I was born in number 10, then we moved to 37 and then to 39, each time getting closer to my grandfather. My parents never stopped fighting over this fact, with my father wanting to move away from the dark, overpowering influence of Grandfather and my mother never agreeing to break the bond.

As a result, I lived a double life. At home with my parents and sister I could develop as an artist, which is what I wanted to be from the earliest age. But as Grandfather's only male heir, I was being trained to be his successor in the underworld. His cronies in the racing community referred to him as Old George and me as Young George. In retrospect, I'm grateful to Old George because I couldn't have survived as an artist in war zones without the thug skills he taught me. Growing up between these two houses – one bohemian and creative, the other callous and lethal – made me a contradiction: a sensitive artist aesthete and a street-smart gangster who can face the worst horrors of war and come out undamaged.

Hard Hat Orangeman, Belfast 6-13 July 1997

In the Garvaghy Road marches a group of men in bowler hats led the way to the beat of drums and heralded with pipes and trumpets. These were the leaders of the Orange lodge, the hardest of the hard Orangemen. One was a double for George Halpin, as I remember him. Someone yelled, 'Salute to the hard men of Orange', and the crowd saluted and cheered. I needed to see this to experience where 'it' came from. There is nothing I hate more than bigotry or bullies, but without the training of a hard Orangeman I couldn't have lived the life I have lived. Watching these men, I never felt so lucky to have escaped Grandfather's influence.

31

Protestant Marchers, Belfast, Northern Ireland July 1997

Nana

My grandmother Lavinia Figtree was what in those days was called a lady. Nana never went outside without a black velvet bow in her hair and dressed in formal attire. She was born in Sheffield, England, to a wealthy family but after the death of her mother she sailed to Australia with her stepmother and father who aimed to invest in coke and coal works in Wollongong. She had an unhappy childhood as her stepmother wanted to assert her own children in the inheritance and everything else.

Nana was, however, classically trained in piano and the arts with private tutors. She saw the handsome and wild George Halpin as her way out. George's father was a master builder and had recently been killed in a workplace accident. He was from a long line of Irish architects and engineers some regarded as geniuses.

Nana's family did not approve of the relationship, so she would position her easel outside the shop where George worked and they would pass messages to each other. One of her paintings of this urban scene in 1904 is now in the Wollongong Art Gallery but no-one viewing it today would know it was Nana's excuse to see George. Nana told me they eloped one night when George put his sulky below the window and Nana passed her few belongings down to him.

The elopement lost Nana a stake in the family fortune but the house in Villiers Street with its horse stables was provided by her family with a monthly allowance until she died. This gave her a degree of independence and was the main factor that enabled George to live a reckless, uncaring life. No matter how big his gambling losses he still had a roof over his head.

Grandfather rigged races but Nana was naturally lucky and once won the lottery. If I wanted a tip on a big race it was Nana I would go to rather than Grandfather – her tips would always win me some pocket money. Nana's tips would always come with the advice, 'George, when you're betting on a race the talent is with the horse and the jockey – gamble on your own talent and you will be a certain winner.'

Growing up with a grandfather who was a professional gambler has taught me to take risks not only with my life but with money. But it's Nana's advice I heed when I make a film without funding, buy a ticket to a dangerous war zone, or fund the Yellow House. Thanks to her I never think, *This film is going to cost me more than it makes me so I shouldn't do it.* Gamblers don't place the same value on money as the rest of humanity.

Nana had a big kitchen table with a white enamel top. She encouraged her five daughters, my sister Pam and then me to draw on it with the broad carpenter's pencils Grandfather and his racetrack bookies used to calculate the odds on horses. Nana would say, 'This is the best way to learn and no paper is being wasted.' Once the drawing was finished we'd wipe it away with a wet cloth. Nana was right. You don't want to ruin a good piece of paper with a stupid idea or clumsy line.

Whenever Mum, Pam or the aunties were there it became a competition of who could draw the best hands or the best rearing horse or one another's portrait. It made me a habitual drawer. My favourites were imaginary beasts, dragons and monsters. The first artist I had a connection with was Aubrey Beardsley. There was a dark strangeness in his line that immediately attracted me.

My great grandparents

Nana with her daughters Violet and Dulcie

Nana on a sulky led by her pony Desmond

Nana's 1904 painting of the former main street of Wollongong is famous in our family. Forbidden from seeing grandfather, she would paint in front of the shop where he worked and have secret meetings. Their elopement cost her, Nana, a stake in the family fortune.

I won the Rockdale Council junior arts prize in the under 12 age group with my painting of hot rod cars racing at the Sydney Speedway. My style had fully formed. Hung alongside later work, anyone can see it is a Gittoes.

Mother Soul

Our original house, number 10 Villiers Street, was convict sandstone, very small and had no modern amenities, so my father decided to upgrade to a Federation-era house: number 37. But at the auction my grandfather played a trick on my father and bid against him, forcing the price up. At the end he told the auctioneer he was bidding for Dad and we were stuck with it. Dad believed Grandfather did this to put us into so much debt we would never be able to sell it and be forced to remain under his influence with his house and stables only a few doors up. We lived there for a couple of years until our neighbour, an old Mr Hedge, died and Dad saw the opportunity to buy his place a lot cheaper and escape the debt.

Mr Hedge's house had become overgrown with a 'jungle of weeds' and even before the exchange of contracts Dad decided that he and I should clear them. The pile of weeds and bushes was huge and I could not resist going and putting a match to it. Within no time the blaze had consumed our neighbour's back garage and police and firemen were banging on our back door to speak to me about starting it.

There was a secret trapdoor in the floor of the old pantry which Mr Hedge had delighted in showing me. I used it to hide and was able to hear the other kids putting the blame on me.

There were only two bedrooms in the house so it was decided that the dining room which adjoined the kitchen could be partitioned off as my bedroom. It was scary because I was still a young kid and it was a long way from my parents' bedroom in this spooky old house. In my nightmares I would often imagine monsters from hell coming up from the underworld via the trapdoor.

Then Mum did something beautiful. She got blue water-colour paint and made a reproduction of the Willow pattern on the partitian wall. This magically beautiful creation and her wonderfully pure brushwork seemed to banish the dream demons.

The best thing about Mr Hedge's house was that he had a beautifully made hobby shed. My father, who always encouraged our artistic talents, put a glass wall of windows in it so Mum could use it as a studio. Around this time Mum had done a course in ceramics at St George Technical College so Dad installed an electric wheel and a kiln. I would sit up in the mulberry tree outside the window and watch Mum make her magical creations.

Mum had incredible abilities and her ceramics sold like hot cakes. Just as my nana taught me how to draw, the other most important lesson of my life was Mum's insistence that 'no work of art can live unless you give it a soul'. Mum would move on from pots to ceramic sculptures – mainly of bush creatures – and the owls, koalas and kooka-burras which I have in my house still follow me around the room with their eyes. They are creatures with soul and sometimes I feel my mother's presence in them, watching over me.

I was always proud of my mum. She was beautiful looking and liked to show off her great figure – always asking me when she bought new stockings to tell her what I thought of her legs. I also loved the fact that she was a true bohemian nonconformist. At one point she decided to make ceramic busts of her own torso. One day I came home and she was topless with skimpy panties, using a mirror to replicate her own form in clay. I had a couple of school mates with me and their eyes almost popped out of their heads but Mum was unfazed and told us to go to the kitchen to make ourselves afternoon snacks, before turning back to her reflection.

When I did the Yellow House with Martin Sharp everyone was talking about the Generation Gap but Martin's mum, Jo, and my mum, Joyce, both contributed. Jo painted the clouds around the mounts of the Magritte lithographs before they were framed and Mum took a book of Magritte paintings and made them into three-dimensional ceramics – including the still-life rock fruit bowl, bottle and book on the table of our stone room installation, leaves turning into trees and a pair of men's boots and women's high heels turning into feet and toes. Mum loved working on our Yellow House experiments. Martin and I agreed we were lucky to have such cool mums.

But Mum's passion sometimes translated into something closer to madness and her screaming and fighting with my father could result in her leaving or disappearing for days on end. I would accompany my father searching for her and this was always very disturbing.

POTTERY GROUP SHOW

They call themselves the Kabin Potters and they are the first group in Australia to make pottery for Ikebana arrangements.

The group, formed six months ago, will hold its first exhibition of pottery tomorrow, Saturday and Sunday at the home of Mr and Mrs Claude Gittoes at Bardwell Park.

Mrs Gittoes is a member of the group. The others are Mrs Harry Webb, of Kyle Bay, Mrs William Self, of Bardwell Park, Mrs John Sandow, of Penshurst, Mrs Thomas Freeman, of Cronulla, Mrs Les Lane, of Penshurst, Miss Margery Hilliar, of Wahroonga, Mr Douglas Mc-Donald, of Beverley Hills and Mr Jock Maxwell, of Bexley.

They have all been potters for many years but didn't seriously consider making pottery for Ikebana until last April when Mrs Webb and Mrs Sandow went to an Ikebana International exhibition at the Wentworth Hotel.

Only three of the 100 containers used were made locally.

"We decided then we would like to see some Australian pots used in Ikebana arrangements," Mrs Webb said.

The subject came up again when several of the women, who are founders and members of the St. George Potters group, asked if anyone there was interested in doing this type of pottery.

Several were, and they decided to form a group.

A friend and associate member of the group, Mrs William Pigot, who teaches at the Sogetsu School of Ikebana, showed them slides of Ikebana flower arrangements and explained what kind of containers are used in these arrangements.

Mrs Pigot, who has studied Ikebana in Japan, feels that their pots have a distinctly Australian character.

"There is an earthiness about them, a feeling of spaciousness and the earthy colours — dark oranges, browns and terracottas — are typically Australian," she said.

Women's Section, Thurs., April 18, 1968

Mrs Claud Gittoes with an Ikebana pot.

Antoinette Starkiewicz with my mother on our back lawn – both bohemian artists they became friends at the Yellow House – despite the age difference.

Shane Robbinson and mum collaborating
Yellow House period.

Mirow and Awliya

MAKUBOY, SOMALIA, 18 SEPTEMBER 1993

I am at Makuboy, a remote feeding station run by CRS (Catholic Relief Services) and set up to save undernourished children. I had heard from Delta Co soldiers on the way here that Makuboy is the most distressing place to be.

This drawing is of Mirow and Awliya. As I write, I am sitting under a thorn bush with them and Awliya is starting to sip some porridge – something the nun and CRS thought impossible when we arrived here this morning. This means she will probably live. Awliya is a beautiful proud little girl. An Australian child as sick as her would not try as hard to relate emotionally and communicate with a stranger like me.

Mirow is the grandmother of three little girls – Awliya (6), Madaye (3) and Mariana (8). All are weak but Awliya is nearest to death. Mirow brought the children to the aid centre after their mother had died. She had to carry them, as none were strong enough to walk. So Mirow would carry Awliya and Madaye (one on her back and one in her arms) for a kilometre, leave them, then go back for Mariana, and so on for the two weeks it took her to reach the aid station. She foraged for food in the night, digging up worms and grubs and collecting droplets of dew from leaves to fill a cup.

The nuns have a rule that if a child can eat the UN-provided protein biscuits then they can be given special attention but those who can not swallow will probably die so they do not waste their limited time and resources on them. Awliya's throat had dried up so I gave her a barley sugar sweet to suck. It was too big to fit into her mouth so Mirow cracked it in half with her teeth. The barley sugar worked and by afternoon she could prove to the nuns she could digest a biscuit. Here the test of living or dying is a biscuit!

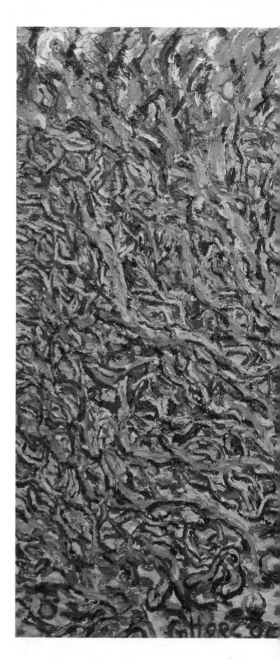

The men of their village took all the food + water and left the old + frail women to die. Mirow's daughter (mother of the girls) stayed because she was sick – she pleaded with Mirow to leave her and take the girls – but she waited until she died + buried her. I've been saving coffee sacks and have given them to Mirow to trade as she journies to the sea

Mirow & Awliya

Puppet on a String

Rockdale Markets were the best place to go on a Saturday. I was allowed to walk there on my own from about the age of six. I loved the smell of the fresh ripe fruit and the scents of the flowers. I started my own little garden from plants I bought there – pansies were my favourites. The markets were where I bought my first comics and my two salamander walking fish – one white, one black. I made a pool for them out of old convict washtubs carved from a sandstone block.

My biggest discovery at the markets was a bunch of puppets. They had rubber, latex-smelling heads and were painted in amazing colours. This was before plastic toys started to be imported from Japan. I built up a cast of characters and started inventing stories for them. Puppets helped me to develop my skills as a showman. Our back lawn was big enough to play cricket on and there was a hump in the middle and a flagpole. This let me place my improvised stage up high enough to be like a theatre.

I don't know how I managed it but one Saturday afternoon Dad came home from golf to see the yard full of local kids being entertained by his son and the puppets. Being an adult, he worried about the needs of so many kids. Back then Dad's mother, Ma, would always bring my sister Pam and I jars of boiled lollies whenever she visited. They tasted weird so we only pretended to like them and would spit them out when she wasn't looking. As a result, jars and jars of boiled lollies had built up in our pantry. Dad handed out these boiled lollies to the unsuspecting kids then he sent a tin around for donations. I proudly gave my 'take' to the Red Cross fund at Bexley Public School that week.

This was pre-television. The local kids were so bored they kept coming back for more puppet shows. Even the adults got interested. When I was eleven some kid's father decided to book my puppet show to play at church and scout halls to make more money for charity. It was okay doing puppet shows on our own familiar lawn but the audiences in the halls filled me with fear. The emotional price I was paying to do the shows made me look more closely at where my money was going and more aware of the suffering of people around the world. My interest in humanitarian causes developed in tandem with my stage fright.

One show in a Forest Road church hall was so heavily publicised a few hundred people were expected, mainly adults. A friend's father owned a new invention – a reel-to-reel tape recorder – and convinced me that if I pre-recorded the voices of my puppet characters as they acted out my scripted stories the stress wouldn't be so great. All I would have to do was operate the glove puppets. I had lots of voices. This was the golden era of radio and I'd grown up listening to and loving radio drama for its ability to conjure other worlds and make the listeners invent a visual experience in their heads. I still remember the strangeness of hearing my own voice played back sounding nothing like what I thought I sounded.

The big night came. Peeking out from the side of my puppet theatre, I could see the seats filling with families chatting among themselves in anticipation. I was unaware that I was about to experience the most embarrassing moment of my young life, something so terrible it still makes my stomach churn and my face blush red. As I began the show the taped voices boomed out on speakers filling the hall in a way I could never have done. But the problem was that we hadn't allowed enough time to change the gloves of the different characters.

My plays were fast, with many characters changing back and forth and only speaking a few lines at a time. The recording was too fast for the turnaround. The glove that was the witch would still be on my hand speaking the lines of the fairy godmother and the ogre was delivering for the hero. It was total chaos. No-one was able to follow what was being performed.

From backstage I heard murmurs and soon everyone was talking and asking each other what was going on. I turned to the technician and told him to turn the tape off but he panicked and increased the volume. That was the end of my Red Cross puppet shows but not the end of my puppets.

I never realised those innocent puppet shows would set my life on a trajectory towards all the horror and suffering this sorry world could offer. My name was inscribed on a merit board and the Red Cross visited the school to meet the child puppeteer and fundraiser and gave me a bag full of books and pamphlets on Florence Nightingale and World War I to take home and read.

Later when I took up puppets again at the Yellow House in Vietnam-era Kings Cross, I was performing to people wanting a good night out. It didn't feel the same as knowing the performances were to benefit people in less lucky countries. The following year I wrote to Mother Teresa of Calcutta asking her for advice. The role of the artist seemed to have become that of a clown and I wanted to know if she thought I should go back to university and study medicine or engineering so that I could make a real contribution to alleviate suffering.

To my surprise Mother Teresa wrote back:

MISSIONARIES OF CHARITY
54 A LOWER. CIRCULAR ROAD.
CALCUTTA 16. INDIA

Pentecost 72
Dear George,

Thank you for your letter.

Yes, the Gift God has given is very great & beautiful because God is such a Great Artist – looking at the beautiful things he has made like the world.

I am happy for you that He can use you to express this love for art & beauty. Use it only to glorify him.

Pray for me.

God Bless you
M. Teresa M

I have taken her advice to the letter and am a very happy human being as a result.

Thanks, and God bless you, Mother Teresa.

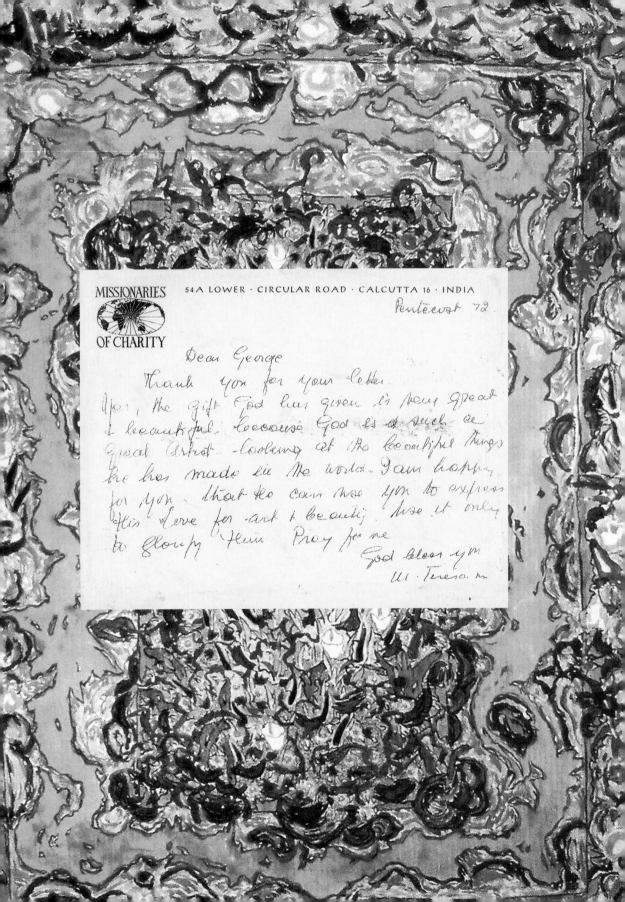

MISSIONARIES OF CHARITY

54A LOWER · CIRCULAR ROAD · CALCUTTA 16 · INDIA

Pentecost 72.

Dear George

Thank you for your letter.

Yes, the gift God has given is very great & beautiful. Because God is a such a Great Artist - looking at the beautiful things he has made in the world. I am happy for you - that He can use you to express His love for art & beauty. Use it only to glorify Him. Pray for me

God bless you

M. Teresa m

The Class Idiot

I was born left-handed but forced by teachers to use my right. I'm also dyslexic, so I had a lot of difficulty with reading and writing at primary school. Most days would start with a spelling test, or being asked to read in front of the class. Being the class idiot was a huge embarrassment. I knew I wasn't stupid, but the difficulty I had with reading and my bad handwriting put me at the bottom of the class. The one thing I was good at was painting and drawing. Every year I would win the school's Book Week painting competition. The paintings were done at home and brought in for judging. The winner would be allowed to choose a book. I loved the recognition.

One year my teacher decided the judges had been deceived and that I was a cheat – that my mother and sister had helped me to do the winning works. I was given a poor-quality piece of paper and asked to paint something in front of the class using the terrible school poster paints. Under such pressure and scrutiny, I panicked. The paint turned watery and merged into browns and greys. I failed to perform, losing my usual sense of form. My work was a mess. The teacher held the disastrous painting up for the class to see and everyone laughed as the wet colours ran into each other. The prize was immediately taken off me and given to another student. The stigma of being a cheat stayed with me, making me hate the class and the school.

Around this time, I did an IQ test. A few days later my parents were asked to come to see the headmaster. I stood in the doorway while he angrily told my mother and father that I was a lazy underachiever because the test had shown I should be at the top of the class not the bottom.

Shortly after this I got sick with glandular fever and was put under strict quarantine at home and not allowed to attend the last few months of school. It was probably the best thing that ever happened to me. I began to go to Rockdale Public Library and borrow books. I began voraciously consuming books, amazing myself each time I finished a book over one hundred pages long. I loved science, history and other non-fiction as much as fiction and began to think I could become someone who could make a difference in the world.

I could feel my brain growing like a melon.

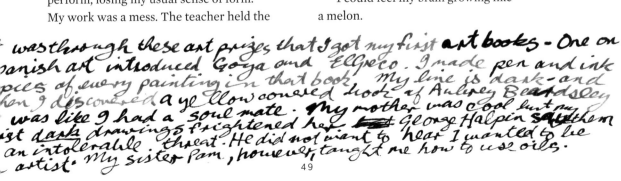

was through these art prizes that I got my first art books - One on
Spanish art introduced Goya and ElGreco. I made pen and ink
copies of every painting in that book. My line is dark - and
then I discovered a yellow covered book of Aubrey Beardsley
was like I had a soul mate. My mother was cool but my
artist dark drawings frightened her. George Halpin saw them
an intolerable threat. He did not want to hear I wanted to be
artist. My sister Pam, however, taught me how to use oils.

Mr NIGHT

The English and history master was a Mr Knight, a Christian Fundamentalist. He was on a mission. Mr Knight reminded me of one of the dark characters from Dickens. He wore unfashionable double-breasted suits wrapped around his bony physique, and his teaching technique was to ridicule other's religious views and use his cane without mercy.

When the day came for Mr Knight to deal with evolution – a subject none of the other kids was familiar with – he started by imitating an ape, hunching his back, swaying his arms and making monkey noises. Everyone in the class thought it was hilarious and they were rolling around at their desks with laughter. Mr Knight suddenly became very serious and said, 'Some scientists believe we came from apes. Hands up who believes this?' No-one put their hand up.

Like most kids of that age I was fascinated with dinosaurs and often dug up parts of the backyard looking for fossils. When I found Huxley's simplified version of Darwin's theory of evolution it became my favourite book. Mr Knight must have sensed my realisation that we were being manipulated. He pointed to me. 'So, Gittoes, what do you think – did we evolve from apes?' I said, 'Yes, I do believe we evolved from apes.' My challenge must have made it clear to him that I was reading above my age and had potential as both an English and history student, but from that moment Mr Knight hated me and caned me as often as possible.

Another day Mr Knight was relishing telling us about the Nuremberg trials of Nazi war criminals. I put my hand up and asked why Americans hadn't been tried in the same court

over the bombings of Hiroshima and Nagasaki. He was furious with me and I was sent out to stand in the hallway.

When I received my exam report at the end of my first year of high school I had been given zero for both my English and history papers. To receive zero was incredible and made my aggregate so low that in the following year I was moved to the lowest classes where the emphasis was on learning manual skills like woodwork. As I walked into one of these classes at the beginning of the year, one of my fellow woodworkers said, 'We thought you were a brain, not one of us.' I reassured him that I definitely wasn't a brain and gave up any academic aspirations, focusing on sports and learning how to make things with my hands.

I learned there was a record for getting the greatest number of cuts of the cane for misbehaviour in one year. I set out to break this record. If I couldn't be one of the best, I would be the worst.

NIGHT VISION

BAIDOA, SOMALIA, 28 MARCH 1993

During night patrols in Baidoa the soldiers use night vision glasses – which give them a weird greenish view through two mini TVs over each eye.

In the medieval streets of this African town where there isn't even electricity, it makes them look like Hollywood robots out of a Terminator *or* Star Wars *movie – totally alien and frightening.*

For the soldiers, their greatest fear is that they will mistake a child playing with a gun for an adult with a real gun. The toy guns are homemade, and look very real – they are confiscated from the children whenever possible. To the children, the soldiers must appear like monsters stealing their toys.

I curled up under a tank to make the drawing Night Vision Patrol Baidoa – *not wanting the soldiers I had been with to see it as I thought they could take insult at the depiction. But the patrol corporal pulled the drawing out of my folder and passed it around. They loved it, comparing it to heavy metal album covers and said, 'That's better than a photograph – you've shown how it feels to be out there.' From that moment* Night Vision *has become symbolic of what I do as an artist – going into the darkness of war and coming back with what I have witnessed. For the sake of my sanity I invented a character, 'Corporal Night', whom I animate in stories like an avatar puppet of myself – drawing* Night Vision *has meant I have never felt the need to consult with a therapist.*

ART PRIZES

The proudest moment of my young life and the thing that proved to me that talent could be recognised was when Mum won first prize at the Royal Easter Show Arts and Crafts pavilion with her Grecian-style Vase. I had just discovered Homer's *Iliad* and *Odyssey* in a children's book with illustrations in the style of ancient Greek ceramic painting – black on ochre. Mum decided to adopt this style and depict farmers arriving with their animals to be judged in the agricultural parade. We all came to the prize-giving, including Dad's mum, Ma. I ruined the formality of the official family photo by putting on a pair of funny glasses with fake eyes. I still have the pot with its blue ribbon. The Art Establishment had shown its first crack for the Gittoes family to enter through.

Later when I was in senior high school I moved from Kogarah High to Kingsgrove North with a reputation as a troublemaker – attracting the attention of its very strict vice principal. One day he walked into the classroom and told every student to stand 'except Gittoes'.

And then he told everyone, except me, to clap. I thought I was in real trouble and would soon be forced to change schools again.

Then in a cynical, flat voice the vice principal announced that I had won the first Roselands art prize with a large amount of money being donated to the school.

My sister, Pam, had slipped the entry in without me knowing. It depicts a boy (a younger me) on the floor of the Art Gallery of New South Wales blowing up a balloon while a house painter with a ladder looks on, incredulous as high society viewers admire modern abstracts on the walls. This tradesman's face was a portrait of my grandfather and in a way the derision he is showing reflects the derision I believed he felt for my ambitions to be an artist. There is also a Giacometti-like sculpture looking on with its head in its hands. It was one of my earliest expressions of social satire directed at the elite of the Art Establishment. I'm still the boy with the balloon, about to burst and shock, always believing art should work for the populace and not just the few.

Monkey Stories

When I was a kid I was very close to my sister Pam who is seven years older than me and was born during the war. The story goes that my father returned from Darwin in a seaplane. When he got off the plane he had a long red beard and my mother was distressed because she couldn't recognise her husband Claude among the people getting out of the plane. The beard was a total surprise but she soon got over it, and Pam was conceived in the short leave before Dad went back up north.

Pam complains that after the war Mum and Dad just wanted to have fun and go dancing and neglected me when I was born. She contends that they didn't want another child so she had to bring me up. I was her dolly and she pushed me around in a pram and played with me as though I were hers.

As I got older I would get into her bed in the mornings and she would tell me monkey stories. Pam had an amazing imaginary jungle world where the monkeys were the heroes. She still tells these stories to her grandchildren. I suppose that's why I love monkeys so much and think it's wonderful to finally get to know the monkeys we have at the Yellow House in Jalalabad. When I got to puberty at about thirteen or fourteen, Dad decided it wasn't a good idea for me to cuddle up with my sister in the mornings. I think he might have seen me lying on top of her a few times and told me it was time the morning visits and monkey stories stopped.

Dad's idea of a holiday was six weeks at Tuggerah Camping Park. He had a khaki tent left over from the war and Pam and I had a double stretcher with her sleeping on the top. Everything came up in a trailer on the back of my grandfather's Ford or in later years our family Holden. It was my job to crawl under the tent once it was stretched out on the grass and put the centre pole in. Everyone, especially my father, was tense from the long drive, when the car would invariably overheat. Us kids just wanted to get into the surf, but Dad always insisted the tent be set up before we hit the water.

Dad would book the same spot at the front of the park every year. For him the ultimate holiday was to sit in a deckchair and watch pretty girls in skimpy bikinis go past. Dad loved the simple luxuries of summer, like strawberry jam with cream on fresh bread, and watermelon. He was an expert at selecting melons and would tap half the melons on a truck before choosing one. Then we would have a competition to see who could eat the most, until our bellies were set to burst.

The most fascinating thing about our holidays was watching Pam's juggling act with boyfriends. Usually there would be the official boyfriend who was allowed to stay in the tent with us. Then there were the others who had their own tent and lived on condensed milk while waiting for their moment in the sun with Pam. I enjoyed the rough mannish way these boys survived without proper cooking equipment or any of our luxuries, and I took advantage of my status as the brother by

making them take me fishing or to see Jimmy Sharman's boxing tent. In the competition for Pam's attention a few went into the ring to fight the professionals and put on a show. Dad would be chuckling up the back of the crowd. Those were the days when everyone in Australia stayed up late to listen to the radio if there was a world title fight. The big ones were Jimmy Carruthers' fight in South Africa and, later, anything featuring Cassius Clay (Muhammad Ali). Fist-fighting was big.

When we were settled in, Grandfather Halpin would arrive with Nana and his bodyguard/driver. These young drivers were usually in love with Pam too. One, Ted Clark, a champion bantamweight, actually proposed to her. This didn't go down well but Grandfather didn't have him killed, as he warned he would do to any man who threatened his darling granddaughter's honour. Grandfather always brought a heavy presence with his transistor radio to his ear, constantly listening to the races wherever they were held and organising bets at SP bookies.

I didn't make many friends in the camping ground but there was a family of intellectuals – I think they may have been nuclear physicists – in one of the tents deeper into the grounds. The boy was my age and they were there every year, just like us. One year he got a giant toy cannon for Christmas. These cannons had a spring in them that could be pulled back to fire. I used to shoot small fireworks called tom thumb bungers out of mine, the trick being to shoot them skyward and see them explode in mid-air, but mine was much smaller than his huge cannon.

We were playing with our presents in his tent when he put a meat skewer in the chamber and fired it at his sister. It got her in the eye and penetrated right through. He did it in stupid fun but she was blinded. The sight of her with this skewer in her eye is still one of the most traumatic experiences of my life.

The big event of the holidays was going to the movies at Long Jetty. One year a movie came along that gave me nightmares. *On the Beach* had been made in Australia with Hollywood stars Ava Gardner, Gregory Peck and Fred Astaire and was based on Nevil Shute's novel. It's a post-nuclear war story about a US submarine, captained by Peck, that pulls into Sydney Harbour after all humanity 'up north' has been killed. Only Australia is safe, but everyone knows nuclear clouds of radiation are coming and will eventually kill everyone in Australia as well. This thought terrified me.

FIVE DAUGHTERS MAKE A FIST

Grandfather had five daughters and didn't want any of them to leave home as he used them all like slaves. Aunty Violet was his best horse trainer and married late by elopement. The first time she visited with her new husband, Grandfather 'punched and kicked the shit out of him'. To make it worse, he was a Catholic.

Another daughter, Dulcie, who'd married a war veteran with a plate in his head from a battle wound, had a great market garden and fruit stall business on the road to Rooty Hill. They made enough to retire and sold the business and moved into a house further up the road in Villiers Street.

Grandfather was delighted to have two of his daughters back in the street but he hated Dulcie's husband, Jim Whiteoak. Jim was proud of his business success and his status as a war hero.

The first Christmas came around and my mother hosted the whole family in our dining room. The women out-did one another with the cooking and by the end of it everyone was as 'full as eggs'. But throughout the dinner there'd been continuous verbal jousting between Grandfather and Uncle Jim.

At first they were making jokes but then the jokes got personal. Uncle Jim was incredibly fit with abs like a weightlifter. He pulled up his shirt and told me to punch him in the guts 'with all you've got'. I said, 'I don't want to hurt you, Uncle Jim', and gave him a light tap. Uncle Jim was worked up and said, 'Come on, George, you can do better than that.' I refused and he and my grandfather got abusive calling me a poofter, a sissy and a girl for not being willing to throw 'a real punch'. I said, 'Okay', and gave Uncle Jim a serious punch, but still not as hard as I could hit. He went down in a heap and I immediately felt bad. Aunty Dulcie was shocked and said, 'Come on, Jim, it's time we went home.' Grandfather was smiling – 'A kid put the big man down'.

Within an hour we heard that Jim had died. The combination of Christmas dinner, his war wounds and my punch had killed him.

Dulcie moved to another house in Rockdale, unable to stay where her beloved Jim had died. Grandfather had won – Dulcie became an unpaid helper to Nana until the day Nana died. For years after, to fill the hole left in Dulcie's life by Jim's death, I would pick her up in my St George cab and take her to and from Nana's house. I did paintings of her favourite flowers to hang on the walls and helped her plant a garden, but nothing was enough to erase the memory of that punch.

BIG SHOT

It is dark times. The world is near its end. I'm in a cabin built into the side of a cave. Everyone I have ever loved is in here with me. We notice a figure pass in the outer dark. There is no sense of threat so the door is open. It's the resurrected Jesus who enters. He invites my family and friends to follow him. A cave wall opens. Now I'm outside wondering why I chose not to follow. I try to re-enter the cabin but the door is protected by angry dogs that tear at my legs.

Investigators are finding evidence to connect me with past murders. Evidence builds until I am hunted by accusers convinced of my guilt. My chasers transform into wolf-like dogs. By the time they catch up with me I have returned to the crime scene – a Hansel and Gretel witch's house of horrors. I try to run to the room where my parents are sleeping but the long dark hallway has a paralysing effect on my muscles. I fight to move forward, heart pounding against invisible forces. I find my sleeping parents but they vanish as soon as I approach them. Then I'm in the terrible place where I remember the victims murdered – it is sick and evil.

An accuser appears wearing bloodstained clothes. The dogs are barking and tearing at my legs. There are now three accusers who bear no resemblance to dogs or humans – they are demons, grotesquely assembled from decomposing bodies. One has a stick with a crescent-moon-shaped hook – it pokes at my chest to gather my soul. My fear is so extreme I force myself to wake.

My perpetual nightmare of being chased by angry dogs to a scene where the bodies of victims are being uncovered was a dream shared by my mother – possibly the result of Grandfather telling us how he'd disposed of bodies in the Cooks River. The day after Grandfather died Mum went to his house, to where she knew he'd hidden the guns, hired a speedboat and dropped them to the bottom of Botany Bay.

When I was a really young kid I'd found one of the guns, a small submachine gun of the kind issued to commandos, and snuck it onto the roof of the shed. I had my friend Richard on the roof with me and was pointing it at him, trying to pull the trigger, when Mum screamed. There was a bullet in the breech but my chubby young fingers didn't have the power to pull the trigger.

The night Grandfather died I was seventeen. He asked for me but Mum decided she could prevent him from dying if she could prevent him from seeing me. I was told not to come – that he would be okay. In fact, there was nothing our family doctor could find wrong with him. Age meant he was losing his grip on the racing scene. He was told a horse was a 'sure thing', meaning a race had been rigged, and he'd bet a huge amount of money on it. This had been a lie to get his money and let him know he had lost what power he had – he was being put in his place.

Afterwards he'd felt so humiliated he came home and said, 'If that's life, then I've had it', and lay down to die. He literally willed himself to death. Mum's bluff didn't work and I never got to say farewell to this most influential force in my young life.

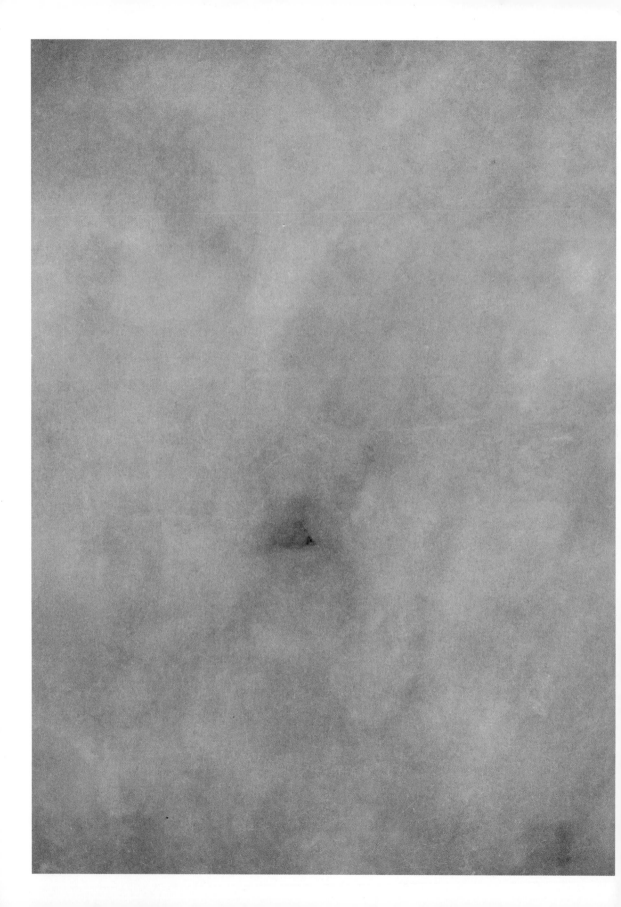

AMERICA

To the amazement of teachers who saw me as a rebel and troublemaker, I had won a Commonwealth Scholarship to Sydney University. But my hunger for direct experience meant the slow pace of formal study would not hold me.

In my first year at university my professor of fine arts, Bernard Smith, brought the influential art critic Clement Greenberg to Australia to give the inaugural Power Lecture. Bernard introduced me to Clem and I showed him three of my paintings.

Two of them were on round canvases with a single shaped patch of colour. The third was like looking into a green mist with no definable shapes in the composition. Clem liked them and told me I was wasting my time in Australia and needed to come to New York.

To get the money I took a job as a chainman, a surveyor's assistant, on the Cahill Expressway. Dad worked at the Department of Main Roads and was able to pull a few strings. He said, 'It's time you got away from your mother.' It was good, fast money. The expressway was on a deadline and we were working double shifts seven days a week with generous overtime rates.

My writing in the margins of drawings goes back to being bored by schoolwork and passing drawings around to my friends. But the visual diary style where I combine writing with drawings and found pictures goes back to this first trip, alone, to America when I was eighteen, turning nineteen. I wrote letters and postcards to my mother, sister, nana and girlfriends.

I travelled across America from Los Angeles to New York in a Greyhound bus. When I arrived I only had ten dollars in my pocket and used this on a taxi to the Bowery. Dad had helped out a Salvation Army guy, Colonel Mackenzie, on a visit to Australia. The colonel took me to his apartment at the Vermeer on 14th Street near Seventh Avenue. His wife, also a colonel, welcomed me and put me up in the bedroom of their daughter who had recently left home.

I was lucky and landed a job with IBM helping to illustrate their reports to investors. One day I was in the building's lift and an amazing-looking older woman got in. She reminded me of Greta Garbo. I spontaneously asked her if I could paint her portrait but she made fun of my request, telling me she had been painted by all the great artists of Europe. I got off at my floor, embarrassed. A couple of weeks later I ran into her again. This time she recognised the Australian accent, made a joke about kangaroos and agreed to the portrait.

She told me to meet her at a restaurant in the Village. Over a meal I learnt her American name was Marie Woods but she was born Baroness Von Lebzelten. Later, when she opened the door to her apartment my eyes bulged and she laughed. The apartment was littered with portraits of her as a young woman painted by Derain, van Dongen and Picasso, among others. These artworks sat amidst rotting food and ancient Greek sculptures. Yet, with a collection worth millions,

the Baroness lived in squalor and slept on a striped mattress on the floor.

I had tired of Greenberg's minimalist abstractionists. As I set to work on the canvas it was the great early twentieth-century portrait painters Soutine, Modigliani, Otto Dix and Oskar Kokoschka that were in my mind. I thought the painting was going well and turned it around to show the Baroness. She fell backwards like she had had a stroke. By showing the Baroness herself as an old woman it seemed I had killed her. When she recovered she told me it was not too bad but I had given her too much forehead and joked 'I haven't got that many brains'. She suggested I go back to my studio and fix it before she saw it again.

When I went back to her apartment it was snowing, there was a gale force wind which blew the canvas around behind me. I gripped the stretcher frame with one hand and let it blow back behind me like a sail. I was confident it was good. And this time the Baroness was also happy with the portrait. I didn't

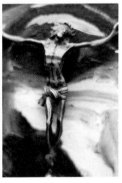

expect anything in return from someone who had known the masters I loved but the Baroness astonished me with three priceless gifts – a rare Kitagawa Utamaro woodblock print of a mother and her child, a beautiful medieval bronze crucifix and an original photo by Etienne Carjat of the young French poet Arthur Rimbaud that belonged to his lover, Paul Verlaine. The photo was signed by Rimbaud and he had cut a cross into the face with a razor blade.

On my way back through the Village I could not have been happier and decided to drop in to an occult bookshop where I had already purchased a few books on mysticism. The owner had silver hair, pale skin and was a self-declared warlock. I hadn't realised how much the bookshop owner looked like Andy Warhol until now, when I saw the real Andy Warhol was standing next to him. Both of them found me very funny – a young surfie type from Australia clutching a medieval crucifix in one hand and a book of Julian of Norwich's mystical writings in the other. They kept me talking and made jokes about everything I told them. I realised I'd unconsciously turned the crucifix upside down and was swinging it like a pendulum with the feet squeezed between my thumb and forefinger. The two of them laughed like they'd won a bet.

Andy's Factory was near Union Square, which was on my way back to the Vermeer on 14th Street. We walked back together and had what was, for me, the most exciting conversation of my young life. I remember two important bits of the advice he gave me. Firstly, he told me I needed to 'invent myself'. When I asked him what he meant, he stopped and looked at me. Flakes of snow had begun to fall on the shoulders of his coat and he flattened his hands out and put them up, like someone with a gun pointed at them and said 'Do you think I was born Andy Warhol?' His second piece of advice was this: 'If people tell you they love you, you're fabulous, a genius ... it isn't because you are, but because you bring home the bacon.'

Joe and the Black Panthers

The Baroness and I were in her apartment drinking a cup of tea when the door burst open. It was the African-American artist Joseph Delaney and it was clear from the expression on his face that he didn't like me being there. The Baroness had been his patron for many years and he was jealous of someone moving in on his territory. I countered by suggesting I go to his studio and do his portrait. Joe was taken aback by my presumption, but agreed.

I arrived a few nights later with a canvas and paints. It was January in New York and icy cold, but when Joe pulled the door of his Sixth Avenue loft open he was shirtless. He pointed to bullet wounds he had received in World War II as a way, I think, of further intimidating me.

Joe was the right influence for me at this time. He was a figurative artist influenced by all the painters I loved, especially the German Expressionists. Along with his many portraits and nudes there were large history paintings with themes like the celebrations in Times Square on V Day when peace was declared. His new work documented the Civil Rights Movement. Joe had been friends with Jackson Pollock at the Art Students League but had resisted the move to abstraction.

As I took up my paints and set up the canvas, Joe put an LP on his turntable. Not music but the great speech of Martin Luther King Jnr. It was only months since Dr King's assassination and the recording made the atmosphere in the studio intensely black and white.

Once I finished the portrait I took my brush and wrote in oil, onto the background, 'I have a dream' and then turned it to show Joe. He liked it well enough to accept it as a gift and invited me to come drawing with him in Washington Square Park.

Joe taught me to stop strangers and offer to draw them, advising, 'You have to draw and draw and draw from life, and that's how you learn to draw. That's how I've learnt to draw.' Joe then asked me to meet him at a Civil Rights rally at Harlem Temple and to bring my charcoal and sketchpad.

When I arrived I was surprised to see Joe on stage as a kind of MC. I was the only white person at the rally and tried to make myself as invisible as possible. But at the end of proceedings Joe announced there was a special guest in the audience from Australia – he was an artist and was happy to draw the babies of any mothers who would like a sketch of their child. I was immediately surrounded by women with babies. As I sketched I was aware of tall men standing behind me who I suspected were analysing every line for a hint of racism. But they found no problem and I sent all the women home happy with their baby portraits. Joe later told me some of the watchers belonged to the Black Panthers.

I had gone to New York with ambitions to become an abstract painter but left committed, like Joe, to making my art a witness to history and the many faces of humanity.

I arrived in New York in 1968, the year when I got over abstraction I started a ser suite. They took 2 years to finish – no one

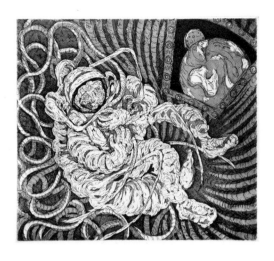

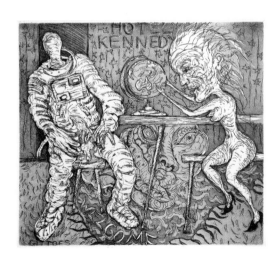

Kennedy had been killed leaving a Hotel.
etchings (20) which I called the Hotel Kennedy

Marie

While in New York I made a lot of friends like Joe but didn't enter into any intimate relationships. All my passion went into writing my letters home to Mum (and my teenage girlfriends).

Once again I hopped on a Greyhound bus but this time took the northern route back to the West Coast. I had the treasures the Baroness had given me in my bag and sketchbooks full of notes and drawings. I had decided that the art that Greenberg had advocated I come to New York to experience was shallow and had lost its connection to humanity. Arriving in San Francisco I went to a huge exhibition of photography, stacked with powerful photo-journalism shots from around the world.

The photographers were doing the job I wanted to do. I found the images of photographers like Henri Cartier-Bresson more exciting than any of the contemporary painting I had seen in New York.

One day I was walking back from Fisherman's Wharf and was struck by the beautiful Slavic face of a dark-haired girl passing by. I turned and asked her if I could draw her portrait. Her name was Marie Magdalene Briebauer. Marie was an artist and poet and it was love at first sight. I didn't think I would see her again until I heard a knock on my door at the Shaw Hotel. I was in the bath and wrapped a towel around my waist thinking it was someone from cleaning.

Marie pushed me down on the bed and that was it.

When I returned to Australia I began writing an experimental novel called *The Romances* and for two years Marie and I corresponded. We were in some ways closer than had we been together. Marie was pregnant to one of her university professors when I met her. She had the baby, a girl, but gave her up for adoption, then dropped out of university to travel the world. I got a job as an assistant librarian at Rockdale Library and also my licence to drive a St George cab. The painting continued but the book and Marie were my main obsessions.

MEETING MARTIN

EXTRACT FROM YELLOW HOUSE DIARY, 1970

My sister Pam's friend Diane Draffin picked me up today in her silver convertible. It's a Datsun Fairlady, not James Bond's Aston Martin, but it feels just as exciting with Diane at the wheel, her long blonde hair flowing in the wind. Diane is married to Peter Draffin, who wrote POP, an experimental novel illustrated by Martin Sharp, a Sydney artist who has found global fame with his posters, OZ magazine graphics and paintings.

Martin's exhibition in the old Clune Galleries is the most exciting show I've seen in Australia since returning from New York. It's unlike anything else – bright psychedelic colours, often painted on the back of perspex with flying saucers blending into Vincent and Mickey Mouse and lots of question marks. It's a finger-up to the hard-edge minimalism of the New York School and plays a very subversive and psychedelic game to combat the pop of Warhol and Lichtenstein.

Diane arranged for Martin to meet us at a Lebanese café not far from his show in Macleay Street. Diane told me it was Martin's favourite place. When he appeared in the doorway his eyes did something strange – they were cerulean blue and glittering like his internal inner light was beaming outwards. Blue – Martin's aura is the deepest blue.

Martin's natural charisma is astonishing. It was like being greeted by a rock star – as if Mick Jagger was walking up to our table. He sat down and I began to shake with excitement – the impact of the meeting was electric. Martin ordered cinnamon toast and strong Turkish coffee. We both knew this was the beginning of a special collaboration and friendship. Sydney was dead. Compared with London, New York and San Francisco nothing was happening here.

If the building where Martin is showing his work can be secured for art, we can create something like Warhol's Factory or Van Gogh's Yellow House. It's listed for demolition but Martin knows the owner, Ian Reid, and he's going to see if we can have it until the wrecking balls come. If I cannot do something like this, I will go mad from the boredom and oppression of Askin's Sydney and the pro-Vietnam Establishment of puppet PM John Gorton, or find a way to head back to New York.

Today is the beginning of something new.

This is not a pipe

The Little Prince

EXTRACT FROM YELLOW HOUSE DIARY, 1970

The Yellow House was really happening tonight.

Julian, Moth and I worked the last few days to adapt the aristocrat-pilot Antoine de Saint-Exupéry's book The Little Prince *into a play to be performed in the cloud room as a special surprise for Martin. Martin loves* The Little Prince *and to us he is the Little Prince – a stranger in this strange world seeking something that can never be found.*

I'm playing the fox, Moth is the rose and the desert flower while Julian, of course, played the prince. As well as our prime roles of fox and rose, Moth and I were required to act all the characters on the journey. At the climax Julian morphs from the prince into the yellow snake who bites the prince, and back to the dying prince again. It works like a suicide scene where the snake (Julian's arm) bites the prince, letting him leave the shell of his body behind and return to his asteroid with its three volcanoes and most importantly the rose that he loves.

As a way of welcoming our audiences and attracting passers-by, we do a street performance early in the evening. Tonight Little Nell joined us as she has done before but the big shock was that Martin, who is usually very shy, made a sudden appearance wearing a huge black fur coat – possibly bear – and performed a dance in the manner of the kind of dark spirit the coat had transformed him into. Then, like a wolf from a fairy tale, he whisked Nell back into the Cloud Room, leaving us and the onlookers a bit stunned.

We then rushed up to the puppet theatre to do our make-up. I didn't have anything for a fox costume so decided to go for full body decoration.

Our performances never go as we expect. Under pressure from Julian not to vocalise, Moth decided to do something between silence and speech for the rose – the strangest slow-motion voice, like something from another dimension. She also added lines not in the book or our script, lines of longing and hope that her prince will return. Moth left a real career with an Elizabethan touring company to join us – normally she would be doing Shakespeare. You could have heard a pin drop – the audience were spellbound. I knew this was really directed at Julian. Moth is obsessively in love with him but it is impossible for them to be anything but stage partners – Julian is completely gay. She thinks I am her rival for his affections but she should realise that's never going to happen.

Martin expressed his gratitude by taking Polaroids, like an Australian Warhol – the camera and its flash were his way of reacting. Jonny Lewis was there with bowler hat. Jonny is a natural-born enthusiast and gave the kind of appreciative feedback we craved after all the hard work.

After doing The Little Prince I had to jump into another role. Albie Thoms had persuaded me to perform in one of his plays for the Ubu collective. I had to make a special crocodile puppet. There was no make-up removal cream left back stage so I took both hands and streaked my fingers downwards – ending up with a brown-striped face, which was perfect, once I'd added a silver velvet cape. Albie is a great organiser and puts together the programs for each night of events. He chalks these on a blackboard which is displayed at the entrance to the Yellow House. I always feel that what we do is too far out for Albie, while we find his Dadaist and Absurdist productions boring. I am, however, going to do Eugène Ionesco's Rhinoceros in the puppet theatre next week. It is nothing like his The Chairs (which Albie directed), it is fanciful and full of lunacy and humour and fits our style perfectly.

After the Ubu play I had to transform again, this time into Khadir the Sufi Storyteller. I put my green turban/hat on. Still unable to find the make-up remover, so layered thick gooey white sandshoe-cleaner straight out of a tube over my previous make-up. It cracked and made me look ancient. This fitted my 'Seven Swords' story in every way. I performed with my face next to the dragon puppet whose tale it is. At the start, Moth played Julian's dulcimer and I made low tones on my flute and Julian emerged like a snake charmer's cobra from our large woven cane trunk. He has been unable to shake the yellow snake persona of the little prince. He freezes at the end of each show and waits for me to put him back in the cane basket and that's the end of our show. The puppet theatre was packed with people looking through the doorway so it was hard for me to get back in and grab Julian. I pushed my way past people squeezed together on the floor but, with Julian over my shoulder, I couldn't see myself making it to the corner where the trunk has its own little stage. I turned slowly around and carried him back out into the hallway. No-one was meant to follow but everyone did, so I placed him down and commenced my whirling dervish dance. Soon people began to spin with me – images from Magritte … Whiteley … Powditch … Martin and Bruce's strange chaise longue with polar bear skin … all flashed past like a surrealist dream movie. We were ecstatic and it was hard for me to wind down enough to perform my money-making role of a Kings Cross taxi driver. I couldn't find any normal clothes so pulled on the silk Chinese dragon jacket which had been a present from Bruce Goold, exchanged my turban for an orange beanie and once again searched for make-up remover. Impatient and pestered by audience members who always want to join our in-house circus, I headed for the taxi parked outside, thinking I would drive the cab back to my parents' house and find something to remove the make-up and have a good bath. I still had on full body paint.

My old St George cab was sitting there, patiently waiting. As soon as I pulled out from the kerb a few drunks opened the back door and insisted I take them to an all-night pub in Newtown. When we approached the Enmore end of King Street they claimed they didn't have any money. But when I turned around and they saw my horror movie face they couldn't get the cash out of their pockets fast enough and insisted I let them out short of their destination! Rid of them, I headed for Bardwell Park. I was low on petrol but sure I could make it. It was about 2am, so most garages were shut. When I hit the steep hill up to Earlwood, the engine started spluttering and stopped. Out of gas. I had no alternative but to lock the cab and walk up the hill to the Shell garage. I must have looked really convincingly monstrous because girls in a passing car screamed as if they had seen a werewolf and the car swerved like the driver was equally startled. When I got to the garage I filled a two-gallon tin from the bowser but when I went in to pay, the guys at the register were so terrified they told me to keep it and gestured for me to leave. This made me laugh which made them even more frightened.

Back at Darley Road, my parents' place, Mum and Dad are asleep in bed. I have a couple of cups of tea and am getting hyped up to go out on the road again. It is early Sunday morning – a good time to pick up passengers who have been partying and are too drunk or stoned to make their own way home.

One minute the fox in The Little Prince, *the next an Ubu crocodile, then a Sufi who turns into a werewolf and now a clean-cut taxi driver heading for the corruption and strip clubs of Kings Cross.*

While soaking in the bath I got an idea to adapt the old John Barrymore movie Svengali *for our next production. Through hypnotism and telepathic powers, a Rasputin-esque maestro controls the singing voice of the woman he is obsessed with, but his love is not returned.*

Experiencing the monster I became tonight makes me think I'm ready for this role.

Phantasmic Mr Fox

Martin and I were working on a Yellow House installation that needed some props. I decided we could possibly find them at the Salvation Army depot called Tempe Tip. Martin gave me the keys to his Mini Moke, an open-top, jeep-like vehicle that was the rage among the fashionable elite. A girl came with me. She did the occasional high-class escort gig for money and played around at the Yellow House with modelling and bohemian art but had no specific talent other than being incredibly beautiful. I put on my 'pimp' clothes from Carnaby Street and we set off looking every inch the fashionable young couple.

Tempe Tip used to act as a halfway house for prisoners close to release. It was a gradual way of introducing them back into society.

When I was young the notorious Fox Brothers were among my grandfather's circle of friends. They ran an army disposal store that was a front for an illegal bookie operation. I would sit and play with all the bits and pieces of military gear while my grandfather went inside and did business with the Fox Brothers. I was always told the Fox Brothers were hitmen. Then after I'd lost touch with that world came the news that they were gunned down on the front verandah of their home. I didn't know that one of the Fox Brothers had survived the shooting and gone to jail.

I was in the used clothing section with my companion when I came face to face with the remaining Fox brother. He was smiling wolfishly from ear to ear to see me – but mainly to see me 'doing so well'. He had seen my stylish vehicle as I drove in and liked my clothes. Then he looked at the girl and made a low whistle. 'Well, George! Old George would have been proud of you.'

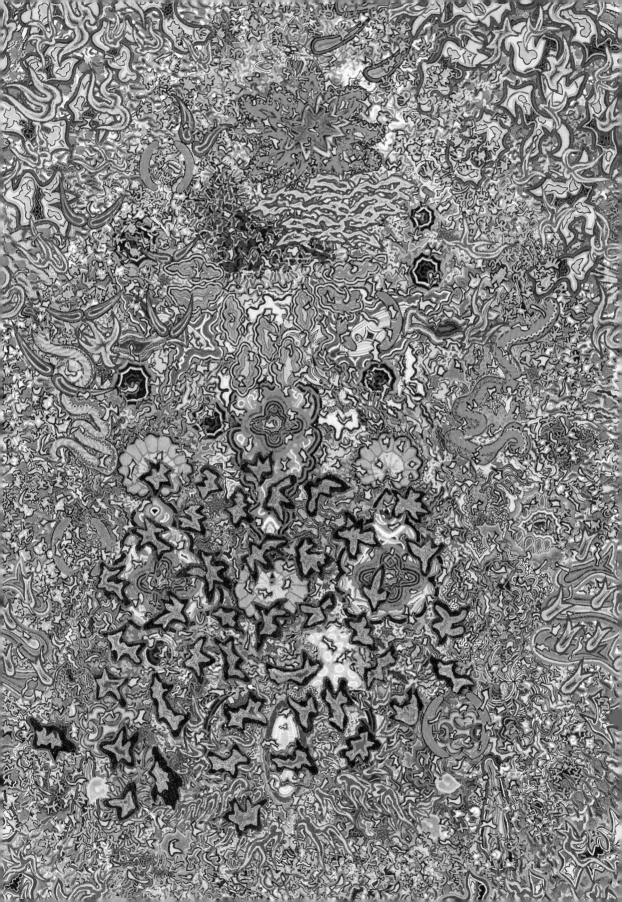

Arrival of Marie

This period at the Yellow House was one of the happiest of my life. With all my new friends I became less dependent on the letters to Marie. Marie had begun writing that we needed to come together and be married. I was only twenty-one, so I wrote back telling her I needed my freedom. The day my sister Pam gave birth to her daughter Selena, I was at the hospital and got a call from Bruce Goold. Marie had arrived and had come directly to the Yellow House where he had found her in the puppet theatre.

Just the day before I had sent her a telegram telling her not to come, that the circumstances were all wrong.

Marie and I rented a small apartment in Ross Street in Glebe, and I introduced her to what we were doing at the Yellow House.

When physically together everything was against us. Everything. A partnership with Marie meant too much loss of *my* self. She demanded a union from within, which, for me, was a terrible loss of clarity – it threw me into the dark.

TELEPHONE BOOK

EXTRACT FROM YELLOW HOUSE DIARY, 1970

All Sydney knows Kings Cross cops are among the most corrupt in the world and even our Premier is often described as 'Mr Big'. Sydney is becoming more like Gotham than New York. The Texas Tavern nightclub can overflow unchecked with prostitutes and drugs for visiting American GIs on R & R from Vietnam . . . yet artists like us aren't allowed to bring some fun and culture to the streets. Busking is common in NYC, but not tolerated in Sydney, even though we don't put a hat out for money. This is Askin's Sydney.

If strip club spruikers can get people through their doors, why can't we spruik for Yellow House? We decided to stage a love triangle on the main street. I was to be the tough roustabout to whom Colombine would give her heart and break Pierrot's in turn.

The Cross can be as dangerous as the Mekong jungle. Fuelled by speed and other drugs, partiers turn quickly to violence. Our way of psyching ourselves into it is to apply make-up, like soldiers putting on war paint. Julian wore his monochrome white face and I drew blue petals below Marie's eye, a pointy, blue cross on her forehead, and purple lips extending into fiery shapes.

Marie isn't a performer and was very nervous but when she looked in the mirror she said, 'It's like a mask– you have made me invisible!'

We left the Yellow House with a sense of 'fuck the police'. People smiled as we made our way up Macleay Street bringing art and a touch of the surreal to this dull city. By the time we reached the strip clubs we had collected a crowd. Bikers, who are part of the protection rackets and drug supply, joined a mix of street prostitutes and exotically dressed transvestites.

The atmosphere was electric. Drunks bantered with girls who saw potential clients. Trannies joined the act. We knew it might flash into violence at any time and it did when two cops appeared and grabbed me. When Julian came to my aid the sergeant said, 'That's the one we want'.

We were dragged around to the Victoria Street cop shop, taken to a back room and bashed with telephone books. Most of their abuse was aimed at Julian, calling him poofta, creep, pervert. We were both hit repeatedly over the head, arms and back and punched in the stomach. Julian was hit twice in the groin as a screaming Marie kept breaking into the room to let the cops know she was a witness. I think this is what got us free – otherwise it was going to be a night in a holding cell and more of the same.

We aren't masochists, but we were ecstatically happy. We had faced down the devil. Julian was so high on the experience he tried to walk like a tightrope walker on the fences of the terraces as we made our way back.

It was the happiest I've ever seen Marie.

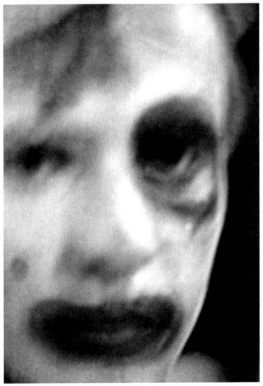

The Last Kiss

I can't blame Marie's despair on our poverty, or separation from her daughter. Her despair was caused by my refusal to commit.

We'd rented a room at Ross Street in Glebe and spent our time going to job interviews that failed. Our relationship had doom written all over it. On our final night together the room wasn't filled with butterflies but demon visions out of Grünewald's crucifixion triptych.

I was away the night when she took the pills. Marie had gone to a string of pharmacists then wrapped herself in a beautiful tapestry quilt she'd sewn as part of the glory box she'd sent ahead to celebrate our marriage.

On the train that day, I had seen a poisoned field of long grass and a road disappear into it and thought of Vincent's *Wheatfield with Crows*. I knew something tragic had happened.

On my arrival at the Yellow House, people were frozen like wax dummies. When I got to my puppet theatre, Martin came up, his face wet with tears. He said, 'Marie has gone'.

Glebe police took me from the Yellow House to the morgue. A metal drawer was pulled out, as if from a filing cabinet, and there she was. I kissed her lips before the cops could restrain me. Her face looked as if she'd been through terrible agony. Sleeping pills do not act like an anaesthetic and put you into deep sleep – as the kidneys fail there is torturous agonising pain. Some fluid had solidified on her lips and run down the side of one cheek. Her face was distorted like she'd been through a traumatic struggle – blue-black patches. Unforgettable. Unforgivable. My own torture through self-blame had only just begun.

All the dead bodies I have witnessed since are eclipsed by Marie's dead eyes – her face has made the realm of death my alternative home. My life is like Orpheus searching the underworld, returning with words and pictures but never able to reunite the part of me she took.

The night Marie killed herself I was madly trying to finish everything needed for the grand spring opening show at the Yellow House. I was in the studio fabricating a flying dragon when the blade I was using slipped and slashed the palm of my hand. I rushed myself to the doctor, but fainted in the reception and was hospitalised for the night. Which is the reason I wasn't with Marie when she made her fatal decision.

I was thrown into tortured darkness, but my sense of obligation saw me go to work on a set of Magritte-inspired murals in the entrance hall. I had just cleaned the paint from my hands with turpentine and was about to leave, when David Litvinoff approached me. He looked me straight in the eye and suggested I take my own life, that I follow Marie to be reunited in death.

David was a friend of Martin's from London, a court jester to the Chelsea set of the sixties. More famously, he inspired the Rolling Stones song, 'Jumpin' Jack Flash'. He was in trouble with the notorious Kray brothers, so Martin offered him a ticket to Australia and sanctuary at the Yellow House.

Either he wanted a poetic end to our romance, or he just wanted to get rid of me – I had never been able to put up with his bullshit monologues. But soon after that he went back to the UK and committed suicide after asking all his friends to a banquet at an expensive restaurant, knowing he wouldn't be present to pay the bill.

I threw myself even deeper into my work at the Yellow House.

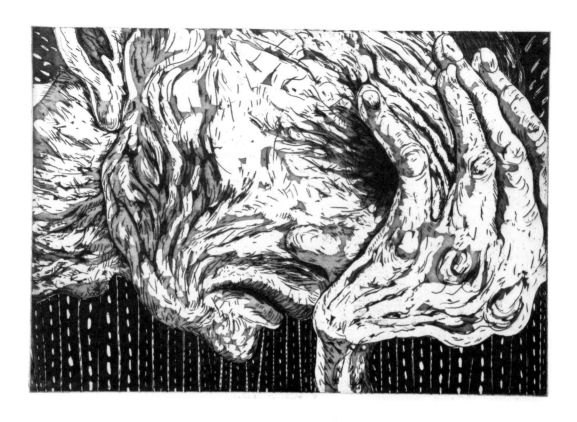

End of Yellow House

The spring show re-opening on 1 September 1971 at the Yellow House was its greatest moment – the total fulfilment of Martin's and my original dreams. People entered through our doors and left humdrum streets of Sydney behind, finding themselves in a dreamland of art installations, original music, theatre, puppets and avant-garde film screenings. It was totally immersive. The artists had put down their brushes and turned into performers in full face make-up, exotically costumed and interacting with the audience in a way guaranteed to open the doorways of their minds to unimaginable experiences.

But after this peak moment we were invaded by a barbarian horde of freaks and hippies pushing to convert the Yellow House into a commune. One night there was a meeting, or rather coup d'état, which Martin and I were excluded from. We were brought in at the end to be told it was more important to create living spaces where the new age lifestyle could be flaunted, naked and free, than to have spaces dedicated to art. Their plan was that the Yellow House could help to usher in the new Age of Aquarius. Art would be substituted for tie-dyed clothes and beads – that there was no need to paint walls and sculpt environments when a tab of acid could transcend straight reality, totally.

A few nights later the Yellow House was packed, not with art lovers but with performing freaks, cult leaders, gurus and runaway kids high on drugs. Standing out from the rest of the throng was Fred Robinson with a white beard

and hair resembling Michelangelo's God from the Sistine Chapel. Fred had his followers surrounding him, including a couple of our most serious Yellow House artists who were recent converts to his cult. Fred prophesied the world was about to experience a second coming of Jesus who was actually an alien and would re-enter our world through the clouds in a flying saucer.

My mother had made beautiful hanging ceramics which held candles and projected flickering shadow patterns. One of the hippies, while balancing on a table, hit his head on the lamp and went into a mad frenzy of revenge, smashing it to pieces before our eyes while several others cheered. To me this moment marked the end of our art experiment. Drug-induced hallucinations didn't need the art of the Yellow House to find revelation – a storm water tunnel could be as interesting as the Magritte Stone Room and a bus terminal as uplifting as my Puppet Theatre.

Martin turned to me and said, 'It's over'. He was right and we both moved on.

A few days later, Martin and I were having a late breakfast in a café across the road when he looked up from a newspaper listing new statistics of casualties in Vietnam and said, 'We should be doing the Yellow House in Hanoi – that's where we're needed'. Neither of us knew how this could be achieved but now, when I return to Australia with photos and films of our Jalalabad Yellow House, I know Martin's dream is alive and well and functioning in Afghanistan.

ALBION'S WOMB
OVER THE ARCH.

I came to George with
faith in God + ...

It would be the exit — to stay. But perfection is not here.

I see without awareness.

God Bless

Yellow House Jalalabad

Kabul sits high in the mountains of the Hindu Kush, which is the back end of the Himalayas.

As we swerve around hair-pin bends and pass through roughly hewn mountain tunnels, I always think of the British retreat in 1842, the worst defeat in British military history, when 4,500 troops and over 12,000 civilians under the command of Major General William Elphinstone were slaughtered in the snow and ice by the mountain tribesmen. Only one European officer, assistant surgeon William Brydon, made it to Jalalabad.

The harsh grey granite rock face is impervious to mercy and still seems to hold, imprisoned, the spirits of lives lost here. Present death is everywhere with burned-out wrecks of oil tankers, tanks and cars from recent Taliban attacks appearing from a failed Jurassic Park of twisted metal monsters.

But any trepidation about the journey is swept away by the sublime magnificence of the fertile valley plateaus that appear like dream landscapes. No matter how many times I do this drive I always gasp when I first see the fields and ancient adobe villages spread out

below. I turn to Hellen and smile to be sharing it – there is no greater sense of adventure than entering this ancient world – knowing few outsiders will ever take the risk to see what we are seeing. In the valley rims there are ancient cities made from mud brick and stone and built around deep caves full of amazing secrets which I yearn to explore.

Fish from the mountain river streams is caught and cooked in small roadside restaurants above the valleys. Hellen and I choose one where we can sit, eat and watch from one of these eagle perches as the farmers and shepherds with their flocks move about ant like below – nothing about the way they live having changed in thousands of years.

As we finish lunch Hellen places her burqa back on and the wind catches in the blue fabric, billowing out, allowing this oppressive garment to take on a cloud-like beauty against the rich green of the rice fields below.

Hellen has been testing herself with me in the tribal belt of Pakistan and Afghanistan for a few years now and has more than proven she is up for this gig. We met at an artist's squat called the Gunnery, in Woolloomooloo. It was 1991 and I had been invited to come and support a group of punk artists who had taken over a former Navy training building and turned it into one of the most exciting creative spaces Sydney had seen since our Yellow House twenty years earlier. There is nothing arts bureaucrats hate more than artists working outside their influence, free of constraint. The Australia Council for the Arts had decided they wanted the building to expand their administrative headquarters and were using the law to turn the artists out.

The Gunnery artists were hoping older artists with a similar history of creating creative spaces would rally to their side and help defeat the grey monster.

I walked into a domed space which had been used for testing weapons. Hellen stood in the spotlight of a dark stage singing a haunting abstract song, without accompaniment. Her super high stiletto heels showed off her showgirl legs in fishnet stockings rising to tight leather shorts and top. She moved like a panther and when she turned to me I was smitten, but I was a father with two small kids. It would be two decades before we came together as a couple.

Now, as we approach the checkpoints, at the entrance to Jalalabad city, Hellen tightens her burqa and tilts her head down in the abject manner expected of women when coming under the gaze of men and I slip into my persona of an old white bearded local wearing religious pill box cap and typical Pashtun clothes. Mohammad's car is anything but foreign looking with its metallic stickers praising the Name of Allah and we are waved through without being searched or requested to show passports.

The stretch of the road from where we had lunch is one of the most dangerous for ambushes and attacks. The villages on either side of the road are sympathetic to the Taliban.

Today we make it safely down the road but a truck thirty minutes ahead of us had been hit by rockets and we pass it, burning, its tyres melted into the bitumen. Afghan special forces are all around it. The driver has been kidnapped.

In Jalalabad, the painted faces on the backs of the little motorized rickshaws that transport people around the city make us feel at home. One rickshaw shows an old election poster of my neighbour friend the general, and below it a painted action scene with my friend the actor Abbaz who starred in our film *Starless Night*. Half the rickshaws have paintings on the back of the drivers' favourite actors, with guns and knives and handlebar moustaches and a lot of blood, from the kind of Pakistani films I've helped to make. The bizarre thing for me is that I know all these actors intimately and I've gradually become more a part of this culture than I am of Australian culture.

As always in this bustling city built for horse and donkey carts the traffic is bumper-to-bumper slow but I never mind as every sight on the way has a memory of a day of filming in its streets. This whole city has become a giant set for the many movies we have filmed here and most of the people I see wave and call out 'Hey Bubba', reassurance that I'm still one of its best-known personalities. We never enter Jalalabad as outsiders but as members of the community.

Once, for our movie *Love City*, we had a large banner made with LOVE CITY or MINI HAH (the same in Pashto) printed on it in white on a pink and rose red background. Hellen sang 'What the World Needs Now' from the back of an open rickshaw and we drove it through Jalalabad to rename it 'Love City'. Those we passed responded with cheers and smiles and supportive gestures – what we feared a dangerous gauntlet became

A GITTOES FILM WITH BURAQ PRODUCTIONS

MOON LIGHT

مون لائٹ

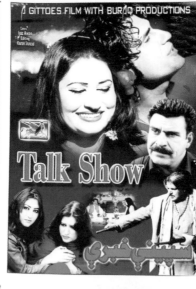

A GITTOES FILM WITH BURAQ PRODUCTIONS

Talk Show

سپین خبرې

A GITTOES FILM WITH BURAQ PRODUCTION

گډوونکي کيسه

THE TAILORS STORY

Moon Light

مون لائٹ

Directed by
George Gittoes

Design by
Dalton & Gittoes Production

A GITTOES FILM WITH BURAQ PRODUCTIONS

دميس سبار
LOVE CITY

A GITTOES FILM WITH BURAQ PRODUCTIO

STARLESS NIGHT

ستارليس نائٹ

A Gittoes Film

نوکرات

SABAH CD HOUSE
CHOWK NISHTRA BAD PESHAWAR Ph:2217777

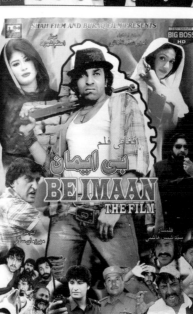

SHAH FILM AND BURAQ FILM PRESENTS

BIG BOSS
HD

افسانتی فلم
بی ایمان
BE IMAAN
THE FILM

The Miscreants of Taliwo

A Gittoes Film

GEORGE GITTOES' EXTREME TOUR OF TERROR CENTRAL

a celebration of joy. We wanted to declare the time of war over. A new time of peace, love and art was about to begin.

Turning into the street of the Yellow House I am thinking we will come up to our big blue metal gate and surprise everyone, but this is not to be. Mohammad, our driver, has rung ahead and everyone is out on the street with arms open to welcome us.

Ishrad our cook, rotund with a waxed moustache, is the most profuse and as well as a hug he plants a big kiss on my lips before I can turn my cheek to avoid it. All our principals are here – Neha the beautiful movie star originally from Pakistan, Amir Shah the Action Hero and co-founder of the Yellow House, Waqar, my close friend and assistant from the beginning, Majrooh the director of Afghan Films for Jalalabad, a true gentleman with blood links to the former king and royal family, and Ashid, the small person who Hellen and I love like an adopted son and who I pick up and carry with me into the Yellow House Garden.

Hellen can only begin embracing everyone once she has entered the protection of our high-walled garden and is no longer under the judgmental gaze of our neighbours and the street. Neha has been waiting for a few days, a lone woman surrounded by men in a culture that demands women always be chaperoned by a male relative, so she is relieved to see her 'sister', Hellen. Our Kuchi dog, Ezmarai, is now huge and, standing on her hind legs, she licks Hellen on the face. I saved Ezmarai from the streets when she was a pup – covered in ticks and just skin and bone.

The two peacocks prance up, extending their necks to inspect our attire. Our roses are in full bloom. Our white rabbit now has a male friend – probably a mistake – and a tabby cat has made the Yellow House home.

Our artistic family is relieved to have their matriarch and patriarch back. As usual we have lots of presents and surprises to share. Plus, we are bringing new equipment like Apple computers for editing, a camera drone and new digital movie cameras which everyone with their thirst for technological development is keen to start familiarizing themselves with.

I tell them the truth is that I really do not know what the film we are going to make this time will be about but I know it will be a good one. As usual the whole team will put in their ideas until we have found our subject. Everyone agrees that Daesh (ISIL) – often referred to as IS or ISIS, particularly in the press – is spreading its message and having talks with militant elements of the Taliban. This may not be good for us. We've gone from the Arab Spring to a kind of contagious fire that's jumping borders like bushfires jump roads.

The Yellow House building has never been inhabited by anyone before us – it had been built and left semi-derelict until we took the lease and fixed it up, so there are no ghosts or past vibes from previous residents.

Our kitchen looks out onto the garden and relies on gas burner stoves. We do not have refrigeration and our water comes from a well in the garden and needs an electric pump to keep it flowing.

Ishrad, or Itchy as we all call him, is preparing a homecoming feast and has the kettle boiling and a plate of sweet cookies and cakes ready on a tray.

AMIR SHAH

Amir Shah is why I'm back in Afghanistan. I had done such an impassioned talk after the screening of my film *Miscreants of Taliwood* at the International Documentary Festival Amsterdam, that people from Oxfam asked me to look at other forms of aid beyond the necessities of food and clean water. I said the threat from the fundamentalist Taliban to the livelihood of film workers in Pakistan was causing real suffering. They agreed to help fund three Pashtun dramas and I returned to Pakistan to work with all my old friends.

The wild adventures I had filming *The Flood*, *Moonlight* and *Starless Night* would require a book of their own. I was mopping up these projects when Amir Shah arrived at the SS Club where I stay in Peshawar. He made an impassioned plea for the filmmakers of Jalalabad.

Amir Shah is the youngest son of old parents. As the baby of the family he's been indulged in atypical ways for Pashtun culture. He's from Laghman Province, outside Jalalabad, and his father is a respected elder. His dad reminds me of my father, who believed in my artistic ambitions and tried to assist me in every practical way.

Amir Shah is a self-taught filmmaker. He's had to finance his career from what he can earn. He would labour, unloading bags of cement and grain from trucks at night, and use the money to shoot his movie in the day.

When Hellen and I are back in Australia he not only maintains the Yellow House but pushes it forward.

The word for Amir Shah is *indomitable*.

On the first day of shooting for Amir's new action movie, *Be Imaan*, we met him on top of the mountain near circular ruins of a Buddhist temple. He was in an heroic stance with his arms stretched out in triumph.

When Amir saw our drone he immediately wanted to use it for the spectacular opening sequence of his action-chase movie. In the first phase Neha and Amir Shah are being chased by their enemies, then Neha is captured before Amir Shah chases her captors to save her. These scripts are like Marvel Comics with Amir Shah as a superhero. Using his martial arts skills, he overcomes enemies vastly superior in number. In his last film, he fought a gang of twenty enemies, having already disposed of fifteen with martial arts moves. With a tyre in each hand he spun around like a dervish, mowing them down with the force of a Mack Truck. But Amir can overestimate his abilities.

Seeing Neha push the envelope of what a woman can do in this rigid society by rollerskating, Amir Shah decided to purchase speed skates for yet another chase scene in his movie. He had a bad guy tie Neha up, riding pillion on a motorbike, and speed down the road with their heavy machine guns, like a scene out of *Mad Max*, while he chased on skates. It looked fantastic . . . for a few seconds before the bikes got too far ahead. But with each retake Amir Shah got slower and more dishevelled.

Between takes, large US military convoys, fuel tankers, Afghan Special forces and farmers drove by. None seemed at all surprised by seeing action man Amir Shah on rollerskates.

ENTER THROUGH DRAMA

I agree with Picasso when he advised, 'I do not seek, I find'. My documentaries use a mix of fiction and real events which audiences can find unsettling, not knowing what is real and what is invented. I have probably come up with this style as a way of processing the bizarre situations I keep placing myself in. As Itchy pours tea, I tell the Yellow House crew my idea of the film.

Snow Monkey will open with a small monkey foraging for food in the snow against the majestic backdrop of the mountains above Tora Bora. Two figures will trudge past and the monkey will watch them curiously before scuttling to catch up and springing up to the shoulder of the taller man, who allows the monkey to hitch a ride. They stop and look down on the city of Jalalabad.

Night has fallen. The camera moves down an ancient walled street in the Old City of Jalalabad. A fist pounds on the blue gate of the Yellow House artists' collective. The artist occupants are sitting around a gas fire listening to musicians playing traditional instruments. The music stops when the knocking is heard and pump-action shotguns taken from the hoojrah wall as volunteers go to check the gate. The two men we have seen coming from the mountains with the monkey are asking to be allowed in from the cold.

As the tall man bends to enter, the hosts gasp with surprise. The man is unmistakably Osama bin Laden. He's with a young Saudi prince and they're quietly asking for sanctuary and protection. They are welcomed in and offered a hot tea and a meal. Gittoes is delighted to see the monkey. It is his monkey, which had been stolen and he never expected to see this little friend, named Dali, again. Bin Laden is pleased to have been able to reunite them and tells how he has converted to Buddhism. He now wants to help bring about an era of peace and love. This is compatible with the aims of the Yellow House artists and thus the story begins as Gittoes and Bin Laden agree to collaborate.

KAGAME

I went to the Congo to research a documentary I was calling 'Heart of Darkness'. I ended up in Bukavu when the Rwandan Patriotic Army, under the instruction of their president, Paul Kagame, was killing Hutu.

My sidekick was Patience Lamumba, a former Jesuit priest studying Political Science at Durban University. All around Bukavu City were mass graves but these were too dangerous for a white man to film, so Patience introduced me to a priest who was politically active on behalf of his mainly Hutu church congregation. He told terrible stories of burning embers being forced into women's vaginas before they were buried alive.

I gave the priest a small video camera and he began filming this kind of atrocity for my documentary. Intermediaries were supposed to get the tapes to me secretly but the priest filmed something so brutal and therefore so dangerous he couldn't wait to get it to us through an intermediary. He drove out to where we were staying, unaware he was being followed by a vehicle. While we were sitting at the table with the camera and tapes visible I looked up and saw soldiers pressing their faces to the window. Fortunately, Patience was out visiting the cathedral, the door was locked and it was a very sturdy door. As the soldiers banged on the door and tried to push it in with their shoulders and gun butts, I had time to hand the offending tapes and camera to the children at the back door, tell them to take them to Patience and warn him to stay away. When I got back to the room the soldiers had broken in and put me under house arrest. The kids with the evidence vanished into the night.

Knowing something like this was on the cards I'd met the previous night with Horhe Holly, the Venezuelan UN representative in Bukavu, and the only other foreigner, a brave Australian nurse who was running a clinic nearby. Horhe Holly had been found by the children and had received the tapes. Still, the chances of my surviving this wasn't good. My photographs and stories about the Kibeho massacre were well known to Rwandan intelligence and Mossad. And what we had witnessed in Bukavu pointed the finger of blame straight at Kagame and his merciless RPA soldiers.

A Rwandan officer walked in with what I thought was my death warrant and put me in a car with two other soldiers. Throughout the drive I expected at any moment to be shot and my body dumped in the jungle. But to my surprise the officer drove me to an airport on the border, let me free and even walked me to the office with my passport, Holly's bribe snug in his pocket.

I got a message to Patience that I would wait in Kigali until I knew he was safely in Nairobi with the tapes. If he was caught I told him he was to tell his captors he was carrying the tapes for George Gittoes, did not know what was on them and that I could be arrested in a certain hotel in Kigali where I would tell them of his innocence. I probably should have told him to burn the tapes. If they had gotten into the wrong hands everyone on them would have been arrested and killed.

On my way back from this meeting I bumped into Kagame's private secretary. When he saw me his eyes popped out on sticks

ot enough
back to
wrong
together in layer upon layer of heavy drapes.

like a cartoon character. Utterly exposed, I improvised and told him I was about to visit his office to ask permission for an official portrait sitting with President Kagame. This was so outrageous a lie it caught him by surprise yet he told me he could 'arrange it for tonight but as you know the president likes the dark. Someone will come for you at 8pm sharp.'

I was bracing for a trap and my heart was in my mouth when the knock came precisely at 8pm. The soldiers were accompanied by a very smart woman who described herself as Kagame's personal assistant. In the reception area of the Palace the screen was frozen images I'd taken of Kibeho and shown on my website. Not for the first time, I realized a google search could be my downfall. It was certain now Kagame knew my work had been used in the case against the officers who carried out the Kibeho massacre and would later be used at their trials.

I was led down a series of long corridors. Finally, Kagame himself met me at the door with arm out-stretched for a handshake

and a big smile as if he was being reunited with an old friend. He showed me an ANZAC hat which had been given to him by an Australian general and pointed to a chair for me to commence work. He asked if I needed anything but I had all I needed. Kagame began to talk as I drew, getting things off his chest – admitting to all sorts of things to do with this terrible war.

My fears receded. Kagame just needed someone to talk to. In this very Catholic country the president could not count on any priest as his father confessor so an artist would do – someone interested enough to want to do his portrait and who had witnessed his killing machine in action. Kagame said, 'George, I was in Uganda, just a day's march away, and I had the most professional, best-trained army in Africa. I told the Americans just to give me the okay and the genocide would have been over in less than a week – but they wouldn't. A million or more died and they needn't have – you and the world saw how quickly my army took control.'

He didn't talk about the retaliation that started at Kibeho, or the millions who have been reportedly killed by his men in the Congo. I was painting a portrait of evil personified; he just wanted me to see him as a reasonable guy.

After Kagame talked through the night, with my drawing finished I persuaded him to come outside for a photo. But once in the light he was in real and obvious pain, like a vampire. After just a few photos he needed to get back to the dark. But we re-entered at the wrong point and found ourselves trapped together in layer upon layer of heavy drapes. The curtains were the length of the Presidential Office which was the size of a basketball court. The more we struggled the more frantic Kagame got. I was lost in the dark with a man responsible for the soldiers who were responsible for the deaths I had witnessed at Kibeho, whom hours before I had feared would have me killed.

Back inside we shook hands.

If Kibeho was a horror movie, it's possible I'd just met Count Dracula himself.

Kibeho was a refugee camp around a Catholic
Mary, mother of Jesus, had appeared in va
all over the country because they t
Mother. The Rwandan Patriotic Army is
this as an opportunity to slaughter the
herded together like cattle, and woul
knew they were going to die. Much o
were used rather than guns. The moth

ALIVE

tral and girls school. For many years
ty form to the girls. People came from
they would be protected by the Virgin
and commanded by Kagame, they saw
mass. When I arrived they were
their fingers across their necks – they
killing happened at night and Machete
oats were cut and babies left to die.

DEAD

APRIL 21–24 1995

Waqar

Over the last nine years Waqar Alam has become my closest friend and best mate, risking his life for me on more occasions than I can remember. When I met him in 2007 he was a University of Peshawar student working with the International Campaign to Ban Landmines (ICBL). At that time George Bush was describing the tribal belt as Terror Central and bin Laden was thought to be taking sanctuary there. It was and still is where the Pakistani Taliban are based. It's not possible to go to these places now and aid is out of the question. Continuous American drone attacks have made the militants totally paranoid about foreigners, even the Red Cross.

After I'd made *Soundtrack to War* in Iraq through 2003 and 2004, and then its partner film *Rampage* in Miami through 2005 and 2006, Raza Shah, the Pakistani president of ICBL, was annoyed with me that I hadn't used my knowledge of Pakistan's North-West Frontier Province to shine a light on the many misunderstandings about the Pashtun world.

I knew I admired the proud, courageous and generous nature of Pashtuns, but I arrived without a plan. The Pashtun film industry was unknown to me until Raza gave me a bunch of their DVDs. None of the actors or directors had been to film school or had any training yet they had invented a unique style of filmmaking full of colour and pathos.

Every day, in Peshawar's *Frontier Post*, I'd been reading of bomb attacks on video and music stores. All through history bad guys like Hitler and Pol Pot have come down on artists and freedom of expression, and the Taliban had joined that club. If I was going to get into this fight I should take the side of art. Whenever the Taliban blew up a video store they would leave a note describing the filmmakers as miscreants.

Raza introduced me to his friend Tariq Jamal who owned the largest furniture store in town and used the profits to finance his films. Tariq is an imposing character with the persona of a grand Shakespearean actor and is regarded as the most serious producer in this business. We hit it off and, as well as agreeing to let me film his new production titled *Family*, he wanted me to play a role as one of the patriarchs in a feud between families. There was no problem with my looks as I pass as a member of the Shinwari (Blue Eyes) clan and he was happy to coach me with the lines I would have to deliver in Pashto. He gave me a script and told me to prepare as in a few days we would be filming in a former ski resort in Kalam, high in the mountains.

I'd arranged to meet a militant professor at the University of Peshawar and a student of his to guide us to a clandestine location. The guy that jumped into the back seat introduced himself as Waqar Alam. He was small and handsome with pitch-black hair and very

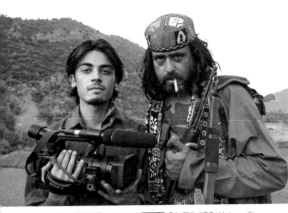

Halt! No.

intelligent eyes. I was ignoring him while discussing the Kalam shoot with my assistant when Waqar broke in, telling me the advice the assistant was giving could get me killed. I listened to Waqar and immediately offered him a job. When we met the radical fundamentalist professor I watched Waqar make him feel comfortable with a foreigner and his cameras. The professor treated us with extreme civility, answering questions about bin Laden that would normally have made him highly defensive. Waqar even got him bragging about his influence on extremist thought, which was exactly what I needed.

Waqar is a charmer and a genuinely devout Muslim. These two aspects have engendered trust from the most unlikely people.

Waqar was in the early days of becoming my right-hand man and second camera cinematographer. On a day when I wasn't required to act we were filming some love scenes in a forest – involving Rheema and the male lead miming a song played on a boom box. The loud music echoed through the trees, attracting an ever-growing audience of locals. Tariq and the cast were too involved with the shooting to sense the tension building in these simple and devout forest folk. Suddenly a group of Taliban sympathisers arrived to put an end to what they saw as gross decadence. We were told that what we were doing was un-Islamic. Tariq argued his cause of freedom of expression until the oldest and most vocal man in the group took out a revolver and pointed it at Tariq's heart, shouting they couldn't allow their wives and children to see such immorality. Tariq said, 'Okay, it's a wrap', and told everyone to pack up and get ready to leave.

Waqar and I had kept rolling throughout – this was exactly what we needed for our documentary. I decided to follow the group of nasties with my camera and try to get them to explain their action, but a younger man now had the revolver and turned on me.

He pointed it at my head while putting his hand over my lens and pulled the trigger. If the gun hadn't misfired I wouldn't be here writing.

Muslims in the tribal belt are strong in their belief that death only comes when Allah decides – this misfire was seen as a sign and I was left to survive with my camera. My first reaction was to check that Waqar had been rolling on this. These guys weren't going to tolerate a retake and my luck might not have lasted for a second pull of the trigger. I got the thumbs-up from Waqar that he had it 'in the can'. Filmmakers are a bit nuts. I should've been traumatised by this near-death experience but I was just incredibly excited that this encounter had gotten my doc over a hump – footage like this is a diamond in the crown.

The first big test of Waqar came with the siege of the Red Mosque in Islamabad. We had returned from Kalam and Tariq was shooting missing scenes in rural areas outside the city. It was a big day for me because it was the day where my character gets shot. There's a lot of blood in Pashto films and it's done the old-fashioned way. A small explosive is fixed with a detonator to the target's chest, or wherever they're going to be hit by the bullet, and a plastic bag full of blood is taped in front of it – a wire leads to a battery trigger. The special-effects guys who wire up the actors are usually professional technicians who come down from the big studios in Lahore to do the job. Tariq had used one of these guys in Kalam and I was impressed. But Tariq couldn't get them to travel and so the guy wiring me up was a low-cost local with homemade equipment.

The explosive put on my chest seemed huge, as was the bag of fake blood. As he fiddled with the detonator, I heard in background chatter that one of the other actors had refused to do it as someone had recently died when his heart stopped after being blown backward by an over-powerful explosion. I gently suggested the technician move the device closer to my

stomach than my heart. Ultimately, when the blast happened and I realised I was still alive, I was so shocked I forgot to act, making my death look fake and hammy – great for my documentary but not so for Tariq's drama.

While this was going on I'd noticed people taking calls on their phones and huddling around a radio broadcasting the news. I walked over to Waqar with fake blood dripping through my clothes and asked him what was going on. He told me the Taliban had taken control of the Red Mosque in Islamabad only a few blocks away from the seat of government.

I decided we needed to drive to Islamabad straightaway and film as the government's forces surrounded and laid siege to the mosque's compound. This was a huge moment in Pakistan history and coverage of this bare-faced attempt at taking power by the Taliban, whether symbolic or real, would be essential to our story.

Once in Islamabad we found many city blocks cordoned off by the military and the Red Mosque area declared a war zone. All media were being turned away and told it was a sealed operation. I now saw a different side of Waqar. He didn't accept no for an answer even when it came from heavily armed soldiers and police. He'd been working for me only for a couple of weeks but was as dedicated to getting to the heart of things as any seasoned frontline journalist.

He told me to follow him through a shop then took me through twists and turns around back alleys until we were on a very wide road. I didn't expect to see cars because of the road-blocks, but there were no people in sight either. It was spookily quiet. Waqar kept marching on, his shoulders bent forward, his steps full of determination. My years of experience in war zones told me something was wrong – the hairs were up on the back of my neck and I could feel unseen eyes watching us.

We arrived at high walls painted a dull red and heard a banging on the gates behind us. Then there were heads calling to us from above the wall and four men jumped down in front of us. I was startled, expecting them to display weapons. Instead they put their hands up like in an American movie and surrendered themselves to us. Only then did I realise Waqar had taken us right up to the gates of the Red Mosque. I could be certain many sniper rifles were pointing directly at us and officers were watching every move we made through their binoculars. Waqar and I were wearing traditional Pashtun clothes with prayer hats and had nothing to distinguish us as journalists other than our cameras. The men who'd jumped from the wall were deserters from the jihadists in the mosque, so it was just as likely the mosque's defenders could also open fire on us.

Waqar began explaining that they'd made a huge mistake. We weren't Pakistani special forces soldiers sent to help them escape. When that realisation hit them I could see absolute terror in their eyes and they seemed to be saying, 'We are all going to die'. Waqar told them to keep their hands up and slowly walk to where we guessed the army and police would be taking cover from the snipers in the mosque. We could go with them, which would mean the confiscation of our cameras and a lot of interrogation, but we braved the marksmen and took the huge risk of crossing back over the road and disappearing into one of the side streets.

Once out of range we turned on our cameras and filmed the four deserters slowly making their way to the fate that awaited them. The stress and summer heat hit us and we walked to the shade of an abandoned mosque. Inside, the compound was peaceful. We washed our faces and hands and took our shoes off and washed our feet as worshippers do before prayer.

The big doors of the mosque were closed so Waqar told me to rest while he searched for a high vantage point where we could film the siege. I was grateful for the chance to rest but soon became worried when he didn't return. I went to look around, leaving the cameras and gear on the bench. There was no sign of Waqar and I knew in the pit of my stomach something had happened to him. When I returned to the bench my alarm went deeper – both cameras had disappeared. Hours passed while I waited. I started forming things in my head to say to his parents. Finally, some senior police officers appeared to tell me Waqar was okay and had been detained with the cameras.

We were in a lot of trouble but I didn't care because Waqar was alive. I was told I would be charged for trespass in the mosque, disobeying a police cordon and not having a film permit from the Department of the Interior. These were heavy charges that could see me deported. I argued my case but I think it was my genuine concern for Waqar that won the officer over. Waqar arrived smiling with relief and the cameras over his shoulders and we were freed.

Waqar later told me he'd made his way to the top of the mosque only to bump into a special forces squad of snipers using the position to observe the Red Mosque. They'd confiscated the cameras and forced Waqar to show them what was on the tapes. He'd cleverly fast-forwarded the tapes so they appeared blank. Then when they got him to wind back he managed to stop at spots where the footage was unimportant, knowing when they ordered him to wipe it nothing of value would be lost. Waqar had acted with the nerve and savvy of a newsman twice his age. I was very proud of him.

SALVAGE

I n some ways Waqar has spoilt me. The period I have worked with him in Pakistan and now Afghanistan has been the longest time I have spent in any single war zone.

Waqar has been my constant interpreter, confidant and protector. It wasn't always this way. Sometimes my guide has their own agenda, as when I found myself being led into a death trap in the Philippines by the person I thought had been assigned to my protection.

SMOKEY MOUNTAIN, MANILA, PHILIPPINES, 1989

For weeks I've been hearing from frightened leftist activists about comrades who've been 'salvaged'. A salvage is when a political prisoner is systematically tortured. Grotesque sadistic techniques are used – the victims are kept alive for days while every part of their body is violated and brutalised. The aim of the perpetrators of the torture is to send out the message 'there is more to fear than death' – that any dissent can lead to a similar fate. The mangled body is left in front of the house of the victim's family or in a more public place where the whole community can see it.

Today I witnessed the result of a salvage first-hand. I'd arranged to meet community theatre activists at Smokey Mountain, the large rubbish dump near the ports outside Manila. These activists have been working with the urban poor who live on what can be scavenged and recycled out of the rubbish. The group have adapted Christian passion plays to become vehicles for social protest. Over Easter, the Stations of the Cross are enacted in places of shame to embarrass the government. I'd taken with me one of the papier-mâché masks of Jesus Christ from the organisation's headquarters as a prop to use in my photographs.

At that time Smokey Mountain was a totally militarised no-go zone. I needed safe passage to get there, so a friend took me to a secret location where I met with the leader of the Sparrows, an all-female terrorist group. When I entered, my friend was told to stay outside. He instantly warned me not to enter but it was too late, I went in. I was assigned a young female revolutionary zealot. En route, she stopped our taxi and ordered me to get out. She'd been carrying an Uzi submachine gun in her handbag and used it to indicate where she wanted me to go. Under the road bridge, two girls were holding their noses and pointing to a body saying, 'Dead man! Dead man!' Although his face was smashed, I recognised the body of someone I'd met at the headquarters the previous week. His name

126

was Mark and he was one of the theatre workers I'd hoped to photograph with the Christ mask.

Instinctively I sensed a set-up – if I was kidnapped or killed by these right-wing vigilante torturers, it would draw international condemnation from the media and this would be useful to the leftist revolutionary cause of the girl pointing the gun. I took my photographs carefully, knowing they needed to be published – the world needed to see what was being done. I focused and moved around the corpse while knowing it could only be minutes before these bad people came for me too. The Sparrow woman wanted me to return to the high ground of the road where the taxi had dropped us and where we would be highly visible to the vigilantes – she was prepared to sacrifice her own life so long as I was taken. I refused to do what she wanted.

I went to the nearest shanty hut, somewhere Mark would've been known through his work with the Jesuits. The old man sitting outside was unaware of the salvage and was sceptical, so he got me to describe it in detail. He began to cry and, satisfied I was telling the truth, he called to his two sons and ran the risk of asking them to guide me to safety.

The Sparrow girl was looking conflicted – her gun waving from side to side in her hand. This wasn't the plan, but I could see total fear in her eyes. It's one thing to agree to go on a mission that could mean being tortured like Mark and another to see and imagine the things that were done to him and then maintain resolve. I said, 'You don't have to die here – we can get out of this'. The old man reiterated my pleas and she snapped out of her indecision and decided for life. Within minutes we found ourselves being pursued by machine gun-carrying vigilantes.

Regardless of the conditions I'm unable to cancel my creative directive. I'd come with the mask of Christ and I was going to use it. I stepped into the smoke haze at the top of the mountain and got one of the boys to pose with it. The boy automatically stretched his arms out as the crucified Christ. As I worked with my camera, an old woman was bending over collecting reusables from the rubbish. She had a grey shawl over her head and shoulders and kept her eyes fixed on us. She resembled a goddess from Greek mythology described as an ancient crone. My mind wandered to another time and place, thousands of years in the past – I was in a state of shock and had to shake myself out of it to survive in the present.

The boys indicated that our pursuers had our 'scent' and were getting closer. We followed them, running until we got to an open bog like a lake of black mud stretching hundreds of metres wide. I had to make the decision whether to try to cross it or go around. The boys said crossing was too risky – we could sink and be smothered by the ooze. But the smoke haze that had been obscuring us from our pursuers had lifted and I estimated that trying to get around it would mean capture or being shot. I opted to cross the mud. The boys wouldn't come and I didn't want to risk them further. We could see where we were going and no longer needed guides.

The Sparrow and I headed in, sinking to our chests in this putrid mud formed with fetid tidal water from the decay of garbage and the dead bodies of those either too poor to be buried or dumped by their murderers. This was the most nightmarish situation I'd ever been in. I could see our pursuers – they had opted to go around, so we needed to beat them to the other side.

Finally, we dragged ourselves out of the mud, black with filth. A bunch of recyclers had been watching the contest and came running over to us with buckets of water, splashing them on us to wash off some of the mud. I spotted a motorbike taxi and hailed it. The driver was well aware of our predicament and the danger he would be putting himself in if he helped us, but he indicated we jump on the pillion seat behind him. The vigilantes realised we could be slipping out of their grip and began firing their automatic weapons.

The bike wasn't built with the power to take the weight of a European passenger and our get-away was proving too slow. I knew those behind us would have vehicles and be in hot pursuit so, seeing a large transit bus, I got off the bike and stood in front of it with the Sparrow and made it stop. The driver could see her gun and reluctantly opened the electric doors. The inside was air-conditioned, cool. The passengers looked at us, terrified. I glanced out the back window and saw the vigilantes had caught up but were unwilling to take on something as big and public as our bus. I saw our brave motorbike guy make a safe departure with a wave to us. He was a good man.

We hadn't gone far before the bus started to stink from the mud we'd carried in on our persons. I saw that we'd reached an area where there were plenty of taxis and told the driver to let us out. The taxi driver wasn't pleased with our stench but he was happy with the amount I offered to pay him.

I didn't want to lead anyone who could be following us to where I was staying, so I got the driver to drop us at a huge shopping mall. I'd lost my shoes in the mud and needed to replace them, and horrified the shop assistants as I tried a few stores but found none had a size big enough for my feet.

I took the Sparrow girl to a restaurant with outside tables and got us both a good meal. She told me the failure of her mission meant she couldn't go back. I knew she was from a village on a distant island and suggested I could help her with the travel money to return home and find a new identity. She was grateful and left as a friend, wrapping her Uzi in some food bags and placing it in a rubbish bin before turning to me, smiling and vanishing into the crowd of shoppers.

I've learnt in these situations that it's important to manage my state of mind. I'd noticed a downstairs cinema was showing the Mel Gibson film Lethal Weapon and decided to buy a ticket and spaz out on fantasy violence. It worked, and by the time I left the cinema I'd stopped shaking from the horror of finding the salvage and began thinking of painting a torture victim – modern crucifixion – a believer in liberation theology having had more cruelty inflicted on him than Christ on the Cross. More than a crucifixion – a world humanity bound and tortured.

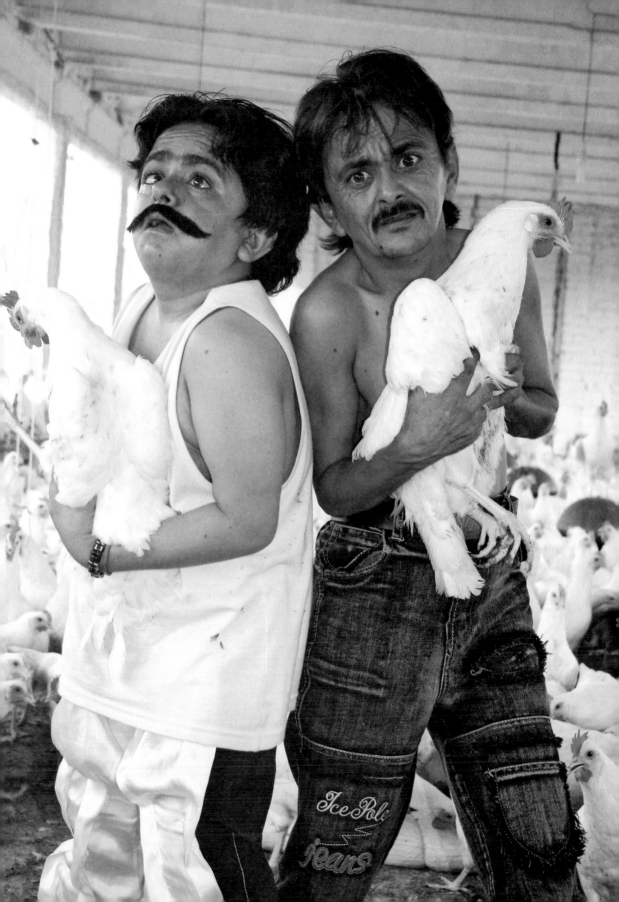

Ashid

I never feel complete unless I'm surrounded by a circle of performers whose veins flow with real circus blood. In medieval times I might have sought the company of troubadours and troupes of Commedia dell'arte mimes, musicians and jugglers. At the original Yellow House it was Julian the mime, Moth and Bruce Goold. Then I formed the TREE theatre group (Theatre Reaching Environments Everywhere) with the dancer Ronaldo Cameron and musician Martin Wesley Smith. Hellen has circus blood, Amir Shah is totally Mr Showbusiness, but the most magical member of the Yellow House Jalalabad is our pixie, Ashid.

A Pashto film isn't a Pashto film without a small person. Ashid is three-and-a-half feet tall and is perfectly proportioned. He could have saved a lot of money for the *Lord of the Rings* trilogy; he is hobbit-sized and a natural hero. If Hellen is right, Ashid also has supernatural powers.

The first two Pashto dramas I made were *Fire* and *Servants*. I used Bul Bul, the tiny star of too many Pashto dramas to count. Bul Bul was from an aristocratic family and one of his uncles was a police chief. Bul Bul was notorious for carrying a gun and being prepared to use it. Legend has it he killed a man who had insulted him and the incident was covered up by his uncle. Even more interesting, his partner was the very beautiful film star Rheema. They lived together though unmarried – something totally forbidden by the ultra-strict laws of this society. Rheema was also from an aristocratic family and her

decision to be an actor was viewed as bringing shame to an illustrious name.

I met Bul Bul on the set of *Family*. There were gangster types backing the film and late one afternoon the cast was sitting around when two of these bullies picked up Isfandear, the small young sidekick to Bul Bul, and held him by his ankles, upside down. Isfandear had originally been spotted by Tariq selling ice on the side of the road. He was from a very poor family but his small size gave him an opportunity to blossom. But Bul Bul wasn't prepared to take Isfandear on as a protégé – the class divide was too great. By now Isfandear's pants had fallen down and he was crying for his exposed nakedness. It had gone too far. I sprang up and knocked the offending gangster down to release Isfandear.

A chill went through the air. These guys were seen as unchallengeable, ruling by fear, and for a few moments it seemed one of them would reach for a gun or knife. Bul Bul's laughter broke the tension. Grinning from ear to ear, he nodded his approval. His star power saved the situation. Obviously he felt this was one for little people's rights.

When I went to my room, I felt very vulnerable to payback and when there was a knock on the door I boosted into a hyperalert state. Partially opening the door, I was relieved to see a smiling waiter with tea and various sweets on a tray. I stepped outside and the gangsters, who were staying a few rooms down, held up their glasses of green tea as a toast to letting bygones be bygones. I'm sure Bul Bul had spoken to them, otherwise I'm certain

there would have been blood spilled. From that point on Bul Bul, Isfandear and I were bonded.

Pashto films are a strange mix of professional actors and amateurs. Gangsters are recruited to play gangsters and policemen to play policemen. There are so few 'good girls' willing to take up acting because of the social stigma, that it's necessary to hire prostitutes to double as actresses and dancers and work beside real actors like Rheema. The prostitutes/actors are all talented vamps and can dance in an erotic way that makes male viewers go crazy, plus their film work is great for business: their clients get a buzz out of being able to purchase intimacy with a star of the screen.

While making these films I become the ringmaster of an incredible circus act – a carnival of extreme characters and situations more entertaining and dramatic than the films themselves.

The most famous real-life gangster and movie star in the Pashto industry is the Iceman. I had played beside him in a Tariq Jamal film and gotten to like this lovable rogue and his henchmen bodyguards. Audiences love him; knowing he 'does the do' in real life makes him more exciting to watch.

All the actors demand up-front contracts and part of their salary paid in advance. I paid both Isfandear and the Iceman and then heard the film would need to be delayed as both of them had gone to Dubai on business. Holding the production up until their return became very stressful and I was constantly on the phone trying to work out what had happened to them when a Dubai police officer answered the cell phone I'd purchased as a gift for Isfandear. I was told the Iceman had been involved in a bank robbery and was in prison. I imagined a Tarantino-style scene where tiny Isfandear stood on a teller's counter with a shotgun demanding they open the vault for

a hooded and grenade-carrying Iceman. The bottom line was that I was without my villain and my small guy.

The next day I put out a casting call for a small guy. Suddenly I found my large apartment at the SS Club in downtown Peshawar full of every kind of hunchback and freak in the region. Bul Bul was there to help me choose, but he looked as perplexed as I felt. It was pandemonium, with each of them doing competing acts, from contortion to juggling and sword fighting, to get my approval. I could find spots for a couple of them but none of them was right as Bul Bul's sidekick. Unlike Bul Bul, they all had elements of the grotesque. Then Javed walked in with a small, perfect, almost supernatural being. In the presence of the others, Ashid shone with a golden aura around him. I had no doubt he was magical – a real-life pixie. I asked Javed where he'd found him and Javed shrugged and said, 'In a forest'. Totally the stuff of fairytales. Bul Bul smiled and nodded and we signed him up on the spot.

Bul Bul became Ashid's teacher, resulting in some of the funniest scenes in the film where the two of them, wearing fake vampire teeth and white make-up, chase Rheema through a forest, with Bul Bul turning to the camera and singing David Bowie's 'Life on Mars'.

Ashid was my discovery but he has rapidly gone beyond our productions to become one of the most famous stars of Pashto film and TV. He came to Australia for the Sydney Film Festival premiere of Love City and charmed everyone. Our dream is to make him a Hollywood star.

Ashid is one of the founders of the Yellow House and he teaches our children's acting workshops. He's a huge asset when shooting our documentaries as everyone, even the potential nasties, wants to come up and shake his hand and get a selfie with him.

Hellen Goes to WAR

I've never taken anyone to war, always depending on my ability to find compatible locals to work with. I felt it too great a responsibility to take anyone who didn't have the level of survival skills I've had to develop. When Hellen decided to join me in Pakistan for the shooting of the Oxfam-funded vampire movies, I cautioned her against it but she proved to be unstoppable. The times we shared there will always be the wildest times of my life. Hellen likes to say: 'I love George so much I couldn't stand to know he was in danger without being by his side'. The truth is that Hellen's presence increases the level of danger many times over. But I'm not complaining as she has made my life a lot more interesting. Apart from Waqar, Hellen has a better understanding of how I make things happen than anyone. When she first arrived in Ayubia, in Pakistan, on the set of my vampire movies, she wrote in her diaries:

HELLEN'S DIARY

George's capacity to work is extraordinary. Being here with him is seeing the real George – a total maniac and formidable force of energy.

He is over sixty but every hardcore gangster and ex-Taliban in the cast fears his wrath. Tossing his mane of hair as he walks along the dusty, run-down streets past dilapidated shops, surrounded by Pakistani Intelligence spies and lurking Taliban and twisted souls, he is always in control. Holding his camera like a rocket-launcher, he shouts orders and laughs loudly to show his pleasure when things go well. This isn't his country but no-one would doubt he is the ringmaster. He takes over – George, king of the jungle!

The cast is huge and many of the actors are actual gangsters, killers and conmen. George couldn't police them all and still keep his mind on directing. His solution was to order in a gunslinger – a Pakistani Wyatt Earp called Abab – with a wild west-style six-shooter in his holster.

At the end of the first day with Abab as enforcer we found ourselves under the blood-red sun, high noon at dusk, filming the 'Death of Rubina' scene. We couldn't get 'quiet on set'. Abab had been asked many times to hush the crowd, yet every time I looked out beyond the cameras he was either chatting or gawking. George was getting angry. I said, 'Abab, what the fuck are you doing? Tell them all absolute HAMOOSH [Quiet]!'

Abab got out his shiny new gun and waved it at the children on the hill. When they were slow to react he fired a couple of bullets which only just missed their heads. I didn't worry George with this as he was filming a death scene with two little girls aged around six. We knew that for one of the girls the tears were very real as she had lost her own mother only a week before. This was close to her tiny heart.

Abab took me aside afterwards and screamed, 'I do not work for you. I work for Mr George'.

This prompted me to tell George how he had fired the gun. George immediately asked Abab, 'How much do we owe you? You're leaving'. Abab looked shocked and made excuses. Knowing Abab was also packing a semi-automatic in his chest holster, George stood up and stared him down with eyes like the double barrels of a shotgun. 'Look, I've been in every fuckin' war you could have heard of, including a Rwandan massacre where thousands of people were cut down with fuckin' machetes, so I don't care if you are carrying a gun, I could kill you in five seconds.'

Abab looked like he was going to cry and couldn't get out fast enough.

The next morning, Govinda the dancer produced the antithesis of this conflict – a fantasy come to life in the form of a puppet show, beautiful beyond belief. The puppeteer uses a simple reed instrument, clenching it in his teeth and blowing through it to create the 'voice' of the puppets, while jangling bells. The drummer, his beloved wife, created the soundtrack. The puppeteer made a hissing cobra sound as the princess is murdered for daring to fall in love with a peasant boy – at this scene, so ancient and beautiful in this rugged countryside, I felt tears welling. I looked at George and tears were flowing down his cheeks and he began to sob. I could see him as a little boy, doing his puppet shows on the backyard lawn in Rockdale. Here in Jalalabad he had struggled for three months to find real traditional puppets and eventually located the last ones left. Seeing the hard man cry brought George and the crew closer. It was what everyone needed to see.

Gul Minah

Last night I saw a very small girl eating something like garbage in front of a closed shop's roller door. She was a six-year-old – Gul Minah. She's forced to make $3 per day before she can go home, even if that means she has to work all night on the very dangerous streets of Jalalabad. She collects recyclable stuff like drink cans and sells them by weight. She's very beautiful but probably has never had a bath in her life. I arranged to meet her and her brother at Burger Chief, a restaurant that doesn't sell burgers, in the middle of the main city drag.

Gul Minah works with her eight-year-old brother who regularly hits her across her face with the back of his hand. They both carry dirty white bags, which, once full, are bigger than they are. Gul Minah has six sisters and five brothers. Their father is in jail for murder.

I took them to the roof of Burger Chief, where the restaurant piles all its garbage, including hundreds of soda cans. The cooking is also done up there and, once you see this, it's difficult to ever order a meal there again.

Gul Minah's eyes were wide at all the cans. I helped her and her brother fill their bags to bursting. Then I ordered a chicken, salad and chips and a waiter brought it up to them with round bread and warm milk tea. Normally they eat what they find in garbage bins or discarded on the street and drink gutter water.

As I focused my camera on her delicate little face I realised I had someone amazing in front of me – film magic. Her hair had been plaited in an elaborate way and she smiled and said her mother had done it for her.

Gul Minah and her brother came back to the Yellow House after their long walk to the recycler with the big bags full of cans. They were nervous but the garden was full of other kids doing lessons with the tutor we'd employed to prepare them to enter school.

Neha had been away for a few days getting her visa renewed. When she arrived back I told her about Gul Minah and she said, 'Does this mean she's joined the Yellow House?' I took a few seconds to think about it and then replied, 'Yes, I suppose it does'. The Yellow House has changed so much since it started out exclusively as an artist collective. It's now more a centre for gifted and talented children from very poor families.

The problem with girls here is that they are programmed from birth to hide their faces. I had been trying for months to get one of these small recycler girls into the film but all had refused until Gul Minah.

Gul Minah is amazingly articulate for an illiterate six-year-old and seems comfortable chatting with Neha as if she is an older sister or aunty.

Neha

Neha is like family to me. Along with Hellen, she is a matriarch of the Yellow House.

Neha's dream was always to be able to ride a pushbike or motorbike. She learnt to ride both in the thirty-metre driveway of the Yellow House. In a society where a woman must wear a burqa outside and walk in an abject way, straddling a speeding bike is unthinkable.

When we got Neha to Australia, the first thing I did was drive her to Cronulla Beach with two bicycles in the back of the car. There she joyously cycled along the boardwalk past women in headphones jogging without male chaperones and surfie girls in short-shorts and bikinis. Neha said she'd never thought women were really as free as this; it was just American propaganda. For me, watching Neha riding along on that bike was like releasing a caged bird and watching it fly for the first time.

Neha's mother is a famous star of Pakistani television and is extremely supportive of her daughter's career, making Neha unique among the dozen or so actresses we have worked with on our dramas. Everyone at the Yellow House loves Neha, but when she first arrived she was nearly burnt as a witch.

Neha has to sleep with the light on – she cannot bear the dark. Something happened in her childhood that gave her night tremors. She also sleepwalks, and at the Yellow House her entranced walks take her into the garden. Hellen and I started hearing strange stories of how the men would come out of the *hoojrah* late at night to see Neha gliding above the ground with a glowing green light emanating from her body. When they tried to catch her she resisted them with superhuman strength. We dismissed these stories, but it got serious when they held a morning *jurga*, a meeting, and decided to get in a specialist *mullanah*, an exorcist, to assess her demons. Overnight the Yellow House became like Salem so we decided to put a quick end to this hysteria.

Hellen got on the computer and printed all the information she could find on sleepwalking and night tremors. She then sat with the men of the Yellow House and explained to them this condition had nothing to do with devils and demons and that Neha wasn't a witch or possessed. It worked and they dropped their cruel superstitious judgements to accept Neha as wonderfully eccentric.

My friendship with Neha started when we cast her as the female lead in our Pashto movie *The Tailor's Story*. One day during shooting she plucked up the courage to ask me if she could learn to use the camera. I was surprised. She told me she actually wanted to direct. Now she edits as well as acting and directing. With Hellen, Neha teaches other Pashtun women in our women's workshops; her ongoing presence at the Yellow House has enabled it to become as much a place for children and women as for ambitious male actors, artists and filmmakers. Our dream is to someday see her win a major international award as either an actor or director.

LATE AFTERNOON GUN DECISION

I was working out some visual ideas for the film when Waqar put a new handgun and holster with bullets in front of me. For a moment I thought the gun was a toy. It was shiny with plastic insets in the handle with a raised star. But it was real – one of the replicas made in the tribal belt of Pakistan. The idea of getting handguns for Hellen, Waqar and myself had struck me in Australia, but now I felt uncomfortable. To give myself more time to think, I told Waqar the gun was too cheap and nasty. Action man Marshook pulled out his gun – old and dirty, cold monochrome metal and no ornamentation.

I will probably go along with the guns, but I'll go to the market myself and make sure they are weapons of substance, not like toys. But if it hadn't been for Waqar taking the initiative, I would have let the idea slip. My pump-action shotgun has been sitting in our room the whole time we've been away and its action is slow and stiff. I'll take it to a gunsmith and have it cleaned and lubricated. It's a beautiful thing but sitting unattended it has lost its power.

My father had a beautifully engraved Spanish shotgun that he taught me to shoot with. On my first lesson I was very young and he wanted me to shoot a rabbit. I tried to pull the trigger but nothing happened. The rabbit hopped out of range and Dad realised the safety was on so flicked it off, instantly triggering a blast. The stock kicked back into my shoulder. Mum, who had been watching, was furious.

It was my uncle Eric who taught me at an early age how to use military guns. He had been a gold medallist in the Commonwealth Games before the war, so when he joined up he was made a sniper. He would be dropped on a Pacific island with a list of Japanese

officers to target. When he returned, he had what was then called war neurosis or shell shock. Dad and their sister Ivy bought him a piece of jungle-covered property to 'sort himself out' in. When he recovered, the army still saw him as an asset and supplied him with as many .303 rounds as he needed to practice shooting at the range. I would often go with him and he would let me shoot at targets. I found I shared his gift and enjoyed the sport.

When I was in my late teens my uncle Eric shot himself. He took his old sniper rifle and put it to his heart, but, for some bizarre reason, the bullet didn't kill him. I felt his humiliation when we visited him in hospital. All those years later he still had not forgiven himself. He took me aside and said: 'You cannot kill another human being without killing part of yourself. Murder is murder – even for flag and country'.

THE Marksman
THE RIFLEMEN'S MAGAZINE.

MAY 1955
Vol. 7, No. 8.

[Registered for transmission by Post as a Periodical]

OUR MARKSMAN OF THE MONTH

H. R. Gittoes

ERIC GITTOES (Parramatta Rifle Club)
Winner of the Riverina Union Championship Aggregate.

Uncle Eric taught me that you can not kill
another human being without killing part
of yourself. He could no longer live with

143

mories.

Yellow House Calligraphy

esterday I started painting 'Jalalabad Yellow House' in huge, looping calligraphic strokes on the back side of the wall that protects us from the street. I needed to renew the space to rejuvenate its spirit. Everyone loves to watch me paint and likes giving advice, but for me it was a reflective moment. It was the way Martin and I both painted words on the walls of the original Yellow House, using our eccentric longhand scrawl we'd developed in our school days back when students still had to write with a nib and ink from an inkwell in the desk.

I painted 'Oh Hello, Oh Lee Ello, my garden grows, my heart overflows, Oh please don't go, Oh Hello, Oh Lee Ello', an ancient Sufi whirling song, high on my Puppet Theatre walls. The song was to spin and become intoxicated with. Martin had pondered a large wall in what we called the Magritte room. We all expected him to do some kind of Artoon combination of Magritte and Vincent or Munch, but I woke one morning to discover Martin had been up all night writing calligraphic text that filled the wall. It was like an extension of his masterpiece, *Catalogue No. 3,* that he produced in London to bring back to the Yellow House. Of all Martin's work it is still this that I go back to for inspiration; it is as important to me as Goya's black paintings and etchings . . . *Catalogue No. 3* was the synthesis of all he had learnt doing *OZ* magazine.

At the Yellow House Jalalabad, I organised for a young artist to be found who could do Yellow House Jalalabad calligraphy in Pashto with Arabic script above mine. His name is Milad and he's another young artist who hasn't been able to get any kind of art training in Jalalabad. Milad did a good job on the callig-

raphy. Once again it reminded me of the young artists who flocked to the original Yellow House and were allowed to take up a brush in some way. The big decision that involves Milad is that I have decided to get him to paint 'The Yellow House Jalalabad' on the outside street wall. Presently we have an ad for a private business school that is in no way connected to us. I got the wall washed and a white base painted over it. Tomorrow our identity will be there for the world to see and we will be easy to find. Hellen is concerned this could make us more of a target for the Taliban and other bad guys, but those who might want to kill us already know where we are. I see our Yellow House name on the wall as a kind of protection magic. Face fear and it's likely to retreat. Show fear and it's more likely to advance.

Burning Fire and Children

EMPANGENI, KWAZULU-NATAL, SOUTH AFRICA, 3 MAY 1994

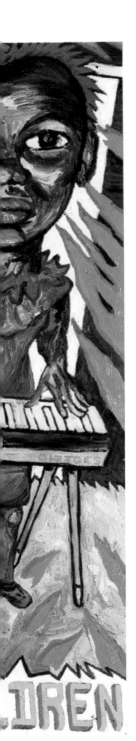

For the last couple of days, I have been travelling around the Empangeni region of Natal with the Zulu poet Madlinyoka. KwaZulu-Natal is a divided region, engaged in a black-against-black civil war between ANC supporters and Inkatha Freedom Party supporters led by Buthelezi. The international press often makes it seem that Inkatha represents all Zulu interests. But many ANC supporters here, like Madlinyoka, belong to Zulu tribes.

Madlinyoka has insisted on having two bodyguards with us in the vehicle at all times. Each has a pump-action shotgun wrapped in sack-cloth. At this stage, while it seems the ANC has won the election, Inkatha has the majority vote in Natal. Leading up to the election there have been a number of ambushes and murders. Here the burning necklace of victory will not provide safety for its supporters in Natal. Most express the fear to Madlinyoka that his celebration could turn into a bloodbath. Many of the musicians are in refugee camps – forced from their homes by the fighting.

Madlinyoka told me he is certain of one group of musicians who will not be intimidated. We swerved off the sealed road onto a dirt track through thick scrub. This was way beyond the fringe of the townships. We pulled up in front of one of these fibro shacks. Painted on the wall in bold red and yellow print was the line 'BURNING FIRE AND CHILDREN'. I immediately thought this referred to necklacing and the violent deaths of so many of the children of Natal. I was wrong – it refers to the musician Petros Bhozas Mithenbu who has adopted the stage name 'Burning Fire'. The 'and children' refers to his own children who play as part of his band.

Burning Fire and his family were happy to pose for me. The whole Mithenbu family, including a very old grandmother and Burning Fire's half-crazy brother, gathered around to watch the drawing. Burning Fire's smallest daughter – nicknamed Pinky – began singing backup vocals for her younger brother, nicknamed 'Vitamin'. Some of the lyrics I remember are 'Let us come together now – live as one – stop fighting one another – we are working the same problem. Why you going hunting out your brother? Giving him the pain I feel – the same blood flows in me as in you'.

These were Pinky's father's words – to me Pinky seemed to be saying 'What has war got to do with us kids? Why can't we be left out of it?'

As we left, Burning Fire agreed that he and his family would perform at the celebration. I was amazed at how casually the children had been committed to something so potentially dangerous – something so potentially dangerous that other adult performers had felt too frightened to agree to participate in. Burning Fire is clearly an optimist!

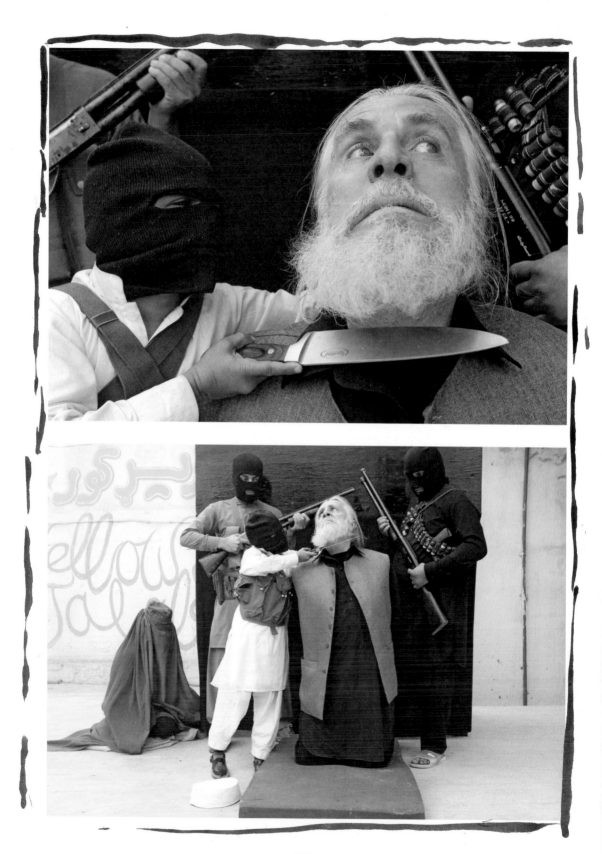

DECAPITATION

James Foley's beheading dominated the news on our way here. The world is getting accustomed to images of ISIL guys with hoods and hunting knives cutting the heads off journalists and prisoners but this has been a real possibility for me for over seven years, and more recently Hellen has shared the threats.

From the beginning of the Yellow House Jalalabad we have half-expected radical Taliban to break through the doors of the Yellow House and behead us on our own garden stage and possibly even film us with our own cameras.

My first experiences of this kind of shocking imagery came when shooting *Miscreants of Taliwood* in 2007 in Pakistan. There I had filmed video stores being bombed and experienced Taliban attacks on local crews but the real horror only struck home when interviewing Shah G Khan, Dean of Political Science at the University of Peshawar.

Shah G Khan studied and has taught in prestigious American universities. He has movie-star charisma – on camera he resembled a Pashtun Paul Newman. He wanted to do the interview where no-one could overhear, so we went to the rooftop of his home and he took his AK-47 with him.

Shah G represents the kind of liberal humanist values which one would hope will, someday, be embraced by Pashtuns throughout Pakistan and Afghanistan.

I wanted him to talk about what the Taliban and Fundamentalists see as suitable entertainment to replace the existing industry that they were systematically destroying.

He explained their use of real-life horror scenes to simultaneously entertain and frighten their audiences. If sporting events were replaced by public executions, audiences would soon become desensitised; unlike a game there are no winners – only losers. This necessitates escalating atrocity – Shah G gave the example of showing a ten-year-old boy cutting off the head of a kneeling man. I was still innocent enough to find it hard to believe such footage existed, or that it could be purchased from one of the many Taliban video and music stores opened in place of those they had blown up.

The next day Waqar and I went to the market to purchase this decapitation DVD. If my film was to be about the destruction of the arts and film industry, I needed to show what the opponents were providing in its place.

The market was in the tribal area where the Taliban have greatest support. I knew if we were going to use this footage I would have to film it being purchased from a shop front and not simply downloaded.

This simple act of purchasing a DVD was possibly the most dangerous thing Waqar and I have ever done together. In this market, cameras are seen as instruments of the devil – if I was caught filming and identified as a foreigner they would immediately assume I was American and I'd be killed on the spot.

Waqar, who normally has nerves of steel, was edgy and suggested we do some general shopping for items we needed so we could eyeball the space and work out a plan. I agreed we would abandon the idea if it seemed too risky. The store we chose was run by two young teenage boys. If they were selling the DVD of a ten-year-old performing a decapitation then it was perfect for our doc. However, it was next to a similar store, manned by guys with long black beards who were obvious Taliban recruiters – they would be quick to blow the whistle on us if we were caught filming. These open-fronted stalls were across the alleyway from a store with a kind of attic roof space where goods were stored. I could see a way to climb up and hopefully film unnoticed. If we had been a special forces team, I'm sure our plan would have been rejected.

The boys happily sold us a dozen DVDs and confirmed the footage of the decapitation was one of them. I filmed their smiling faces as they slipped the discs into a paper bag. Waqar must have felt he was on a roll – instead of making a sensible exit he went next door and chatted with the beards before moving on.

As I made my escape with the footage it was as if we had just successfully robbed a bank and were making our getaway with the loot.

My mood changed when we slipped the DVD into our player and saw the victim being prepared, then the kid with the knife, then the blood as the jugular is severed, and then the hacking sounds as it chops through the spine. Worse than the gore was the absence of horror or any emotion on the face of the child executioner. The boy explains this is what is done to foreign spies as he holds up the head like a trophy. It was exactly what I would have been called if caught with my camera.

When we cut this into our film, the broadcaster refused to show it without some extreme editing. In the final version we see the boy place the knife on the victim's throat and the first trickle of blood before the screen goes black and the audience only hears the sawing and hacking sounds until it comes back to the moment the boy holds the head up high. To retain some of the initial impact I put a box in the corner showing the living face of the victim beside his now very lifeless face.

When the film was shown at festivals people would walk out and in a few cases members of the audience fainted and had to be assisted. At every Q&A I was immediately criticised for including this part of the story. People were passionate about their right not to see what was happening, even in its censored, modified form, regardless of my argument that I couldn't make a film showing the destruction of the music and film industry in Pakistan without what was replacing it.

This footage in *Miscreants* is still the main reason for the death threats to me and what we are doing at the Yellow House. The first death threat Hellen experienced was phoned in while we were shooting. This was the scariest threat I have ever received. Thinking decapitation wasn't frightening enough, they offered to remove my face from my body. At the time, Hellen and I were staying at the SS Club and Hellen, unfamiliar with this kind of intimidation, asked, 'Does this mean we leave immediately?' My answer was 'No – these bastards cannot ever be allowed to think they are winning'. I was proud of Hellen when she trusted me and we stayed.

The latest images of IS decapitation have spooked everyone at the Yellow House. We get Al Jazeera, the BBC and CNN clearly on our TVs here and night after night there have been more decapitation stories.

I've decided to use my own peculiar Gittoes style of voodoo magic – I will dramatise my own decapitation in the garden of the Yellow House, complete with a burqa-clad Hellen, held and made to watch in the background as the whole thing is taped for propaganda.

This will have to be 'in-house' – no one in the community would approve of this being dramatised. The hope is that this will exorcise our fears – by acting it out we may prevent the reality.

OODOO PROTECTION MAGIC

am in the middle of the seige of the
ed mosque and I think I used
all my spare lives yesterday.
I rang a special effects guy
ho rigged me up to be fake shot.
the middle the fighting we
tached blood satchels and small
xplosives to my chest and wired
em to remote detonator box.
pretended to be focusing my
mera on a helicopter. The trick
or me was to fall realistically
ut without damaging my camera.
here could be no retakes - the fake
ne could draw real fire and I
eeded to be up and out of there
fast. As I hit the ground I
ould see both defenders and
ccupiers swiveling their guns to see
here the non existent shooter was.
f I am still alive tomorrow then
his protection magic has worked.

Into the Wilderness

One of my favourite miniatures is "Majnun in the Wilderness - more so because it was created in Herat, Afghanistan the date on it is 1447.

... when I was last in [Bon?] for the Film Festival there was a show called 'The Conflation' at the National Gallery. There were lots of images of aesthetics and mystics alone in [their] hermit wilderness.

I've taken a long time since then to realise the wilderness is where I keep going - but it is war - Rwanda, Bos, Afghanistan, Iraq, most recently the [V?] Tribal Belt -

In the Wilderness

Pakistan + It is being alone in these places with the threat, not of wild animals, but of the front line - a new kind of Melancholia. I used to relate it to Dürer's 'Knight Death + the Devil' but it is closer in spirit to these solitary mystics - like them I'm there to contemplate the nature of reality, and what it is to be Human + if their is a God - what place does he give to this violence in his plan for creation.

THE HISTORY OF WRITING

I write all the time. It's usually the way I start my day and what helps me to sleep at night. I spend more time writing than on any other form of expression, including painting and drawing. But usually it's only intended for myself or to be shared with a few friends and family, unlike my films, painting and photographs, which I promote to the widest possible audiences.

It took a very wise schoolteacher in Durban to open my eyes to the truth of why I write. In 2001 I had an exhibition called Lives in the Balance touring South Africa, a retrospective that dealt with some of my most horrific experiences in places like Rwanda, Bosnia and Palestine. People here have a better understanding of my work because their pain, on the road to the ANC victory in 1994, is still healing. I spoke to several school groups – all black kids. Their teachers were three very large Zulu women who were a bit intimidating for a white Australian talking about experiences in Africa. I couldn't gauge from their expressions what they were thinking, so I did what I always do and told the stories behind the paintings. As usual a hand went up and a student asked the inevitable question of whether my art was therapy to help me cope with what I'd witnessed. Before I could answer, the oldest of the teachers broke in with, 'It has to be the writing, not the painting – you could only have survived all this by writing about it'.

This wonderful teacher had intuitively sensed something I never realised. Just as one of the most healing services a psychiatrist or priest can perform is to listen, I write because I need to write, just as I draw because I need to draw. Unrealised by me, that writing has kept

me sane. In war zones there's rarely the chance to send letters – the personal diaries and margin notes are my outlet. In situations like Kibeho Camp, where I've been alone, without a companion or family or any kind of therapist to talk to, I've found a quiet place and begun to write.

These diaries become my companions. I'm an expressionist in my painting, and the very process of drawing forces me to take in every detail and that only stirs up my emotions. But at some point I discovered that if I slightly transformed my world into a kind of parallel universe and created a puppet character for myself that distanced me from myself, the writing calmed me down better than writing diary-style recollections. It was as though I was turning real experiences into dreams. This opened a door to sleep, transforming the horrid reality into something else; exorcising my mind with the assurance all the worst things had been poured out on paper.

The thing that fascinates me the most about situations where a lot of people are dying violently around me is the sense of doorways being opened. Writing allows me to open up completely to the possibilities of the other side.

The editors of *The Bulletin With Newsweek* cut out any paragraphs I submitted on the supernatural – mine was their first story of the horrific human tragedy in Kibeho. All the reports and articles and interviews I did on Kibeho had to be as factual as possible – I was a witness who could get the perpetrators tried as war criminals, and did so. But during an event such as that massacre or a battle, I swing between cynical, rational atheism and outright mysticism. Rationally, I know that the dead are dead and there's nothing more that can be done for them. It hasn't worried me to walk over corpses to get to a child who needs to be carried to safety. But then, I've also experienced states of totally altered consciousness. I don't think this is unique to me. When I ask soldiers who have been through the same killing zones about this they agree they've felt the same and are often glad that I can articulate it for them.

When the ships of Odysseus approached the rocks where the Sirens sang sailors to their doom, he had his crew put wax in their ears, but tie him to the mast so he could hear their seductive song – the song that made the living want to pitch themselves into the abyss. When people are dying around you, it's like hearing the Sirens' call and no longer fearing death. It's as if the dead are saying, 'This isn't so bad, join us and stop worrying about holding on to life'.

I've noticed over and over again how, early on in a deadly situation, people take cover and tremble with fear. Then, as it continues, they lose their fear and begin to do reckless things that can get them killed. I often wonder how many soldiers who have won medals for bravery have actually begun listening to the dead. The day at Kibeho we were asked to go and do a body count and it felt as claustrophobic as an aquarium. Rather than sea creatures swimming overhead and all around, it was the dead that closed in on us from every angle – their world, that other world of death, somehow felt more present than ours.

Everyone who's been at the frontline of war knows that, when they are walking into the zone, the change of reality is instant. It's as real as walking through the doors from the street into an office building. Inside that zone there's a heightened state of consciousness. This is one of the factors that makes a photo-journalist keep going back to war. There's no buzz like it.

These are the things I can offer from my life at war. I have rarely, if ever, articulated them – but somehow these are still the things which everyone senses in me and wants to know more about. The buzz is what keeps me working . . . but it's something that can send you insane.

From behind things are listening at my legs and claw into my body ... the sound of my progress inching in the hall - not a child's race like Oma's ...

Together there is a chance we can get away - my need to save her is not selfless, she is a shield to fend off my monsters

IRAQ

MARVEL COMICS GROUP
CAPTAIN AMERICA

Past man, Past spider, Past robot.

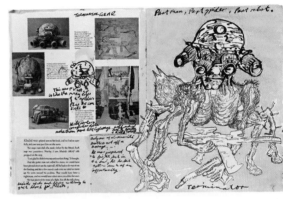

Terminator

MTV WAR

MTV SOLDIERS

The dog and his reflection

COLES

IRAQ

CHARON

NIGHT VISION DIARY, 2001

Walking to the other side of the island I can see the distant fires more clearly. It is obvious from the flashes and bursts that some grand battle is going on – something to be fleeing from.

I drop my gaze to a figure in the water. A giant of a man, he has a large paddle which helps him to move easily across the waters. The black ooze only covers the big man's ankles, but when I try to walk out to meet him I find myself up to my neck in the slush and have to struggle to make it back to the rocks. The man is dragging others behind him who are attached in some way to a harness by hoses. These passengers are submerged up to their necks in the grim fluid. The stench has gradually gotten stronger and I envy the big man the filter mask he is wearing. Then I see semi-transparent gossamer-like wings and suppose this is what is keeping the big man above the mud. Again I wish I had some kind of weapon. The stranger is only fifty feet away and has a handgun strapped to his left thigh.

My hopes rise when I recognise some of the men from my unit, just heads with dirty faces, but their eyes are unmistakable. The giant detaches some of the tubes from the back of his harness and passes them to me and I strain to pull in each of my men, one at a time, hand-over-hand, until the core group of seven are on the rocks with me. The giant has dragged his other passengers up to a pathway and delivered them to the gate where they pass a snarling dog into a shadowy darkness. I remember translating a poem from Latin at school. Finally, I get it. The dog is Cerberus and we have made it across the river Styx and the big guy was Charon the ferryman. Virus Squad is in Hades, which means we are probably dead.

I call my men to attention: We have fought our way out of bad places before. Why should Hell be any different?

Hellen was my guardian angel
from afar. The Ambulance guys
could not find a vein and said
"He has gone cold stiff." I had almost
bleed out and my phone rang.
It was Hellen and suddenly I
was not a hobo of the street but
someone of importance to someone.

NEAR DEATH

I started having trouble with my knees while here in Afghanistan shooting our last film Love City *and made an appointment with a top knee surgeon on my return to Australia. When I went in for blood tests my PSA (Prostate-Specific Antigen) was through the roof, indicating cancer. Within a week I had been operated on by robots and my prostate removed – the cancer with it. Shortly afterwards I had both knees replaced too.*

I was recovering from all this when the good news came from New York that I was to receive an award for social justice. My doctors told me I shouldn't travel – I wasn't fully healed and I was still on strong painkillers, including oxycodone. But I hate letting people down, so I went. In the plane I even had to inject anti-coagulants into my stomach to prevent blood clots and keep taking aspirin to thin the blood. I couldn't understand why I felt so weak. When the award was behind me, I remained in the Chelsea Hotel taking meetings with friends and doing some business. I felt very bad.

I rang my publicist and told her I thought I might be dying. She was convinced I was having a panic attack. I rang a doctor friend from Médecins Sans Frontières who arrived with a bottle of whiskey: the publicist had told him her diagnosis. A friend, David Levi-Strauss, dropped in and we had a small party of drinking and good conversation. But once I hit the bed I felt like death. I finally crawled into the bathroom and began vomiting blood in huge quantities. I slipped down the stem of the commode and was lying on the tiles, dreamily drawing spiral patterns in my own blood when a voice inside said, 'George, if you don't get up, you are going to die'.

I used the wall to force myself up and then, in my blood-soaked tracksuit, dragged myself along the hotel corridor via the wall. Once in the lift, I vomited more blood then emerged like an apparition from The Shining *into the Chelsea Hotel foyer, throwing up blood all over reception. The hotel clerks looked on in stunned horror. Everyone was frozen until I half-shouted, 'Can't you see I'm dying? Call an ambulance'.*

I was rushed to Bellevue Hospital. The plan had been to pitch Snow Monkey *to Screen Australia a few days after my return – instead I did my pitch from a hospital bed. These assessments are always done with the filmmaker present so I felt I had lost my chance. I was on painkillers and pretty wired, so didn't hold back on explaining my wildest, most unconventional ideas for the film including a mix of hard observational documentary footage and totally surreal dramatisations. But they went for it, so I now have as much freedom as I need to make a very experimental and intuitive film, documenting this war-torn country as it struggles to find good leadership in the upcoming election.*

Taliban at the Yellow House

Majrooh, the director of Afghan Films for Jalalabad, had arranged for me to meet Maulana Abdul Zahir Haqqani, a Taliban candidate for the election. The maulana was in charge of Taliban forces in Herat before the American war, so he is huge.

Everyone was so terrified of this visit that I decided that now, before he arrived, was the time to shoot my own decapitation, to ward off the very real possibility of Taliban assassination. My logic was that if this kind of magic worked for me it would also work for the group: Ashid was happy to play a nine-year-old with a hunting knife and Waqar went out and bought balaclavas to disguise their faces. Itchy the cook and Waqar stood either side of me with guns while Ashid made speeches about me being a foreign spy before putting the knife to my throat. The scene was so ridiculous we almost forgot the impending danger.

Once the filming was over, the team tidied the garden and made the Secret Garden Café as presentable as possible. There was nervous electricity in the air.

Maulana Haqqani arrived in a white LandCruiser with two armed bodyguards. I welcomed them in. One of the guards had the supercool look of a war-hardened Taliban in Ray-Bans, an American cam jacket and an AK-47 plus, of course, the beard. The other armed bodyguard was older and seemed softer. The maulana had a tight black turban of the kind only a Taleb leader wears, a grey tweed sports jacket, cream cashmere sweater and otherwise traditional clothes. He's a little man but, like Tom Cruise, projects large.

While I had been welcoming Haqqani into the garden, Waqar had been chatting with his bodyguards off to the side. He pulled me aside and whispered that he had confirmed the maulana does not just share the Haqqani name but is from the same tribe and family as the Haqqani clan in Waziristan. The Haqqanis are the worst of the worst enemies of the US and totally deadly, being responsible for most of the spectacular raids in Kabul and elsewhere. This had become very scary. The Haqqani network would be the prime suspect for sending that letter offering to cut my head off and televise it. They are extremists and have been known as guns-for-hire for centuries.

I sat Haqqani down in our garden café, next to the monkey cage, and Itchy brought trays of sweet cakes and biscuits. Hellen was out in the market, so I got Itchy to phone and warn her about our 'guests'. Normally she would fling her burqa off as she came through the gate, but that theatrical act of rebellion couldn't happen today.

Once seated, Haqqani became very serious and started telling me how they had been investigating me and what we were doing for some time. In light of the death threat we had received, I was expecting him to reel off accusations, but instead he said: 'We have decided you are a good man and what you are doing is for the good of the Afghan people. I'm here to tell you that we have decided to support and protect you and the Yellow House.'

A sigh of relief went through us all.

Suddenly, Hellen and Neha could be heard banging at the gate. Both came in, with appropriate male chaperones and fully covered by their burqas, heads down, not looking in the direction of our male guests. Perfect behaviour to confirm Haqqani's opinion of the Yellow House.

Knowing Hellen would be alone in our room unaware of how things were going, I sent Waqar over to reassure her. I later found out that when he opened the door she was sitting on the bed with the handgun, ready to shoot. She had decided that if things went really bad it was better to defend herself than submit as a victim.

From this point on, I began to feel as if I were on safer ground with Haqqani. I asked his opinion of the major candidates in the upcoming election and he explained the Americans had targeted the older and wiser Taliban leadership so consistently with drones and special forces it was creating chaos – young, inexperienced, uneducated fighters were taking leadership roles. These young, susceptible fighters were joining Daesh (ISIL) and even more radical groups. He blamed the Pakistani Intelligence Agency (ISI) for giving the Afghan Taliban a bad name.

To our surprise, the maulana was very happy I was teaching film and media skills and invited me to his home and village once the elections were over. This is totally contrary to the way the Taliban, when in office, were against TV and media. Obviously they have recognised this was a mistake and want to be able to use media to their advantage.

When I was last in Afghanistan doing work on landmines, I carried special letters from the Taliban allowing me to take photographs and never had any trouble. To be honest, I never had to show the letters and I took thousands of photographs. There are a lot of misconceptions about how strict the Taliban were on the arts and photography. It seems it's all okay so long as it doesn't go into areas that are offensive to their sensibilities. These are easy to identify and avoid.

Then Asam, who drives our blue circus truck, arrived with his six children, including his new baby. Asam has that 'salt of the earth' look all politicians respond to and want to get endorsement from as 'men of the people'. Asam has also been a mujahideen fighter and this is totally expressed in his bearing. The bodyguards would have recognised it immediately. The maulana felt he was part of a village scene and relaxed.

The only discord came from our female monkey. Gala had been caged for the filming and didn't like that she wasn't the centre of attention, so she took her two metal drinking bowls and used them like cymbals to bang together whenever the maulana praised Sharia law.

It ran through my mind that I should make sure I have a Pakistani visa in my passport when I return in August … there might be a slim chance the maulana could arrange for me to travel to Waziristan and interview his clan members.

When we'd explored all these topics I asked the maulana to pose on the stage with me and his bodyguards with the Yellow House calligraphy on the wall behind us. It was totally surreal. Since the creation of the Yellow House, our fear has always been that the Taliban would come in the dark of night, raid us, shut us down and possibly kill us or take us hostage. Now that the maulana has been our guest and posed for photos we come under his protection. It makes us much safer than having professional security guards. We showed this man no fear, there were no guards or guns, no sense of him being the enemy – just our peacocks spreading their feathers in the Secret Garden.

Omar's Rose Garden

When I was a teenager I read a book on Persian gardens and began making a small symbolic garden with miniature roses. This was around the same time as I read *Mysticism* by Evelyn Underhill and, through it, discovered Sufi poetry. I realised a garden could be up there with poetry as a form of expression about a world beyond appearance.

When I first started making films in Jalalabad, I stayed at the Spinghar Hotel. The leasing of the Yellow House came later. The Spinghar enabled me to experience a true Persian garden for the first time and I loved it. The old gardeners there were from the Sufi tradition and every placement of every flower and tree was symbolic and linked to an exquisite little mosque. The joy I felt sitting in the garden of the Spinghar is difficult to express. The roses have had no genetic modifications – they are ancient originals of incredible variety. It was this garden, especially the roses, that got me started on decorative watercolours. The garden opened a door that had been rusted shut in my heart.

One Christmas Day, Hellen and I walked around the garden. No-one but the roses seemed to know it was Christmas. It was one of the most romantic strolls we've ever taken. Holding hands with Hellen Rose in the Sufi rose garden on Christmas Day, with the gardeners smiling back at us, not knowing why we were so happy – it was a moment I will never forget.

A week ago I was searching for billboards to film in the city and I noticed some old men selling roses by the road. We stopped and bought enough to fill the back of the car. The Yellow House XI usually plays a game of cricket with the neighbours at this time of day, but when we arrived with the roses everyone got involved in their planting. Each rose had a place in our garden with the most beautiful yellow rose taking centre stage.

When we were making *Simurgh*, a children's film directed by Neha, at Asam's village, the local teenage boys couldn't stop staring at our actresses. Neha was used to it but Hellen was hiding in the car and started screaming at one boy who just stood there and stared at her as if she was a rare animal in a zoo. Rather than being frightened away, he just stared harder.

I needed to cast a 'bad boy' in our film and he was perfect. My own schoolyard instincts told me that if I got the meanest kid in the pack involved, the others would cease bothering us. He told us his name was Omar. He dearly wanted to be an actor and make films. Our movie stars, Amir Shah and Marshook, generously gave him acting and stunt training. He did a great job in his role and I pleaded with them both not to forget him once I left and to include him in their films. His mother and father had both been killed during the war and he'd been raised by a grandfather who was cruel to him and his four brothers.

He'd never known the love of a mother or sister. Omar had the aura of a dog kicked too many times. He was very thin and bound up with invisible scars.

When I returned to Jalalabad from my last trip overseas, I asked what had happened to Omar. No-one at the Yellow House knew, but I managed to get in touch with him via someone from his village. Omar arrived thinner and sadder than last I'd seen him – it was heart-breaking. While obviously malnourished he was working sixteen hours a day, seven days a week in a job that paid only eighty dollars a month. He had to give most of that to his brothers. His personality seemed to have turned inward – he seemed unreachable.

I gave him a permanent job at the Yellow House. He was very suspicious of everyone at first but after spending a day with me stretching canvases over frames for my oil paintings, we developed a rapport. Now he has begun to blossom.

He gets here before anyone else wakes up and waters the roses before going to work on the rest of the garden. The roses have become his project and we've been out together with Hellen to buy more. His next innovation was when he decided we needed to grow our own vegetables – tomatoes, eggplant, zucchini, carrots and garlic. He has created maze-like irrigation trenches between which he is planting seedlings.

This is ancient peasant farmer knowledge made visible. It made me understand what some American soldiers told me once while travelling in Laghman Province. We'd pulled up next to some heavily armoured American vehicles and I decided to walk down and ask them what they were doing. It turned out these soldiers were all agricultural specialists from Kansas. They'd come wanting to advise the local farmers on modern farming methods but in the end said they had learnt more than they could teach. The local farmers didn't use pesticides and their methods of rotation and irrigation were astonishing.

This garden has become Omar's but it brings joy to the whole group. It's spring and we're rapidly seeing this most beautiful garden, a vision, appear before our eyes. The peacocks seem happy to live amongst an elegance that complements their own and the monkeys are finding the herbs that we have seeded are good to eat. Yesterday both monkeys were in a patch of clover-like green, feasting on the leaves. It feels more like paradise than the larger, more developed garden at the Spinghar.

This is also helping the film, as the candidates for the election and other key figures I need to interview mostly come to the Yellow House for filming. The garden puts them in a relaxed mood and everything flows from there.

I've begun work on the canvases we stretched together and the roses are beginning to creep into the imagery. They will be an extension of Omar's garden.

Long-Awaited Kiss of Freedom

I'm a romantic at heart and enjoy love stories. The greatest celebration I was ever lucky enough to participate in was at Pretoria in 1994 for Mandela's inauguration as the first black president the day he made his 'Rainbow Nation' speech. For me and the huge crowds it was the greatest triumph of the human spirit any of us will ever experience in our lifetimes.

I managed to get a pass into the giant dinner party leaders of the world were throwing for Nelson Mandela on his great day. I did something unusual for me and went out and purchased a conservative suit and tie. I had a chance to take photographs and possibly interview the likes of Al Gore, Yasser Arafat, Fidel Castro and Prince Charles. It was one of the highest points in the history of humanity and I was surrounded by most of the movers and shakers who determine the destiny of the planet. Mandela was going to have to deliver his speech in a bulletproof glass booth and the security fences between the partygoers inside and the populace outside were twenty feet high and the military guard was a shoulder-to-shoulder wall of muscle and guns.

My entry to this elite gathering had been very hard to come by and I was excited when I got it, but my heart went out to the crowds. People had climbed trees for a better view and crowds were a swaying, singing mass of joy. I knew if I exited the inauguration, security would never let me back in. I was torn but the call of the people won. Out I went.

Once outside, an old couple, Jacob and Elizabeth, both in their eighties, immediately approached me. With my suit and my cameras around my neck, they had mistaken me for a commercial photographer.

They offered to pay me to take a photo of them together, telling me this historic day at Mandela's inauguration was as important to them as their wedding day sixty-four years earlier. They had spent their savings coming from Soweto to be here and had their Sunday best on.

I told them they were mistaken if they thought I was a wedding photographer but offered a couple of Polaroids for free. As I lifted the camera to my eye, I realised a photograph wouldn't be enough and asked Jacob and Elizabeth if they would pose for a sketch. The pose made their kiss last for a couple of minutes – long enough for a curious crowd of appreciative supporters to form around us. As the kiss continued, the crowd grew larger and began to cheer and sing with delight.

Everyone was feeling so elated they were searching for ways to express their joy. It seemed this kiss said it all for those who witnessed it. This couple, as old as Mandela, 'created' The Long-Awaited Kiss of Freedom.

The Long awaited Kiss of Freedom

When Elizabeth saw my drawing she
said she had to have it. I gave it
to her but said "This means you will
have to pose again for a second long
awaited kiss of freedom. When they
embraced again the whole crowd
cheered - all the triumph of the day
was in this moment.

Election Day Jalalabad

I'd gone to sleep thinking: *tomorrow is going to be bloody*. My focus for months has been to be here for the first free election. It has shaped itself in my mind as a day of incredible risk. I visualised myself breaking through police cordons to document the results of suicide attacks by the Taliban and dodging bullets as gun battles rage.

The first surprise was that the day was cold and rainy. It has been sunny recently. Yesterday we had candidates on our stage against a backdrop made from their election posters. First, Humarie Raffi, the leading female candidate, who arrived in clothes of dark indigo and sombre blue, her hands nervous. Then Dr Fawad Khan Azizi, an old friend who is tired of the status quo and wants to cure the system from within. Then the representative for Ashraf Ghani – the former general Abdul Raqeeb. He is a neighbour, with his home and headquarters about five houses down from the Yellow House.

As usual I was the first to wake and went to the monkey cage with a bunch of bananas, let the peacocks out and put Tim Tam on my shoulder while I made myself a cup of tea. My nerves settled down until I heard some explosions and gunfire. It seemed the anticipated Taliban offensive had begun.

I had sent teams out to film the politicians casting their votes when I got a surprise invitation from candidate Jahanyar to join him at his home. Accepting would leave Hellen at the Yellow House on her own. The cook, Ishrad, who usually protects her, was at his home and no others, like Marshook, were overnighting in the *hoojrah*. I told Hellen not to open the gates to anyone and I got her the pump-action shotgun and fully loaded it with cartridges. I also gave her our Russian handgun, also fully loaded … both with the safety off.

I thought this would be a quick moment together while I wished him luck and then I would be back with Hellen but, to my surprise, Jahanyar wanted me to document him casting his vote. As the representative for Ashraf Ghani, he is the most likely target for militant Taliban. In the last week there have been announcements by the Pakistani Taliban that they plan to use force to prevent the election happening. It seemed like an ultimate act of courage or faith for Jahanyar to walk to the polling booth without an armed bodyguard. Having a foreigner by his side was an obvious provocation. He was asking me to risk my life with him.

Jahanyar has a crippled hand, but still, we held hands going up the street. It was a long walk to the polling station and at every opportunity Jahanyar stopped to greet people and make speeches. I worried that my presence at his side could be misinterpreted as American support. Many vehicles drove past us with dangerous and unfriendly occupants, but we made it to the heavily guarded entrance to the polling booth. Jahanyar's years as a general, his esteemed status as a military hero, had perhaps made him a little reckless, but I felt honoured being part of this display of courage, as if I were with Gandhi or Martin Luther King on one of their historic marches of unarmed defiance.

Inside the polling compound Jahanyar was stopped by a cripple with two short walking sticks, a ridiculously bent back, and the face of John the Baptist. He and Jahanyar had an

animated dialogue and I was reminded of a Sufi story in which a king looking for an answer to a terrible dilemma is met by a scruffy beggar – but the king cannot see past the low status of the beggar and consults instead with many wise men who cannot help him. Ultimately, only the beggar holds the answer, and the king is humbled, learning that one shouldn't let superficial attributes blind one to truth. Many people joined us – wedging notes between his bent fingers and the top of his stick.

After Jahanyar had cast his vote, I noticed that the garden around us was filled with large blooming sunflowers – it was as if the spirit of Vincent Van Gogh and our Yellow House had extended its protection to the polling station. The walk back was slow, but Jahanyar insisted I stay by his side. My three cameramen were nervous that we were stretching our luck and said we should split while the going was good, but I stayed with Jahanyar until we reached his house. Outside, the Kabul River was flowing strongly from the snowmelt and rain, eddies and surges of small wavelets formed as the snow-covered mountains of Tora Bora loomed above this fertile plateau. In my mind I started entering spaces on the other side of the river and imagined what it would be like to spend half of the rest of my life here – seeing the Yellow House artists evolve and

encouraging newer, younger ones. I could envision planting roses to make a larger garden for my peacocks and monkeys, and making art that wasn't about war or violence, but a celebration of the end of both.

The reporters that evening on TV international news on the BBC and Al Jazeera seemed disappointed not to have negative stories to tell about Taliban attacks compromising the election. The only candidate that got any prominence was Abdullah Abdullah. It was as if Ashraf Ghani didn't count. Either the reporters had done very superficial research or there was a conspiracy to only promote the candidate favoured by the Americans and NATO. My take is that Ashraf Ghani cannot be bought and is too smart to be manipulated by US interests and bribes.

At the end of the day, the feeling at the Yellow House was euphoric, all believing their hero, Ashraf Ghani, had won and this would mean a much, much better future for the arts, women and Afghanistan in general. Ashraf Ghani has a daughter in New York who is a prominent contemporary artist doing performances and installations. His wife is a Christian – these factors alone make our community of artists, especially the women like Neha, excited to see what he will do once in power.

ROCKETS ON THE ROAD

Our documentary *Love City* has been selected for a major film award in Norway. Since the film had been funded by Norwegian Film Institute money, and produced by Norwegian company Piraya Film, we decided to attend in person, and afterwards make a short visit to London to meet with an art dealer and catch up with my daughter, Naomi, whom I hadn't seen in over a year.

We didn't get on the road until about 3.30pm, a dangerous time. I sat in the front, playing the old patriarch for security. Hellen sat in the back with Waqar to sleep.

As we approached a steep mountain pass, I heard gunfire nearby, but there was nothing to see except the back of the large truck in front. Our driver, Nasir, is a tough guy with a deep voice and his scars suggest he's had his throat cut. He has a curled lip and is uncomfortable with foreigners in his car. He'd proved himself to be a madly risky driver earlier in the trip, barely avoiding a couple of head-on collisions when driving on the wrong side of the road to get around trucks.

At the sound of gunfire, he pulled in alongside a truck loaded with potatoes. Rounds ripped into the sacks of the tightly packed load. The truck was taking a pounding and our driver was using it as a shield. Then, without warning he put his foot down and moved ahead of it. I could see tracer rounds spiralling in front of us, mixed in with the sound of regular AK fire. Then there came the loud and unmistakeable sound of an Afghan army fixed artillery piece cannon firing. They were firing into the rocks above us and fragments were hitting the roof of our vehicle. The Taliban fired back with equal ferocity. Our driver sped through, gambling that neither side would shoot at civilians as any car could contain relatives of the families of either side.

Hellen woke to find us in the middle of a battle. As she jolted alert, the car in front of us decided it was safer to turn around. We almost collided as it did a U-turn and just managed to swerve around it when an RPG rocket shot over our bonnet and past our windscreen into the hills above. It seemed to be travelling in slow motion – the whole thing felt more like cinema than reality. We only knew we were through the heavy crossfire when we passed a bunch of very nervous-looking Afghan army soldiers taking cover behind their vehicles.

We flew to Europe sky-high on adrenaline.

The Great Coat

POLISARIO REFUGEE CAMP,
TINDOUF, WESTERN SAHARA, ALGERIA,
11 FEBRUARY 1994

The only regular item of uniform worn by Polisario soldiers are these army greatcoats. Misha's father was home on a very rare visit to their tent in the refugee camp. Misha had eight brothers and sisters who all wanted time with their father. However, their mother demanded some time alone with her husband. He has less than twenty-four hours' leave. They hadn't seen him in three years. I, naturally, assumed he was making love with their mum in the tent.

A sandstorm was blowing and all the tents were shaking and flapping. Unable to have her father in person, Misha tiptoed into the tent and took his coat. Then she proceeded to swagger around in the proud manner of her father. All the kids loved it. Her mimicry then turned from the serious to the comical.

It became a child's send-up of men, war and the plight of their families. The other children laughed so much some had to lie down and roll around, holding their stomachs.

Naomi

My daughter, Naomi, was born just a few months before my father died. She has inherited my mother's creativity, as I did. For good or bad, she got the fearless gene as well.

I got a punching bag and boxing gear to teach my son, Harley, to fight just as my grandfather had taught me. I was surprised when Naomi showed even more interest than her brother. I taught her how to punch, duck and weave and she showed incredible ability. Naomi, like Harley, is a head taller than me and very athletic. One Australia Day, Naomi and her girlfriends were at Cronulla for the fireworks and partying. There'd been news of a local gang of tough girls going around beating up and slashing the faces of pretty girls. I was working late when Naomi and her friend Melany came in flustered and excited. Naomi had been attacked by the leader of that gang, but defended herself so well she'd been pulled off by two witnesses. The scene made it into the media and the next day Naomi and Melany did an interview about it on radio where Mel bragged, 'Naomi's dad taught her how to fight and Naomi taught me'.

Naomi is a very strong personality and highly competitive. Like her mother and my grandfather, she loves horses and spent much of her childhood on the back of her beautiful black stallion, Mirage, winning show-jumping events. For a time, it seemed she would have a career with horses. But Naomi also loved the underwater world and when she left school to attend the Whitehouse Institute of Design, her first assignment was to dress her friend Kalinka in a wedding gown and photograph her modelling it underwater.

It was midwinter and Kalinka had to dive off Bundeena wharf in the long white layered gown. I was part of Naomi's crew with my Nikonos underwater camera. The shoot was going well and we had more than enough images so I swam in towards the beach. Then I heard Naomi screaming, 'Dad, what are you doing? We're still in the middle of the shoot. Get back here!' It was like hearing my own voice coming back at me.

Naomi can draw brilliantly. My personal belief is that there are far fewer people in this world who can draw than can paint and that Naomi has exceptional talent. Recently she has focussed on classical technique and visionary art. But, just as the ocean was my alternative career (for a long time I planned to be a marine biologist), she too has felt its pull.

A few years ago she decided she wanted to learn scuba diving and took a job on a Caribbean island called Utila, off the coast of Honduras. Hearing it was a former pirate island and that the airport there and boats were still used for transporting drugs and other contraband, I became worried and decided to pay her a visit. But when I arrived Naomi was very much in charge. She was dating a former Miami cop of Cuban-American origin who ran the dive school where Naomi had originally come to work. She couldn't have seemed less like some princess needing help from a concerned dad. And the boyfriend, with his history in the Miami Police, was a genuine tough guy with more than enough ability to protect my daughter.

On the island, they called Naomi the Whale Shark-Whisperer because she always seemed to find the whale sharks that most of the tourists had paid to see and snorkel with. It was here that Naomi discovered she had an incredible lung capacity and became a competitive free diver. Her boyfriend specialised in cave diving and that's actually how he proposed. They were coming back from a deep and dangerous exploratory dive when she saw something glittering on the line that the

divers run as a guide back to the surface. As she got closer, she realised it was a diamond ring with a note asking her to marry him. (It's a wonderfully romantic story but the engagement broke off; I assume because both personalities were too strong for one another.)

I used to have a regular gig on a radio station in Texas during 2011 when I was preparing my *Witness to War* retrospective at Houston's Station Museum. The audience liked my true-life war stories, and I was always proud of the number of positive listener call-ins. In one show I asked Naomi to share the mike and she told of her adventures in underwater caves discovering the bones of woolly mammoths, ancient Inca treasure and

the remains of schools of prehistoric dolphins. The lines went crazy.

On one of her adventures Naomi met a professional underwater photographer who has taken stunning images of Naomi posing while free diving in exotic underwater locations. Since she can hold her breath for four minutes, the poses in these photos are magical, she looks as comfortable with the fish as on land.

I'm glad I will have the chance to see her on this trip. The guy she's with now is Canadian and a fellow diving instructor. He has pretensions of writing but has never published. They met in Mexico and travelled from there to festivals in Italy and Portugal where Naomi has had mural commissions. Presently they are in Morocco.

I worry about her. Naomi mentioned he isn't allowed into the US as he's previously been mixed up in drug-trafficking. I let them stay in my studio in Sydney when they were on a brief visit home. The guy was proud of the fact he hadn't worn shoes for a few years. All I could think was, 'If Naomi has a gallery opening full of clients, will this dropkick show up barefoot?'. In my business, observation reveals all; I could see he was streetwise and full of low-class cunning – the kind of individual I call a 'trouble magnet', someone who raises the antennae of cops and other authorities.

I hadn't seen Naomi for eighteen months so I bought her and her boyfriend tickets to London and booked them the room next to ours at the Frontline Club. They'd been hitchhiking through Europe and had made it from Portugal to Morocco.

I was incredibly excited to see her, so instead of waiting in my room I went to a little Somali-run café a block away. I took my diary and was writing in it when I sensed them. It was a very romantic image . . . they were walking towards me, Naomi grinning from ear to ear, the dust of their travels sprinkled in a beige haze over them. They were loaded down with rucksacks from life on the road. They joined me at the table and the nice Somali owner of the café fussed around them. He could tell this meeting was very special.

I got them settled, then took Naomi to the National Gallery. I was keen to give her some one-on-one time and we headed into the swell to surf great art together. I showed Naomi how to view the skull in Holbein's *The Ambassadors*. (When one bends down and views close to the canvas on the extreme right side, a blurry shape becomes a perfect skull.) At one point in my career this work inspired me to do a whole lot of elongated heads – the glitter paintings. Naomi promptly showed some passers-by the secret, to their amazement and surprise.

Naomi soon learnt that in every large room of the National there were two or three great works while the rest of the space was padded out with 'also-rans'. We began analysing what made the greats great and the others ordinary. When we got to the post-impressionists, a crowd eight deep was stuck in front of the Van Goghs. I pushed my way through to show her how Vincent usually drew the work in a crimson colour with dammar varnish mixed with the oil, then it became a matter of colouring with the oils. Vincent liked to get the drawing right and then concentrate totally on colour and texture. He had a light touch and could paint blue over yellow and still retain the blue.

The first artist Naomi became excited about wasn't her dad, but fellow Yellow House artist Martin Sharp. Visiting his studio home in Bellevue Hill as a child, she was enchanted by his juxtaposition of colour and mastery of design that gave his work maximum 'bang'.

We were gravitating towards what was once the most important painting in the museum for Naomi. There was a time when she wasn't interested in art and thought her career would be with horses. We had three horses stabled and Naomi went with her mother most afternoons to ride them and on the weekends they both went to pony club while Harley and I went on surfing trips. For work experience she spent time at the stables of racing legend Gai Waterhouse. A very different world and childhood from my own, with my horse-trainer grandfather, George Halpin, but there were parallels.

The painting we flowed towards as if drawn by a king tide was George Stubbs' painting of a rearing horse on a plain background. On an earlier trip to London, when Naomi was younger, I bought a poster of this painting as a gift and she had it in her bedroom for many years.

Lament for Stari Most

The destruction of the Stari Most (Old Bridge) at Mostar has been a central image in my thoughts about the Bosnian conflict – even before I came here.

The Stari Most once crossed the Neretva river from east to west. It was completed in 1566 by the Turkish builder Hajrudin – a pupil of the famous architect Sinan, who created the famous Blue Mosque, among others, in Istanbul. Hajrudin used master stonemasons from Dubrovnik. A local rumour is that a Croatian millionaire paid a million dollars to the army to be allowed to blow it up. He wanted to purchase his place in history regardless of the negativity of the act.

Today I've been back to the Sarajevo College and Orphanage for Mentally Disadvantaged Children. After telling the tutors of my experiences in Mostar they immediately asked, 'Have you met Inka Catovic yet?' and took me into their music room where Inka was practicing the piano accordion. Inka, a Muslim, had survived on the east side of the Neretva through the siege – experiencing both Serb and Croatian bombardments which started on her eleventh birthday. She has just turned fourteen. Her parents were both killed in 1994 when their roof collapsed on them after a rocket hit their apartment. Inka was trapped for three days under a slab of reinforced concrete with her two sisters and baby brother. She yelled for help for forty-eight hours while comforting her sisters and brother. Her brother (fourteen months old) was the first to die. By the third day all she could do was tap a piece of metal. Someone heard her and motor vehicle jacks were used to lift the concrete. Inka was the only one of the four children still alive.

When Inka was eventually evacuated to Sarajevo she had no relatives so was sent to this orphanage school, where it was hoped she could regain her speech. Her calls in the dark had been her last words spoken. There was nothing wrong with her vocal cords - her loss of speech was due to psychological trauma. The school approached her problem through art and music therapy. It was with the piano accordion they really brought her out of herself. She already knew the basics of how to play it. Gradually she began improvising hauntingly sombre music. Apparently her mother had been a good pianist. The music came first and then the words. She still prefers not to speak.

Inka agreed to play for me. The music swirled and flowed like the blue Neretva river and was so moving it brought tears to my eyes. I asked her teachers to ask her what the composition was about. The answer came quickly – 'Stari Most' – the Old Bridge.

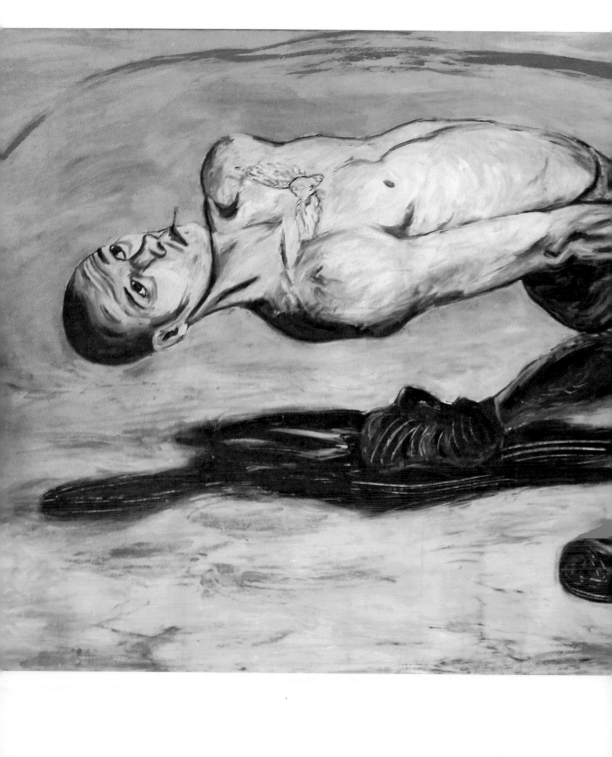

Ohio Farm Boy

The American invasion force is on the outskirts of Baghdad city but already teams of scouts in their Humvees are making quick advance guard probes. A few hours ago, Mohammad (my translator) and I were working on the bridge, filming a dead donkey, on its back and bloated, when an open US Humvee rushed past. I got a glance at the young soldiers inside and they looked terrified – putting the throttle down at break-neck speed – then there was a huge explosion which flipped the vehicle up in the air where it somersaulted. It had been destroyed by one of the many improvised devices which are everywhere, waiting for American targets. I had seen a guy with a cell phone on the other side of the road who had probably triggered the device by ringing the number of a phone attached to the device.

One soldier had been thrown clear of the vehicle. As we approached we passed his severed foot, still in its boot and smoking, and I could see his other leg was almost severed but still partly attached. We both took our belts off and tried to tie off the bleeding.

I came around behind him and pulled him up into my lap by putting my hands under his arms. He looked like my son Harley – big and healthy and only about eighteen. I asked him where he was from and he said, 'I am a farm boy from Ohio. I wanted to see something of the world beyond our small town'. I tried to keep him talking but he pulled his head around and requested, 'Please, sir, I don't want to be a bother to you, if you can just help me back up onto my feet I will be okay'. By the time the medevac helicopter arrived he had bled out.

MEETING Julian Assange

From the time my friend John Shipton first mentioned the possibility of meeting his son Julian Assange in London, I assumed that it would be foolish to connect us in the minds of security agencies, especially when I was about to return to Jalalabad. The one principle I've lived by is not to allow myself to become connected with any subversive political organisations. I know that while I'm a free agent and pursuing my own inner directions I will be safe from negative judgements by the intelligence organisations that monitor people working in war zones. Being linked to Julian when I'm about to step back into the frontline could be lethal.

The radical wing of the Taliban have already offered to remove my head, and this could embolden them to go through with the threat when we return to Afghanistan. The dangers I face in making *Snow Monkey* will be exponentially higher with the rise of ISIS and the success of establishing an Islamic caliphate over the territory they've captured in Syria and Iraq.

But when Hellen rang with news that Julian wanted to meet me, I thought it was meant to be. I never question destiny.

I went prepared to film or paint, putting the movie cameras in my black bag and three smallish canvases which I primed with ultramarine blue. With all this stuff, Hellen and I got a taxi to the Ecuadorian embassy, telling the driver to pull up outside Harrods.

Hellen was determined to buy Julian flowers to bring a sense of the beauty of the outside world in, plus a bottle of Jameson Irish Whiskey and some chocolate. When we arrived, there were three cops outside the doors to the embassy and two big, dark-blue vans that looked as though they could have electronic surveillance equipment inside. Hellen was wearing her black goat fur over her shoulders, a red dress and high-heeled leather boots. While I waited, one Rolls-Royce, Bentley and Mercedes after another picked up rich Arab women from outside Harrods with handfuls of shopping bags. I'd never seen so many luxury cars in one street. Hellen came back with a bunch of gladiolas and some roses and we entered the embassy.

A cop with a bulletproof vest was at a desk inside. I was surprised to see a London cop in Ecuadorian space. He asked for my name and I naively gave it. Julian later reprimanded me for this, saying, 'You need to make it as hard for them as possible'.

The atmosphere inside the embassy's reception, once we'd passed through the security door, was very relaxed and Juan, our contact, appeared. He was dressed in a dirty T-shirt and greasy jeans – not what I expected of Julian's main assistant.

The room had a receptionist and antique chairs with an ornate ceiling grid that brought home the sense of a gilded cage. When Julian

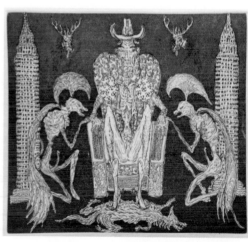

Empire State

My suite of
during

appeared he told us he wanted to talk in the open reception area as a kind of political gesture. The new ambassador had taken away his meeting room and he wanted to make him as uncomfortable about this as possible.

I explained to Julian how I knew his dad and he seemed surprised, but the link to family made him much more relaxed and he took us into his private workroom full of computer screens and keyboards.

He suggested we get something to eat. Hellen asked what he would like and he asked for anything out of the norm. Hellen shot back to Harrods for sushi and Julian and I got into some big-issue items. In the course of our conversation he showed an advanced and deep critical knowledge of film, especially political documentary.

The word 'evil' came up, prompting him to shoot out to his bedroom – he has to punch in a door code. He returned with a new unpublished book and pointed to the word 'evil' on its cover page. It was obviously a topic he was excited about. I asked him how much his situation was preventing him from doing his work and he replied, looking downcast and frustrated, that he was only at about twenty-five per cent capacity.

Hellen sat a large plate of sushi and a bottle of sake on a black toolbox which Julian used to improvise a table. The sake went down very quickly and then Julian jumped to his feet and disappeared again, returning with about eight partially full bottles of spirits hugged to his chest. These were his offerings and he did a spiel on the virtues of each – he went for a chilli rum and I selected an exotic whiskey

while Hellen got vodka. The whiskey was the harshest and strongest I've tasted and it burnt my throat. I imagined the various guests who'd brought him this odd collection. He was proud of its diversity. Every bottle had a story.

Julian stretched out on the floor and slipped his shoes off, showing pink and grey striped socks. I'd lost my shoes half an hour earlier. This was no longer a meeting but a get-together of friends from the same country and culture with similar pasts and professions.

Julian was aware every word was being recorded and I sensed that he was getting messages in for his listeners. A big one was that he was certain he would be in the embassy for another year or more. Only a few days before there'd been a press conference where the media claimed he was ready to leave and give himself up. He explained that this was a set-up and had no truth to it.

At one point he got me to stand up and come over to a side window where he pushed the drapes aside. Here was another big dark-blue van and a fast-looking cop car with stripes and decals. He wanted me to see this and explained that the police had put people in rented spaces in Harrods for even deeper surveillance. He seemed proud that he and WikiLeaks had eaten up an entire counter-surveillance budget originally earmarked for wider applications and that huge amounts of money were being spent on him.

The face I sketched out on my three blue canvases soon acquired the Ned Kelly helmet with eye-slit. To me, Julian is a modern-day Ned Kelly and I titled the portrait *As Game As*.

This image cemented in my mind – Julian, as Ned: defiant, surrounded by officers of the established order but, instead of antique guns, using his hacker skills and computer firewalls as armour with which to repel their bullets.

As Julian lay on his side and made lots of jokes the whole thing felt like I was with a really intelligent hippy at an outdoor campsite at Nimbin or Mullumbimby. I could see this is where this boy from the bush wanted to be and for a short time we'd helped him escape his gilt prison.

Hellen has romantic visions of Julian being let go on the basis of his genius, but I can't imagine the UK, having spent what they have on surveillance, suddenly having a change of heart and letting him go. It's a colonial throwback situation – an Australian bushranger encircled by bobbies representing the Crown. Julian is as self-made as Ned and as brave, but the odds against him are even worse than those Ned faced at Glenrowan.

The most passionate idea Julian expressed to me was about Edgewalkers. He wanted to explain very clearly that people like him and me are what he calls true Edgewalkers. He said most people who think they're walking on the edge are, in fact, a long way from the edge. The real edge is the razor-thin strip next to a steep precipice. Walking that sharp edge takes a lot more than walking some distance from the edge and fooling oneself that the self-proclaimed edge is really the edge when it is far from it. Julian sees himself as an extreme Edgewalker.

We'd talked for five hours. I'm sure Julian was just warming up and would have been happy if we had stayed to 2 or 3am, but if I was to function properly at Kabul airport security the next day, I had to call it a night.

As we left I asked if he would mind if we took some photos. He was happy with this but said we couldn't photograph anything in the room, 'Because I don't want them to build up a picture of this room and what we're doing here – there are clues everywhere that could help them'.

The appearance of the camera put Julian in a jocular mood, a side that's not shown in any of the movies made about him. Julian Assange the prankster came to the fore and he poked his tongue out and made faces while Hellen took shots of both of us. Then I took shots of him with Hellen, who was much better than me at striking poses equal to Julian's. For a moment he was worried the shots with her might be taken the wrong way. I offered to wipe them but then I saw a shiver go through him and he said, 'What the hell, it's okay. You can use them however you like, in the media . . . wherever you want'.

Julian saw us to the embassy's reception. We got our passports back and gave him big hugs. He told me not to give our names to the bobbies outside or answer their questions. Then he explained we couldn't open the door until he was back, hidden in his room. He punched the keypad of his door and disappeared like the phantom he is.

Ancient PRAYER

At the time I painted *Ancient Prayer*, Australia was going through a recession. There were homeless people everywhere doing it tough on the streets during a very cold winter. When I was about twenty, I had the good luck to witness the reformed homeless alcoholic Arthur Stace, Sydney's eccentric zealot, writing his famous message 'Eternity' in chalk on the pavement of George Street. Martin Sharp and I loved Stace's copperplate writing – I adapted it to flow between the walls and the ceiling of the Yellow House puppet theatre, while Martin concentrated on the word 'Eternity' itself. Stace was a near-illiterate phantom of the streets of Sydney, but he showed us that writing in the English language could be as beautiful and significant as Islamic or Chinese calligraphy. Martin maintained that Arthur probably wrote as much, and as significantly, as someone like Patrick White, even though he only used one word.

I was on my way through the Botanic Gardens to the Sydney Opera House, passing Mrs Macquarie's Chair with its convict-built sea wall and views over the harbour. Swathed in blankets and with his back to the wall was an old man who reminded me of Stace. Like Arthur, his face resembled the one Munch depicted in *The Scream* – all hollow cheeks and deep sunken eyes. I felt in my pocket for some coins and asked if I could help him in some way. He smiled a thin smile and told me, 'You can sit down with me and pray for all the poor people of the world who are suffering at this moment.'

I sat down and watched him knit his knobbly fingers together in prayer. His fingernails were thick, jagged and filthy. I did the same with my hands and have never been so moved by the simple prayer he uttered, which I repeated after him. It felt as though we were in a moment where this prayer was radiating around the planet and our hopes could really make a difference.

The first bit of paper I found I used a biro to draw the memory of those sunken eyes and knotted hands. Back at Bundeena, I painted this image of the *Ancient Prayer* in a manner I've never painted before or since. I gave him an aura of blue light, which needed to glow and sparkle, so I used metal flake – a kind of high-quality glitter used in clear duco by automotive spray painters.

William Yang visited that afternoon and suggested I put it in the Blake Prize for Religious Art. I did and I won.

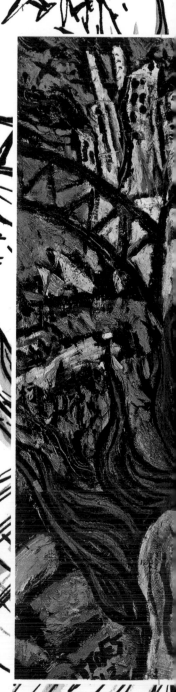

In 2005, Michael Moore was seen as Public Enemy No1. by the Bush administration and Military establishment. Moore's film FAHRENHEIT 9/11 was described as 'a treasonous attack on the Commander-in-Chief at a time when the US was at war'. The pressure put on me, when a number of scenes I had shot with American soldiers in Iraq were included in FAHRENHEIT 9/11, was immense.

BAD NAUHEIM

The US army wasn't worried about how I'd portrayed their MTV-generation soldiers in *Soundtrack to War*, but the scenes Michael Moore used in *Fahrenheit 9/11* were different.

I arrived in Berlin to meet my friend Mayen Beckmann (granddaughter of German expressionist painter Max Beckmann), before travelling down to Bad Nauheim to catch up with the soldiers I had filmed in Baghdad, who were there on R&R. I was planning a follow-up film and needed to know if I had their support.

My cab pulled up in front of Mayen's house in Dahlem and she came out with a worried look on her face. 'Your soldiers are locked up and they're refusing to let them return home,' she told me.

This was my worst nightmare. Those soldiers had trusted me and given me their consent on the grounds they were only going to be in an MTV music film – I'd said nothing about Michael Moore and *Fahrenheit 9/11*.

The advice from my lawyers was I should go nowhere near Bad Nauheim or the American army. Nor should I talk to or trust anyone. I should just keep my head down or serious charges might be filed against me.

I knew what I had to do. I took a train directly into harm's way. It is a long trip and I had plenty of time to think and worry. But my mother always said, 'What is for you won't pass you', and my grandfather had taught me never to back down, no matter how big my opponent.

I booked into a motel in the town Elvis had made famous in his *G.I. Blues* days. As I walked up to my room a couple of military MPs were walking down. They were obviously looking for me but had failed to recognise George Gittoes as he passed them.

I got my thoughts straight, steadied my nerves and went downstairs to face the music.

A group of the toughest, angriest-looking American military and intelligence goons were waiting. The doors were closed behind me by the military police I'd passed on the stairs.

All were strangers except the regimental sergeant major who had helped me to get the access I'd needed for many of the interviews. Obviously he felt betrayed and was the only one there I felt had any right to an explanation.

I was surrounded and outnumbered – but in no way cowed. Then, Elliot, Revak and Dull – three of the men I'd worked with closely – entered and stood behind me for my grilling.

I decided not to pass the buck to Michael Moore and told them, 'You can take me outside and beat me up, jail me or kill me in an alley but whatever you do don't take any of this out on the soldiers. They are all totally innocent. The only one that needs to be punished is me. Just me!' This took them by surprise, so I added, 'And I'm happy to stay here for a week if you need more time to think about it'.

In that week, I caught up with my soldier friends from Baghdad. We did some shooting in the park that surrounds a small lake in Bad Nauheim. There was no resistance from the military brass and I filmed some of the best rap battles I've gotten on tape. Janel, the beautiful singer who featured in *Soundtrack to War*, provoked the guys into giving their best.

I also interviewed Elliot Lovett who sculpted words like Picasso painted but didn't have the money to return to Miami. I remembered his line about Brown Sub being more dangerous than Baghdad and decided to cover his fare back home so *Rampage* could begin.

Happy Birthday

The high-pitched tune of 'Happy Birthday' has been driving me nuts. All day long, it's been impossible to film at the Yellow House without that tune breaking in. Our walled garden is like a small Hollywood sound stage where much of our film recording takes place. I've been sending the crew out to persuade whoever's playing it to take their noise elsewhere. It stops, then it starts again five minutes later. I thought it was one kid selling ice-cream until I went out to investigate myself. The music isn't played from a truck, the ice-cream sellers are teenage boys with barrows, a car battery and a loudspeaker. They sell ice-creams probably made with dubious ingredients in China or Pakistan.

I went out to film them, so we could cut in the footage to explain the noise during the interview we were filming. Which is how I discovered that as one ice-cream barrow boy leaves, another will arrive, which allowed us to film four without moving position, all within ten minutes. It's not a matter of paying a few kids to stay out of earshot, there are whole gangs of them, they number in the hundreds.

I have started to see their barrows all over the city – hundreds of musical ice-cream carts like a vast mobile work of art. This is a new phenomenon here. Refrigeration is unheard of in Jalalabad – we don't have a fridge at the Yellow House – as there isn't a regular electricity supply. So frozen treats were unknown until recently. A few entrepreneurs have started running freezers on generators. The insulated carts contain cooler blocks, so the boys have a limited window before their ice-creams and popsicles begin to melt.

This morning, confronted by the revolting tune, inescapable and continuous, I realised that perhaps rather than being annoyed I should try to include these kids in the movie. The elections had been interesting and we had covered them well, but the footage wasn't that exciting. The real future of Afghanistan was these kids.

We found out where they got their stock, so next day we left at 4am to film them hitting the streets. We drove across the Kabul river bridge and then quite a distance through the rural back blocks to a factory with giant pictures of brightly coloured ice-creams and popsicles painted high above its walls – inside was a cavernous depot for these small wheeled carts. Soon I had befriended a group of the pushcart vendors. Standing among all the teenage boys, there was an older man with a red beard and green eyes that made him a startling double for Vincent Van Gogh. As we waited to cross a road I told him that I thought he resembled Vincent. He smiled and told me he loved to draw. It seems I may have added a painting companion into the bargain. This Pashtun Van Gogh's name is Noor Gul.

I had thought just to film them in the streets, but each of these vendors were incredible characters. After filming, I couldn't resist taking them to see the Yellow House. Hellen was in the middle of doing a mask workshop when they piled in, barrows playing the tune. So the ice-cream boys were faced with werewolves, zombies and devils – they must have felt they were entering a house of horrors. Waqar was able to capture the sense of total surprise and wonder on their faces as Hellen removed her mask and began singing 'Happy horror to you …' at them in a weird witchy voice. This made the monkeys start screeching and the ever-curious peacocks come over to see what was going on.

I had telephoned ahead to warn Itchy, the Yellow House cook, that they were coming. We sat them all down at the Secret Garden Café tables and he served a feast of a breakfast. None of the boys go to school and all leave home hungry. The Yellow House breakfast was like a dream come true with fresh bread, eggs, cake, sugared cream, milky tea and Coca-Cola.

Suddenly I had an idea – it came completely out of the blue but felt as concrete as if I'd considered it for days and discussed it with everyone at the Yellow House. In a comic strip I would have been the character with a lightbulb flashing above my head.

I called everyone to attention and they stopped eating and looked up at me. Then I announced with a flourish that we were all about to go into business together. My idea was that they sell DVDs of our Pashto movies along with their ice-creams. We could go into partnership . . . the movie business and the confectionary business.

The boys loved this and immediately wanted to skip to promotion. I got out the glue and in no time our movie posters had been stuck onto their carts. Then I spent the day delivering bags of DVDs to the ice-cream cart boys and Noor Gul. After each boy received his bag, it was only minutes before they were selling DVDs. Money was filling their pockets. Instant proof this idea had wings.

This could be the solution to our biggest problem: distribution to our target audience. The majority of the films we produce out of the Yellow House have female stars; they are love stories, not action-packed blood-fests. Women aren't allowed into video stores here, so male taste often determines what's purchased. But the ice-cream kids mainly sell to children. The child customers can go in and tell their mothers there are videos for sale. This way we can reach the female audience, which the Peshawar distributors ignore.

What it will mean for our Yellow House filmmakers and their associates is that we will sell enough films to be able to make more. If this works it's a huge step towards sustainability for the Yellow House.

As a start-up incentive we're going to give each kid ten copies of three new films. They can keep all the profit from this original thirty. They should be able to sell them easily for fifty kaldar each. This is a huge amount of money to them; they sell their ice-creams for just five kaldar and popsicles for three. Most of the profit from these sales goes back to the makers of the confectionary. The Yellow House has now become a kind of business school and everyone is very excited about it. This is raw capitalism, selling entertainment and sweet things, bringing joy at a very low price. It is social change in a very sweet pill.

SUPERMARKET

In this medieval society subtle hints mean nothing – a cataclysmic explosion is needed to dynamite the log jam.

When my anger is pushed to white-hot nuclear levels at the Yellow House it has a code name 'Supermarket'. The supermarket story is well-loved here and goes like this . . .

I had a friend who was a soldier in Iraq who'd been helping me with my documentary *Soundtrack to War*. He had a young family and as the end of his second tour approached he couldn't stop talking about how much he wanted to see his wife and three small kids. He'd only had three months with them between two eighteen-month tours. His kids were growing up without knowing their father and he constantly worried that his incredibly beautiful wife – as seen in the photos he kept in his wallet – might start seeing another man. Everyone felt his relief when he got his orders to ship back home.

He arrived home mid-morning and the kids were all over him. His wife asked him what he would most like to do. He said, 'I would like to go to the supermarket, to be surrounded by normal stuff and buy treats for the kids.'

When they arrived in the family car there were no parking spaces close to the entrance to the supermarket so his wife told him to take the kids and she would meet him inside after she found a spot. Once in the aisles he was filled with joy and let the kids take items and open them to eat. His trolley was full of stuff with the smallest girl riding inside it as they queued for the cash register. Once the girl had tallied up the bill he handed her his credit card. It was the same card that worked in army stores in Baghdad but the embarrassed girl told

him it'd been declined. He knew it had plenty of credit but the army had failed to tell him he needed to clear it with his bank before it would activate in the US.

He didn't have another card and the people in the line behind him began to get impatient. He couldn't return the goods because the kids had opened several packets. The girl at the counter was turning red with embarrassment and called the manager, who appeared with two security guards. As this was happening he looked out the glass front doors and saw his wife having a dispute with some young punks who'd taken the parking space she'd been waiting for. One of the security guards came around the register and put his hand on his shoulder and insisted he come with them, and two of his kids began to cry. He slipped his arm around the security guard's, broke his shoulder and slammed his face into the tile floor. Then he took his kids outside and went back in to trash the supermarket. It took a squad of eight SWAT police to restrain him. His hands and ankles were cuffed and he was frogmarched into a police van in front of his shocked family. From that point it was a one-way trip via the military brig back to Iraq.

I have learnt in this patriarchal society that 'supermarket' is expected of older males at the head of a clan or family. I always claim I don't suffer from post-traumatic stress, but like that soldier, I am triggered to explode when enough pressure converges on me. My rational decision-making processes shut down and become pure rage. For me it's all bellowing of theatrical insults. I'm not physically violent, but the violence of those words is such that no-one who's experienced it ever wants to again.

BULLETS OF THE POETS

My son, Harley, was born in 1986, only a few months before I headed to Nicaragua to make my film *Bullets of the Poets*. This was the first international conflict zone I worked in so, in 2016 when Harley turns thirty, I'll be able to say I've been covering wars with my art, film and photography for three decades.

Bullets changed my whole life and approach to art. Meeting the Sandinista women poets who'd fought in a bloody revolution made me realise one can remain sensitive and creative through the worst of situations and not become hardened by what you see. Their brand of poetry was called External-ism. Its laureate was Ernesto Cardiale, a Jesuit and liberation theologist who knew every-thing that could be known about the direction post-modernist poetry had taken, but had chosen to ignore it.

Cardiale's own work inspired others, as poetry always has, to live life to the fullest. Under his influence, and that of the Sandinista, all the baggage, affectations and fashions of the contemporary art world I'd carried since I studied fine arts in the late '60s fell away. I was free to make art about life and not worry if it fitted anything other than my own sensibility.

Back in 1986, we were told the number one person on the CIA and FBI's most wanted list was Commandant Dos, Commander Number Two of the Sandinista, FSLN, rev-olutionary army of Nicaragua. Reagan was in power, drumming up fear of a communist threat to the US from this tiny Central American state, recently liberated from its sadistic dictator – Somoza. There was even a 1985 Hollywood movie called *Red Tide,* which showed communist forces successfully invading the US and going on a spree of rape and pillage. In fact, the opposite was true, with the American-backed contras (right-wing rebel groups) committing thousands of human rights abuses in their CIA-supported clandestine war in Nicaragua.

After arriving at Managua I was met on the other side of customs by US State Depart-ment people who wanted my film to be pro-American, or what they would call 'white propaganda'. They offered all kinds of assistance for cooperation but I refused. I was hauled in to see the American ambassador who told me what I was doing was 'un-American'. When I told him I wasn't American and would continue making the kind of film I was making, he made serious threats. I left knowing I would have to watch my back. Nothing could have pissed-off the ambassador more than the meeting I'd arranged the next day with Commandant Dos.

The commandant was a tiny woman, six years younger than me, with a boyish figure. Her name was Dora Maria Tellez. She was Minister for Health in the Ortega government and one of the greatest guerrilla commanders and strategists who's ever lived. She'd stopped

THE BULLETS OF THE POETS pg

NICARAGUA

A film by
GEORGE GITTOES
PART 1 of the
'Where She Dares' Trilogy

Las Balas De las Poetas

her studies as a medical student to join the revolutionary fight to 'heal a country made diseased by the dictatorship'. She wanted to turn Nicaragua from the country with the highest infant mortality rate in Central America into a model of excellence in health care.

To the CIA Dora was the bin Laden of 1986 and there was a price on her head. I was stunned when she parked a beaten-up Datsun sedan on the kerb outside the National Assembly building and put her hand through the window to open the damaged driver's side door from the outside. I'd expected her to arrive with a military escort or at least some bodyguards.

She wore a khaki military uniform, cropped hair and black army boots. She told us to follow her up the stairs of the Assembly, where she would relive the capturing of its 1500 members, getting a ransom of one million dollars, the release of political prisoners, and a plane out – the most spectacular terrorist action until 9/11.

This meeting was only possible because her girlfriend, the great revolutionary poet and very beautiful Daisy Zamora, had given us, and the film, her blessing.

Daisy tells a beautiful story of how they prepared for the raid. They painted trucks to look like army vehicles with all the military insignia printed onto them. Daisy didn't participate in the raid but she helped to cut Dora's hair to make her pass for a male soldier of Somoza's feared Guardia.

I sketched Dora holding a cigarette – she was a chain smoker – and her thumb hooked into her gun belt. It was hard to believe this tiny figure was seen to be such a threat to the United States. But in the revolutionary war she had been the commandant to take Leon, the first major city to fall to the Sandinistas. I was drawing a hero, a woman and a poet who had defied all stereotypes.

My next subject was Miriam Guevara. Miriam was one of the peasant artists and revolutionaries from the islands of Solentiname, inspired and taught by Ernesto Cardiale. She and her mother, Olivia Silva, were painters like myself, which gave us an instant rapport. Miriam agreed to take me to San Carlos, where she'd led a force that took the barracks from Somoza's vastly superior, trained and equipped army.

The islands of Solentiname are like an illustration out of a fairytale – just green hills that look like they're floating on the flat waters of the vast lake. There was an old record player that hadn't worked in years. The sound recordist, Chris Thompson, got it going again and Miriam appeared with a box of LPs that had brown sleeves but no labels. The first three albums were all Bee Gees covers sung in Russian and played by an unknown Russian band. The LPs must have been part of a Russian aid package to their comrades in Nicaragua and for us it was bizarrely appropriate party music. My mate, the Australian poet Jeff Cassel, was the third member of our team. Local girls arrived from around the island and we danced and drank rum like the night would never end. Before the sun rose we all went swimming in the lake and Miriam took me for a morning walk around the island. She picked up a tiny turtle the size of a snail with orange markings and for a moment I knew I could easily fall in love with her. That day we took a long wooden canoe fitted with an outboard motor back to San Carlos and Miriam told me her tragic story.

Miriam had been the leader of a peasant revolutionary squad that had trained in secret on the island. At that time, she was in love with an aristocratic young man from one of the cities. He'd never been attracted to physical sports and liked reading and cultural pursuits so hadn't volunteered to train with Miriam. In the early morning of the day of the attack on the barracks, he turned up and demanded to come 'to protect Miriam'. It was very typical Latin machismo but not practical. Miriam relented and he joined the group who travelled in their canoes to surround the fortified garrison. Their first priority was to free the political prisoners housed in its jail.

They'd been told by FSLN headquarters that on this glorious day the whole country would rise up and overthrow the dictatorship as a united force of the people. Miriam's plans worked perfectly and they were able to overcome the Guardia in the barracks and set the prisoners free. But back in Managua the Sandinista command lost their nerve and the only uprising was hers in San Carlos. Soon Somoza's air force and navy were on their way to confront her small group. Somehow in the confusion her boyfriend was captured.

Miriam had to give the order for her unit to escape through the jungle, as planned, to the Costa Rican border. She stayed behind, hidden in the long grass of the marshes. The cruel Guardia, knowing they had her lover, tied him to a pole in the courtyard of the barracks and began torturing him in the hope Miriam would reveal herself and they would have their revenge. They tortured him for hours before he finally succumbed to pain and loss of blood. Silent and in pain, Miriam returned to the

jungle and joined the others in the sanctuary of Costa Rica. She can still hear his screams and has been with no other man since his death.

Miriam was still an active soldier and her new fight was with the American-backed contra. They'd been terrorising the local villages – often cutting victims to pieces and scattering their body parts so it would be hard to identify what belonged to who for burial. She had agreed to let us come 'hunting contra' with her.

The Miriam I met that day was a very different Miriam. She was in command of a female unit – amazing Amazons with AK-47 assault rifles, dressed in commando uniforms mixed with feminine touches like small bows in their hair, some with lipstick and make-up and pieces of jewellery. It was clear they all idolised their legendary leader.

We headed into the jungle where the villagers had reported contra activity. But this was not a commando patrol in the silent way patrols are supposed to be. Miriam was singing as they marched – the kind of crazy song of Hamlet's poor mad Ophelia – half humming and half nonsense lyrics. If the contra with their American advisers were waiting in ambush then Miriam was making no secret of their position.

Suddenly Miriam dropped to one knee and began firing. All the others followed her with their AKs set to full automatic. They discharged so many bullets the rainforest trees were lopped and began falling. If Miriam had detected an ambush I didn't like the chances of those waiting for us.

The Captured gun

There was an old hunchback in the fighting patrol and unlike the others with their AK47 Chinese made guns - he had a new M16 American assault rifle.

His village had been attacked by Contra with American allies & he was out gathering wood. After they killed the whole village they cut the bodies up - mixing up the parts so relatives would find it hard to piece together their loved ones for burial. To join the sandinistas he needed his own gun. He tracked the killers to a night camp. Quietly he murdered them all as they slept using a knife and his axe. He took the gun from the corpse of an American special forces officer. He is proud of his captured gun.

Oct. 1986

Tea Addict

In Siem Reap my love of tea nearly got me executed.

After documenting peace keepers around the country I decided to rent a grass hut in a Khmer Rouge-controlled village to get an idea what the upcoming UN-supervised elections would mean to the Cambodian people in a time of flux.

Pol Pot's regime had erased formal education and most skills, including agriculture. Things were desperate. People were starving and would collect flying bugs from night lights to eat. The woman I rented my grass hut from had three daughters and they moved out to let me in, grateful for rent paid in US dollars. Out of gratitude the landlady would catch and fillet rats which she would leave on my front steps as a delicacy for me to cook.

Homeless people started living under my hut on high stilts. One was a fat former Khmer commander who had lost both legs to a landmine. He strung a hammock between my floor poles and hung there night and day. I had to listen to him making constant harsh demands of his wife who was the only 'soldier' left who would obey him. I tolerated him out of sympathy for his wife.

I was craving tea. To get a cup I had to do a long walk to a UN signal base and use their electric jug. One day I found a Hexi stove, a small gadget into which you could slide a combustible tablet to boil a mug of water. I rushed back to my hut and hurriedly boiled water on my floor and dropped a tea bag in for my first homemade tea in a long time. But when I went to pick up the pannikin the handle snapped off and the boiling water went through the

floor directly onto the stomach of the sleeping commander below. He was seriously burnt because, being legless, he could not react quickly to wipe away the hot water.

I was unaware of this until two Khmer Rouge soldiers with AK-47's came to my door to arrest me.

These were the same soldiers who had shot and killed their paymaster the previous week. He had been accused of creaming off money from their wages. I had seen the incident as it was only a few huts away from mine. There had been a quick people's trial in which the man's wife spoke in his defence. The verdict

was death. To my shock I discovered all crimes were punished with death – jail sentences did not exist. Once found guilty the man was shot point blank in the head and then they sprayed his wife's legs with bullets as punishment to her for supporting him. She lived but would always be a cripple.

These soldiers pushed me down steps to a crowd waiting below. I tried to convey my innocence and explain this was an accident but no-one believed me. I was painted as a cruel foreigner who had scalded the commander to make him leave my under-house. People began to spit at me, something Cambodians do when they are very angry. Desperate now, I scanned the crowd and noticed a man who'd been smiling at my predicament. I guessed he understood English as he had chuckled at my telling of the story mixing English with Khmer. I appealed to him for help.

Under Pol Pot anyone who spoke a European language or worked for foreigners was killed. This man must have kept his secret for decades and I knew he would be reluctant to reveal it now. But my pleas reached him and he admitted to speaking English. Those around him showed shock and surprise but my new friend translated my story with much humour, mimicking me making the tea and spilling it and the reaction of the fat commander. He had everyone in stitches. Sensing the moment, I held up $15 and declared I would give it to the commander as compensation and that I would personally travel over the border into Thailand to get him burn cream to ease his pain.

I had just survived a Khmer Rouge people's trial and made a brave new friend.

Harley

Dear Harley,

Today I was cleaning out my paint box and found the small herd of kangaroo creatures you made at Nan's when you were a kid. I must have brought them to Afghanistan for good luck.

There is one very small young boy at the Yellow House who has been working very hard as helper to our cook for the huge amount of catering required for the women's workshops Hellen and Neha run. He is a good kid but comes from so terrible a background he cannot talk about it. He has seven brothers and eight sisters, all below the poverty line.

I decided to give him your little toys. A tear came to my eye thinking about you and Nan and how she used to treasure these things you made with your little hands. I'm sure she would approve of them being passed on in this way to a kid who has never owned a toy in his life.

The boy has them hidden in his pocket as he knows if any other kid sees them they will steal them. He is small and not likely to defend himself. He loves the kangaroo – when you touch the tail the head wags.

When are you doing the big drive up to the Northern Territory?

The first time I made the trip was with Mum and Dad when I was about your age. When the Yellow House ended I was totally broke and could only get a couple of days work every week teaching art therapy at a psychiatric hospital. In those days, no-one bought my art. The Yellow House had given me a profile and I had been in the news but this did not translate to sales. Martin and the others had rich parents with rich friends who bought their work out of social loyalty.

Your grandfather had a caravanette – a small, old, egg shaped van made of plywood. It had a kind of kitchen box and two small annexes, one for the kitchen and one for standing up in. I slept in this van and went on the road with it, despite the fact I was too poor to have a car and relied on kind people to tow me from one caravan park on the South Coast to another.

I had to hitch-hike to railway stations to get to the therapy workshops at Strathfield. I remember my mum would come and pick me up to save me from hitch-hiking and we would sit in the little annex and eat the meals she'd cooked at home and brought down. I did not have a fridge, so everything had to be eaten while it was fresh. Needless to say I ate a lot of pies and fish and chips. But they were good times.

In those days there was a law that no-one could stay in a caravan park for more than six weeks, so I kept coming back to the park at Bonny Vale and

Bundeena became my stopping place. I grew to love Bundeena and dreamt of buying a house there one day and, as you know, I finally did find one – the house you grew up in.

My first time north was an accident. My Dad had retired and I was fresh out of hospital. A wave had picked me up and dumped me, scraping my knees across a coral reef and infections got into my bursas and there was even talk of amputation. This was when I was still shooting underwater films and photos like Rainbow Way.

Mum and Dad were on their round-Australia trip, the one Dad had dreamed of doing. But I was in such a bad way Mum flew down from Cairns to look after me then persuaded me to come back up to Cairns with her. It helped that I got a commission from Cinema Papers and Philippe Mora to shoot outback phenomena for a movie they wanted to make. This was after Philippe had become famous with his bushranger film with Dennis Hopper, Mad Dog Morgan. Their science-fiction film was based on an Arthur C. Clarke book. So I had my 16mm camera and a purpose.

Dad took the longest route to Darwin possible. We took every side road and devious route imaginable. You should visit Douglas Hot Springs. Mum went swimming naked there and got frightened out of the water by a wild buffalo and Dad caught his first barramundi and reeled it in only to be confronted by a large crocodile. I got amazing early morning footage of the steam coming off the water like ghosts dancing.

At Mataranka we met David Gulpilil who was dancing for the tourists. He had been in the films Walkabout and Storm Boy but was treated as a 'boy' by the older dancers. Visiting his reserve he introduced us to David Banassi, the most famous didgeridoo player ever. I bought a didg from David that he'd made from logs hollowed by white ants. We still have it.

For me, visiting Oenpelli and Roper River and seeing the Aboriginal cave art was the most wonderful experience of my life. I climbed high up into the escarpment and found remote paintings on the walls, many tens of thousands of years old.

I desperately wanted to see the great Wandjina paintings but Dad did not have a 4X4 – just a Falcon station wagon with a split differential – and we often bogged in sand and mud. When I got to Derby I was lucky enough to meet the great Wandjina painter Sam Woolagoodja. Sam took me into the bush and to Wandjina Caves, singing to the spirits all the way there. I purchased the Wandjina painting that hung in the house through all your childhood. It was painted with Sam's own blood.

I drove all the way down to Perth with Mum and Dad then flew home, leaving them to drive the Nullarbor. When Dad finally got home he had lived his greatest dream to drive completely around Australia. I was about your age on that trip but you are braver because you are doing all this on your own. It is exciting for me to know you are repeating these adventures in your very different way.

Of course there were many more trips north for the outback films.
Warriors and Lawmen was the first, then Frontier Women *and* Unbroken
Spirit. *The last was* Visions in the Making. *I also shot a film on Jimmy*
Pike in the Great Sandy Desert and another one on bush medicine for
David Attenborough.

The plan on Tracks of the Rainbow *was for your mum, as sound recordist,*
and the four Aboriginal kids we sponsored to meet us at Alice Springs.

Our pup, Gundie, was part dingo and would howl along with the wild
dingoes at night. The stretch from Kununurra to Winton was underwater
but I risked it. At times it was hard to figure out if I had left the path. That
road was just mud and not sealed for a few more years. It resembled a giant
inland sea or lake.

I had a tape player but only a few tapes. One was Willie Nelson and
I played it so many times I knew every song by heart by the time I got to
Alice. At one really rough road stop there were prostitutes working the bar.
They serviced the lonely stockmen who came in to the roadhouse for a drink
and bit of R&R. One of their clients stole Gundie and I was distraught but
a prostitute went and got Gundie back. It was a very kind thing she did.

Your mother and I had the happiest times of our marriage making those
outback films. Gabrielle had grown up in the country outside Yenda, near
Griffith, and loved horses. The oldest of three, she was in her element making
Unbroken Spirit – *about the last days of the Australia's wild west with*
legendary stockmen and cowboys, wild living rustlers, bull riders and bare-
knuckle boxers. Gabrielle showed her prowess on horseback and was more
fulfilled than I think she had ever been before or since.

You were born just before I headed off to Nicaragua to make Bullets of
the Poets *in 1986. By then we were in debt. Documentaries always cost more*
than they make. There was no choice but to sell the house and edit suite in
Baltic Street, Newtown.

After he retired my father had combined golf and travel but he always
helped me with everything so he came in to assist me to prepare the house
to go on the market. I found him sitting on the front step. I asked what was
wrong and he explained how his foot had gotten caught in the garden hose
and he had fallen and hurt his ribs.

I drove him back to his house at Cronulla but Mum was out shopping so
he asked me to drop him to the doctor as he 'may as well wait in a doctor's
rooms as at home'. There was nothing wrong with his ribs but the X-ray
found a dark spot on his lung and he was booked into St Vincent's Hospital
to get it removed. His doctor was to be the great Victor Chang, the famous
heart surgeon, so we felt he was in good hands.

The morning Dad was to go into hospital I had a cup of tea with Mum
while she played with her new little granddaughter, Naomi. Dad took you,
almost two by then, down to the beach. I went down to join you and have the
indelible memory of him helping you to dig a tunnel under the sand castle.

You were both having so much fun I did not want to have to remind Dad it was time to go to hospital.

Back at the house Mum joked about how Dad could not be in better health because he'd made love to her twice that night and had wanted to do it again in the morning but she had refused, telling him to 'conserve your strength for the operation'.

The next morning, I took you kids to see him before he went 'under the knife'. There was a balloon seller and we bought a heart-shaped red balloon with 'I love you Dad' printed on it. No-one expected anything to go wrong. I went for a snorkel at the ocean inlet of Curracurrong. It was beautiful.

I claim to be a mystic with psychic predictive powers but my sister Pam's phone call caught me by total surprise. She simply said 'Dad has gone'.

Apparently he'd had a fall when being moved from his intensive care bed to a regular hospital bed. The operation had been successful but the fall killed him. Mum was there when the stitches in his chest broke open. He looked up, fixed his eyes on hers and apologised for not being able to hold onto life. He was only 74.

I drove to your Aunty Pam's house. It was one of the worst waits of my life. I was expecting Mum to be inconsolable but she got out of the car very brave. I spent the next week in the house with her, helping her adjust to life without Dad. They had been inseparable – true lovebirds. None of us thought she would live long without Dad but she made it to 96 – and got to be a wonderful grandmother to both you kids.

Most of my life my mother had been a ceramic sculptor with her own studio, kiln and pottery wheel in whatever house she moved to. But the essential ingredient in her art turned out not to be clay but Dad. Whenever she was excited about her latest creation or just needed advice the familiar call would go out, 'Claude, come and have a look at this'. And Dad would be there in a flash to admire her handiwork. But after Dad died, Mum never went down to the studio or made a single new piece.

You can be certain I will come up north again and relive memories with you. I always loved it when I left the Queensland roads and hit the Stuart Highway. The air, the light – everything felt different. There is something about the Territory that talks to my soul. I hope it talks to yours too.

Lots of love,
Dad

IT ALL WORKED OUT

My mother died in her sleep after a good day out with her friends from the nursing home so I didn't get to speak to her in her last hours. She had a smile on her face when she went and I gave her a kiss hoping she would find her way back to Dad.

Mum had become too frail to live in her beach apartment and moved into a serviced village for old people. Most of the time she was clear-headed and we could have good talks but there were times when she would begin hallucinating and go into advanced dementia. An ambulance would have to take her to hospital where the ward had security doors to make sure the patients didn't wander off.

When I arrived at Mum's room a nurse was trying to get her to eat but failing. I offered to take over. Mum was in another dimension. She was holding her arm up as if touching roses or hanging fruit in an imaginary garden. It was clear she was somewhere beautiful and was happy. I didn't want to interrupt her reverie but gently got her eating some food from a spoon.

Suddenly she snapped out of it and realised I was there. She was back in my world, happy,

and gripped my hand. I decided to run through her life with all the good memory stories I could think of – her childhood with Grandfather and Nana, our family holidays in the tent at Tuggerah, her trips overseas with Dad and her wonderful times going around Australia and up to the Northern Territory in a caravan, culminating in her large ceramic show at the Museum and Art Gallery of the Northern Territory. I talked about her grandchildren and the Christmases in the house at Bundeena and some of the successes her children and grandchildren have had. Mum held a beautiful smile throughout this telling of her life and made occasional comments letting me know she was getting it. Right at the end she looked into my eyes and reached the very deepest part of me and said, 'Well! It all worked out'.

I thought of all the worries this woman had faced, many created by me. No words will ever mean more to me than *It all worked out*. Our lives as a family were, in her mind, a success. What more could a child ask for?

SHAPING the DARKNESS

What I do is take the darkness and chaos of a place like this and shape it into something. Not just in a painting or film but in reality.

The needs of the children of Jalalabad have been forgotten in this never-ending war. Every problem faced by Afghans is reflected in their stories. I have singled out three of the ice-cream boys who are happy to be included in our documentary. Saludin's father is an invalid named Brave Lion who begs in the street; Irfan's father is an abusive addict; and Zabi's father has been blinded in a botched American raid on their home. These three boys, their lives and ambitions, will become the central characters of the film.

These ice-cream boys are aged between eight and twelve and are the main breadwinners in their families. When asked why they don't go to school they all say they have lots of brothers and sisters who won't get fed if they do not work. Irfan has lots of scars on his forehead and face. He told me his father is an alcoholic and beats him and his mother when he cannot get enough money to feed his habit. The brightest of the boys, twelve-year-old Zabi, has been stabbed by thieves and left to die. The youngest, Saludin, has a crippled father and a baby brother in a similar condition.

I have found them a better, less exploitative ice-cream company, so tomorrow they will glue our movie posters to shiny new red carts which have been sent down from Kabul and begin selling DVDs with their ice-creams with a good take-home profit.

It takes a lot out of me to make this kind of miracle happen.

ZABI, THE COUNTRY BOY

Zabi told us he'd been stabbed and robbed for his meagre ice-cream takings, so we went with him to the site of the incident on the road to Asam's farm, next to a graveyard, to re-enact it. Peasant women were planting seedlings in the fields in a landscape resembling the nineteenth-century countryside depicted by Millet and Van Gogh.

Zabi acted out his story like a professional storyteller. He told us how bad men had come up to him and asked to buy ice-creams which he supplied, but when he asked to be paid they said they didn't have money and wanted his.  They struggled with him to find the money and he resisted until they got inside the cooler and found his takings. He protested and one of them stabbed him in the stomach with a long blade. He was left to die but bandaged himself by tearing up his shirt and stuffing it into his wound. A passing car got him to hospital.

I asked him why he wasn't frightened of this happening again. He chooses to sell on remote country roads because there's too much competition in the city. He said, 'My family is poor and if I don't do it my younger brothers and sisters will go without food.' Such courage from a twelve-year-old.

Some nasty-looking street punks played the part of the robbers. Amir Shah always gets several takes when working with amateurs but these guys didn't know they needed to hold their slaps and punches and not make real contact. Amir Shah expected Zabi to be able to take this abuse without complaint but after the sixth loud slap to his face, I stepped in, 'Enough! Get on with the stabbing and we will be out of here'.

When it was over, a crowd of farm kids cheered Zabi as he passed by them with fake blood down his tunic and a grin from ear to ear. In an afternoon he had gone from victim to a movie star. To celebrate I told him he could open the cart and let the kids help themselves to the iced sweets inside. There was a scramble but everyone got one in a moment I am sure Zabi will never forget.

Irfan, the Karate Kid

I met Irfan on my way to his house – he was buying a single cigarette for his father. Irfan's house is as humble as it gets. Twenty to thirty family members squeezed into two small mud-brick rooms with rags for doors, an outdoor fireplace for cooking and a chopping block wet with blood and animated by maggots. I could hear a newborn baby screaming and I assumed his mother was hiding inside once she had been told a male visitor was coming. There were no glass windows, just a hole punched in the roof with smoke billowing out of it.

Irfan's father's name was Joseph and had a badly damaged face that had once been good-looking. He was clearly drunk. I asked him if he was a musician and he replied, 'No, but I like hashish'. Irfan is a thinker and has a way of resting his chin in his hand and getting lost in his own thoughts. Of all the ice-cream boys who have presented themselves at the Yellow House, Hellen thinks Irfan is the most talented and wants me to make a special effort to help him. I trust her judgement as she has taught many gifted and talented children as a senior drama teacher in Australian schools.

His dad told me Irfan memorises lines from TV dramas and has learnt to fight from watching action movies. Down the road from is a gym for middle- and lower-middle-class kids. Irfan has admitted he often peeps at what they are doing but the tuition fees make it impossible for him to consider attending.

This afternoon, Amir Shah and I took him down to this gym which is in the basement of a shopping complex. It's run by a former military officer who trained in Pakistan and learnt karate at the academy. He's about thirty and has a manicured beard like a musketeer.

When I told him I wanted Irfan to join his school, he lit up with joy. He'd been watching Irfan looking in on the class and his heart had opened wanting to teach him, but as he is only an employee he has not had the power. Still, he has felt Irfan's keenness from a distance.

I kept looking at Irfan's smiling face as he watched these well-dressed, pampered boys doing their kicks and punches – foot and fist making slapping noises against the red leather punching bags held by devoted instructors. I could see in Irfan's eyes that he was saying to himself, 'I can eat this up'. Even if some of the scars on his head are from his father's beatings he is still in a lot of street fights. Only eight or nine years old and already a street warrior.

These well-fed and well-dressed boys wanted to make Irfan aware he was among his superiors. I bought him a uniform and made an announcement that 'Irfan is training to be a movie star in our action films'. I then gestured to Amir Shah to step out of the shadows. Amir Shah is a black belt in Taekwondo and he did a spectacular demonstration of twirling kicks that even impressed the master instructor. I told them that Irfan needed three months of training to be able to appear as a co-star in a new action film. What little boy wouldn't be impressed by that and wish he were Irfan?

Perhaps someday those responsible for Irfan's beatings will be made to regret what they did. For now, he is helping me remove staples from the canvases I'm rolling and taking back to Sydney to be exhibited. I wonder if those who buy them will ever sense the hands that have touched them and the other world they've been painted in.

I'm an uneducated man,

In dreams, I can always walk.

SALUDIN, SON OF BRAVE LION

I make it a rule that all the kids that come to the Yellow House have their parents' approval, but Saludin stalled for weeks before letting me meet his dad, the crippled beggar who calls himself Brave Lion.

I picked Brave Lion up in a cab and brought him to the Yellow House for morning tea. He is a very proud man and wants to see his son succeed more than anything.

Saludin's little brother is two years old and has a crippled foot similar to the crippled feet of the dad. The family believes both the father's and brother's disabilities have been caused by polio. What doesn't add up to me is that both of them were born with this problem.

From what I know, polio is something you catch and not something you are born with.

I arranged for Saludin to bring his brother to Dr Fawat's surgery at 4pm. He was a beautiful little kid. His mother had dressed him up for the doctor in a little brown velvet suit with gold braid and put henna in his hair. The great news is that Dr Fawat agrees with me that it's probably a genetic problem and not polio. Saludin's brother is not nearly as disabled as Brave Lion and it seems possible that orthopaedic surgery could fix the twisted foot. We have an appointment with a specialist and our fingers are crossed.

LOT

The most repellent beggar at Angkor Wat is a little girl I've come to know and love – her name is Lot.

There is an ugly old man who begs near her, only metres away. I don't know what their relationship is, but he acts as if she is his property. Perhaps he bought her. She has been deformed since birth, unlike most of the other young beggars who have been deformed by landmine injuries.

The old man often leaves Lot out in the sun, directly in the path of tourists. Lot has no hands or feet, just one finger, a little finger, which she puts to her nose to depress her nostril. This accentuates her deformity and makes her more grotesque. It is a conscious device. Beggars are professional performers, all have an act and routine to get maximum sympathy. Still, Lot never seems to get any gifts. People are too repelled by her to place money in her lap. She has no bowl, and the moment after people see, then try not to see, Lot, they meet the eyes of the old man. He clasps his hands together and bows his head up and down. The combination rarely fails. Almost every visitor places money in his bowl.

When Lot is not acting her part she seems prim, neat and not at all grotesque. The first time I drew her she looked at it and traced hands and feet onto the drawing with her one little finger. So I added hands and feet, and gave it to her. She was delighted, and hugged it to her breast and swayed as if dancing.

Whenever I came to Angkor Wat I would see Lot jump for joy and wave to me. Yes, somehow she could jump off the ground like a dancer.

229

UDAY'S PALACE

BAGHDAD, IRAQ, 16 APRIL 2003

Uday was Saddam Hussein's gangster son. A playboy with a perverse taste for little girls who he would trawl the streets for in one of his many sports cars, getting his men to scoop them up and bring them to the palace or to a dungeon under the Olympic committee officers' mess.

Saddam had stripped Uday of all responsibilities other than running the Iraqi sports and Olympic teams. In revenge, he would rape and murder these young girls in orgies of sadistic sex. If their families protested he would order his thugs to bring them to grief. Uday was into drugs, rap music and as many dark and illegal enterprises as he could get his hands into.

During the heavy American bombings of the city my driver, a former tank commander, got a call from the gardener of the Olympic Centre. It had been bombed and the gardener was worried some of Uday's sex slaves were trapped in the dungeons. We went there to discover one of the grimmest sights I have witnessed. Crawling down through a hole made by the bombs, I saw a bunch of rags and Ahmed flashed his light in that direction. It was a dead girl in a chequered dress. She'd been beaten and then shot before the bombings. The dungeon doors were open and the scene was horrific.

On the way out the gardener held up the dead girl's clothing and I took a photo as tears ran down his cheeks. He told us he had been a university professor but had refused to join the Ba'ath Party so was demoted to the job of gardener. His son was a brilliant accountant forced to work for Uday. One day he reported on the losses and failures of Uday's enterprises. Uday dragged him out onto the lawn and, in front of his father and all the other employees at the centre, pissed on him.

Uday's men had left the palace in three beige Mercedes. We found the cars abandoned and already being looted. After making a lot of additional enquiries we got to a house where we were told the men were. Ahmed took out his service revolver and cautiously entered a room in the way cops are shown to do it in movies. The girls were in there with a couple of frightened minders. To my relief, Uday's heavily armed bodyguards had vanished. The girls were all twelve or thirteen with simple cotton dresses and scarred faces. Their skin was pale from being kept in the dark dungeons.

It was easy for Ahmed to get local people to assist the girls back to their families. What wasn't easy was preventing the local men lynching the two minders. As I'd crawled out of the dungeon I'd found a piece of a photo next to the dead girl. In the daylight I saw it was a torn photo of Uday and his bodyguards. A rat had clawed at the image with its tiny talons. I was holding a fragment of hell. I still have it, glued into one of my diaries.

Gittoes 2011-16

THE ICE-CREAM PARLOUR

The boys came to the Yellow House with their movie bags empty and their latest supply of DVDs sold. They wanted a meeting about something very important so I decided I could make it a special treat and took them to the biggest, flashest ice-cream parlour in town.

There is this one huge ice-cream parlour in the centre of the city. It's all coloured lights and mirrors, and from the street it resembles a giant pinball machine. The boys in their ragged clothes could never afford to go in there nor would they feel welcome, as most items start at 200 kaldar, which is about three dollars and they only make, maximum, three dollars a day selling their ice-cream. In this place, all the customers are men – women aren't allowed in. Most men buy thick fruit milkshakes, and rather than using straws to sip them, they slowly spoon the contents of the huge glass mugs into their mouths.

Here you will see bearded Taliban quietly at peace with uniformed members of the Special Forces squads that normally fight them. An unwritten agreement allows a truce within the mirrored walls of the parlour. A visit here is also a very special treat for rural visitors when they come to town.

We are six days from Eid, which means the country folk are coming into the city bazaar to buy presents and delicacies for the celebration. Most of the men in the ice-cream parlour regard this as a once or twice a year treat and relish the lights and glittering decorations. Today is even more special as there are three flat-screen TV sets mounted high on columns broadcasting the long ritual of the presidential inauguration ceremony.

The boys had hardly sat down before they made their big announcement. They told me they now call themselves *sha'warrie*, which means 'snow monkeys', and they want to make their own drama by the same name. Their eyes became huge when the ice-cream arrived. It is hand made at the front of the parlour by muscled men who beat and pound it into ice-cream with heavy wooden bats. There's a high pillar of ice next to them, which looks totally exotic in the heat of Jalalabad. The ice-cream arrives on a silver tray with two high peaks like white unicorn horns and is delicious. Some kind of white rind is around the base – possibly shredded coconut, but hard to identify.

The boys articulated their idea for the drama perfectly. They made it clear that if they were going to sell films they wanted to know the whole business so they could make and sell films based on their own stories. They wanted their first production to be autobiographical. I shouldn't have been surprised: in order for these kids to become ice-cream sellers they had been motivated and entreprenurial enough to earn deposits for the carts and the sweet merchandise, and aggressively gone out with their 'Happy Birthday' tune and peddled enough to keep their little franchises going.

I saw this as a chance to convince them of the importance of going to school. Explaining that while they don't need much education to sell ice-cream, if they are going to write, direct and read film scripts they need to become literate.

The Yellow House has changed so much since it started out as an exclusively artist collective. It's now more of a centre for gifted and talented children from very poor families.

we'd make our own movie
and call it Snow Monkey.

Mohad Jabary

HEBRON, WEST BANK, PALESTINE, 13 MARCH 1994
(END OF RAMADAN)

I am not sure of Mohad's age – Madji (my friend and translator) tells me he is only nine years old, but compared with my son – who is about to turn eight – Mohad seems much older. He belongs to a family of thirteen children.

He was in the Hebron Mosque praying with his father, Abed Alkak Jabary, his uncle, and brother Salman when the shooting began. He tells us how his father saw the gun muzzle turning towards them and put his body in front of Mohad – to shield him. He felt the impact when his father took the bullets for him, and was soaked with his blood. He tells us how there was more than one shooter – but I cannot get a clear answer from him on the exact number.

He mentions grenades being thrown and Israeli troops shooting people as they fled from the mosque. There are vertical scratches on Mohad's cheeks which make it seem as though his tears have worn paths down his face. When I first saw him his face had an unearthly, ghostly paleness to it. He was surrounded by mourning women – his grief and pain brought out all my fathering instincts. I was pleased that I had an elaborate Swiss army knife in my pocket which I could give him.

Doing the drawing also helped. I felt terribly inadequate. Nothing I could do seemed to help, seemed significant enough.

Through a translator I promised Mohad, and his adult relatives, that should he ever wish to gain higher education in an Australian school or university, I would be happy to sponsor him.

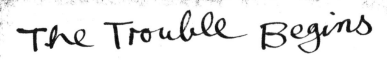

The Trouble Begins

Today is 9/11 and there is always tension here with the possibility of the Taliban launching actions to mark their defiance.

I got my own 9/11 via email this morning.

My daughter Naomi is in jail in Croatia. She and her boyfriend were arrested at the Outlook Festival – one of Europe's biggest music gigs. If I do not do something quickly they will hold her for a month before there is a chance to ask for bail. There are no other English speakers and her hardened female cellmate is already asking for protection money.

She has been in jail since the fifth, including five days without contact with the outside. Another cellmate was released and told the Australian Embassy, which is how they knew to tell the family. The police have not let her contact her family, lawyers or embassy.

The Australian Embassy is doing all they can.

Dear [Name obscured],

I just received an email saying that my daughter Naomi is being detained in Croatia after attending an arts festival. I spent a week with Naomi in London, just prior to her departure for the Outlook Festival. Naomi had a commission to do mural work during the festival and was there in a professional and official capacity. She was a featured artist on the Outlook Festival website. Naomi is a highly regarded mural artist and has done many commissions of this kind.

I am presently in Jalalabad, Afghanistan, making a film for SBS with funding from Screen Australia. My partner, Hellen Rose, is doing a project – for the Department of Foreign Affairs and Trade (DFAT) and the Australian Embassy in Kabul – involving media workshops for Afghan women.

I am prepared to do what it takes for Naomi and if necessary will fly to Croatia to be of assistance. If it is necessary to pay an English-speaking lawyer to represent her, I am more than willing to fund this request.

This is a very worrying situation. I do not have any details of the reasons for Naomi's detention. Naomi is of flawless character and has a clean record on all counts. Naomi has never taken or been involved with drugs of any kind. Naomi is a yoga teacher and champion free diver as well as diving instructor. Basically, a clean-living sportswoman working in the arts and specialising in large-scale public murals as well as her own gallery shows.

I will try calling in the next hour,

George Gittoes, AM

13 SEPTEMBER 2014

I flew Naomi and her boyfriend from Morocco to London. I should have twigged that going to Croatia via Amsterdam and then driving rather than flying was suspicious. I have always felt the boyfriend was using her in some way. The fact that he cannot enter the US due to a past drug smuggling arrest has always cast a shadow over what I thought of him.

I am an innocent when it comes to these things.

Hellen is a lot more worldly. She compared the boyfriend to many of the creeps she has known who preyed on talented musicians in bands. She put a scenario to me while we were in London that suggested something like this was inevitable. But knowing Naomi's hatred of anything dishonest or illegal, I told her it couldn't be true and dismissed it.

Naomi is being held for investigation. No charges have been laid against her. I have no details of the accusations against either of them.

The embassy is telling me to hold back on leaving until they know about the bail. But what I am certain of is that my daughter is innocent and I have to get her free.

14 SEPTEMBER 2014

I'm on flight 797: Istanbul to Zagreb to get Naomi out of jail. The bail is $40,000.

There is only one visit per week to the jail. Her boyfriend is in a separate prison and Naomi says he has been badly beaten. If the bail is set at $40,000 the judge must see the crime as serious. Naomi is claiming her innocence. I am going to have to find a good lawyer who speaks English.

Sniper Alley in Sarajevo is a haunted place. The high rise
concrete and glass towers are perfect protection and vantage
points for deadly sharp shooters with telescopic sights.
Even now, at the end of the war, they continue to pick people
off. The old couple who live in the apartment above mine
have every window barricaded so that shooters can not kill
them in their living room. But yesterday the old man Hasan
went to visit their married daughter. He was late getting
back so his wife, Salma, cleared the window to look out.
A sniper bullet went through a tiny vent in the bathroom and
hit her in the back of the head. The glass was laminated so
did not shatter — leaving a perfect 3D mask of her face in
the glass. I cleaned up the mess and waited for Hasan to return

CROATIA

I was last in Croatia on my way to Sarajevo in 1996, near the end of the Bosnian War. I took a bus from Zagreb past thousands of bombed-out homes and farms to the besieged city of Sarajevo. I was running a gauntlet with others returning to the city. They were fearful for family members left behind in the bombardments and sniper bullet storms. I travelled with them never knowing the concern in their hearts for their loved ones.

Now it is me on the bus, alone with my fears for my daughter, surrounded by passengers who have no reason for concern.

The bus arrived in the ancient city of Pula. Naomi was in a prison behind the Pula courthouse. My ex-wife, Gabrielle, had made contact with a paralegal, a Mr M., who was waiting for me in the hotel lobby, an obvious vulture, preying on foreign parents unfamiliar with the laws of his country. He had a super-thin moustache, almost invisible along the rim of his top lip, and beads of cappuccino froth caught in it as he sipped.

When the judge saw Mr M. follow me in, it was like I had walked dog shit into his office. But he was impressed that I had travelled all the way from Afghanistan. He said, 'I have a daughter too.'

The ancient prison was made from sandstone blocks and was a space where time stopped. I stood with tattooed girls who looked like the friends of imprisoned prostitutes or junkies and a pimp sporting large skull rings on every finger. His collection of skulls was hypnotic to my tired brain – they moved like a band of tiny ghost-puppets when he used his phone or checked his wallet. A turnkey let us into a smaller containment area one by one

and I was told I would have to wait one hour for a meeting with Naomi. I was told Naomi's boyfriend was visiting and it would be another hour of waiting. I prowled the stone courtyard for a very long hour – interrupted only to hand over the items I had brought. They okayed croc shoes, shampoo and sanitary napkins. Soap, conditioner and toothpaste were all rejected.

When I finally got to see Naomi it was through glass and we both had old-style phones to talk through. It looked like a scene out of a movie but it was horribly real. I told Naomi to be careful what she said as our conversation could be recorded. She told me one of the big bully prisoners was setting up to fight her. I promised to get her out by tomorrow.

The judge had instructed me on what she would have to say at the hearing. She had to promise to return to Pula for the trial. She also had to dismiss her court-appointed lawyer and drop all the appeals he had launched. I would not be present before the judge to help, so she needed to get this right or not get out. Naomi looked pale and her skin had broken out in small pimples which she had scratched. She cried a lot on seeing me and I shared her tears. I had many questions but decided it was better to leave them. She told me all the prisoners were forced to take sedatives to keep them passive. At the end, Naomi shuffled away like a zombie – slouching her shoulders and shaking.

Mr M. with the tiny moustache took me back to his office. On the wall across from his desk were two tacky black velvet souvenir hangings with symbols of Australia and New Zealand. I wondered if he had a box full of these things for all the countries of victims of the Pula justice system.

CROATIA: NEXT DAY

I woke this morning knowing with absolute certainty that I had to disconnect from Mr M. I have seen and experienced too much in my life to let an opportunistic creep like him bully me into making a bad decision.

A friend had given me the contacts for another advocate, Lawyer B., and his assistant K. They agreed to see me outside the court at 9.30 and the hearing was set for 10am. It was going to be very close.

Mr M. and Lawyer S. had arranged to come to my hotel at 9am. I rang Mr M. and told him I no longer wanted him or his lawyer. He was very angry.

I got a taxi to the courthouse and found Lawyer B., a very tall guy and a compulsive chain smoker with a nice honest face.

The judge got me into the room alone except for his translator. I told him I was going with Lawyer B. He smiled with a sense of relief and told me this was wise.

A fat young guy appeared with investigation papers for the judge and fixed his very blue eyes on mine. He had a bum-bag around his middle and a pink T-shirt – his clown-like appearance immediately identifying him as an undercover cop.

He was defensively flexing – getting ready for me to attack him either verbally or physically. He knew I was Naomi's dad and I knew I didn't look like the kind of man who would take this passively. But I realised there was a chance to get him to reduce the charges against her. So I let him know that, in my mind, Naomi was innocent. If any blame existed it should be directed towards her boyfriend.

Naomi appeared in handcuffs. It is a terrible thing for any father to see his daughter in 'cuffs. She saw me with the cop and, for a moment, I could see she felt I had let her down by not pushing him up against the court wall and beating him senseless. I winked to remind her this was about getting her out of jail and not revenge – she smiled back. Then she was led in to see the judge.

The judge set bail, asking me to return to his office with $40,000 in cash. Naomi would be freed the following day.

From the minute I arrived I knew there was something wrong. I waited hours beyond the time I had been given. Finally an angry guard appeared to tell me my daughter had been re-arrested on new charges and was at the police station. It seemed Naomi's fat arresting officer with the bum-bag had decided to make more mischief. I wondered if it was to get a bribe.

Naomi looked like the sky had fallen on her. We could hear Lawyer B. having a fierce argument with the senior cops. He won the day and, to my and Naomi's relief, we were allowed to leave. Lawyer B. drove us back to my hotel and on the journey told Naomi, in English, that she was lucky to have such a good father.

The old Russian-era resort hotel was no luxury destination but as the car pulled up, it looked like heaven. Naomi took a shower and we went to the cafeteria where, after a week of bread and water, Naomi piled food on her plate like she hadn't eaten for days.

Naomi showed me the cramped stories she had written in her jail note pad. She and her boyfriend had been separated into men's and women's cells but they worked out they could leave notes for one another in the exercise yard. Naomi would write fantasy love stories set in a romantic past on tiny pieces of paper and wrap them in rubbish – her boyfriend would find them and leave similar, child-like stories. She copied his tales into her pad, combining them with her own.

Naomi was torn by her need to protect herself and her love for her boyfriend.

The following day nervous exhaustion had set in – Naomi wanted to visit a dive shop she had been at when the cops said she was elsewhere and find some other witnesses who could corroborate her story and help prove her innocence. She told me that she had been with them during times when the police claimed she was with her boyfriend.

I decided it was safe for her to do this with my driver friend, Robert. I started to regret this decision when Naomi was gone for hours longer than expected. To quiet my nerves, I decided to go for a long coastal swim and let my mind wander, imagining being here in Roman times when this was a gladiatorial centre. I was swimming back and was about sixty metres from the steps, when I thought I saw Naomi wading in.

I waved and shouted but she did not seem to hear or see me. She was swimming out to sea – directly towards the horizon. I swam towards her, following, but she was much faster and the small waves made it hard going.

Suddenly I thought this might have all been too much for Naomi, *she's decided she can't live without her boyfriend … she can't take the stress of knowing he is still in jail.* Just prior to leaving Sydney a friend diagnosed with Parkinson's disease had ended his life by swimming out to sea – preferring drowning to a slow death in hospital. I started swimming harder but she was too fast and too far ahead for me to catch

up. I made the decision to swim back to shore and get help.

With the tide against me I struggled to make it back. No life guards were on duty. Time was running out. I knew that if I hesitated, too timid to make a scene, there was a chance of her drowning. I must forget about the possible embarrassment of being wrong. If she drowned, I would know I could have saved her, there was no option but to declare my daughter was out there and needed help. I ran around to the hotel reception, entering the front lobby dripping wet in my swimmers and told them that my daughter was trying to commit suicide by swimming out to sea. The reception called two security guards and they went to the roof.

I could see a head bobbing around a long way out. They saw it as well and decided to call the police. The cops came to my room – they still hadn't called a rescue boat. They wanted to check my passport and Naomi's. I said that they had to hurry. They asked me if Naomi was on medica-tion or seeing a psychiatrist. I said, 'She's just been in jail and is very depressed'. It was at this point they rang the police boat. I saw it speed from the other point of the bay and circle the bobbing head. I wondered why they were not helping Naomi into the boat. Then I realised the bobbing shape was a buoy, not a swimmer.

At this moment, Naomi arrived. She thought the police had come to take her back to jail – I had to go to the beach and tell the cops Naomi was back and okay. They were pissed off at me for wasting their time and boat fuel. The hotel was annoyed that I had involved them with the police – but what if she had drowned? I would blame myself forever for failing to say the right things to see her through her depression.

Released from jail Naomi grabbed
my diary, paints and brushes...

ESCAPE FROM BAGHDAD

People constantly suggest I have more than nine lives and must be protected by guardian angels. Not wanting to show ingratitude to my guardian angels, I have to say a lot of that is due to putting in place exit strategies. I've got plenty of them in place here, from the loyalty of Najib, the king of the Kuchi, to my network of trusted drivers. The best example of one of those exit strategies is the story of my escape from Baghdad.

I went to Saddam's Iraq prior to the American invasion and Bush's shock and awe bombing. Saddam was preparing for his 'mother of all wars' and the Iraqi Ambassador to Australia was under house arrest in Canberra. One morning I returned to the Andalus Apartments to find the reception staff terrified out of their minds. A notorious squad of Saddam's intelligence agents were waiting. They took me to the headquarters of the Department of Information. I was told to wait in a room with a TV crew. I came to the conclusion they were there to film me. They nervously confirmed that my guess was correct.

Soon I was ushered into a studio space where lights illuminated some heavily padded armchairs. A man in a military uniform – one of Saddam's ministers – was heavily made up and waiting. He smiled in a wooden way, shook my hand and directed me to sit.

He told me that I was expected to endorse Saddam's regime, praise him as president and denounce George Bush and his allies.

When I refused to do this, even through the thick flesh-coloured make-up, the minister's face reddened and steam almost appeared to be coming out of his ears like a Disney character. It was obvious no-one ever said 'no' to this guy.

The silent dark men who took me back to the Andalus would not speak but their every movement and gesture was threatening. When the door of their black Mercedes slammed behind me, the men in the other two vehicles that had accompanied them rolled down their tinted windows and glared at me through their Ray-Bans. One ran his finger across his throat before the vehicles sped off.

The Kurdish desk clerk had concern all over his face. He asked, 'What did you say to them?' I told him the truth, that I'd refused to cooperate. He looked embarrassed and said, 'Mr George, you have to get out of Iraq fast'.

It was time to speak to my safety net. Since arriving I had befriended the Baghdad mayor. He was a one-armed hero of Saddam's wars and a very intelligent and cultured man. I'd suggested to him that it could be possible to save his beloved city and stop the bombing by getting respected peacemakers like Mandela, Gorbachev, Jimmy Carter and Desmond Tutu to come to Iraq as Angels for Baghdad. If figures of this stature were in the city, the Americans wouldn't be able to bomb and there was a chance for a peaceful solution. He loved the idea. I explained that I'd already put the idea to the Christian Aramaic Archbishop of Baghdad.

He organised for the archbishop and I to talk to various people, including Madam Huda and the Minister of Religion. All agreed that it could work but when the mayor put it to Saddam, he refused to give his go-ahead.

Although the mayor only had one arm he loved to swim – as do I. He invited me to join him at an Olympic pool and we bonded during regular aquatic sessions. He was very close to his teenage daughter who would accompany him to the pool. She wanted to be an artist. I critiqued her portfolio and began giving her drawing lessons. She was thrilled and began calling me uncle.

Our best day together was when the mayor and his daughter took me to visit the ancient city of Babylon – he had been the main force behind its restoration. We arrived as a rally was being held in support of Saddam. A small boy was sitting on the shoulders of a tall relative and he was stirring up people to fight against the American barbarians, shouting they were coming to destroy the ancient culture of Iraq. The scene reminded me of Goya's *The Burial of the Sardine*.

The mayor and his daughter weren't interested in this propaganda and hurried me on. They wanted to show me the Lion of Babylon, a huge granite sculpture. The mayor said, 'This is how Iraq has always been and this is why I have never challenged Saddam.'

Under the foot of the great lion was a small human. The message couldn't be clearer – that the leader, the lion, must keep the people firmly controlled.

The mayor continued, 'When the Americans force Saddam out of power there will be chaos and much blood. He has been a cruel leader but he has saved us from ourselves. This country with all the tribes and sects will never allow democracy.'

I saw a man, a hero, who'd lost his arm in war for his country and worked on visionary projects, but he was a man who knew his legacy was about to be destroyed.

The next day I called the mayor's home, but each time the phone would either ring out or a private secretary would tell me he wasn't available. I persisted and got lucky. His daughter picked up the phone and agreed to get her daddy to speak. Deep down the mayor was an honourable man. He told me there was a Jordanian Airlines plane leaving the next morning and I needed to buy a ticket and he would pick me up and get me there.

I was packed and ready early the next morning, praying the mayor would arrive and not the black Mercedes.

He was good to his word, personally walking me past airport security and the passport checking counter and to the stairs leading up to the open door of the plane. I hugged him and hoped there would be no retaliation from an angry Saddam, frustrated at not getting my endorsement of his presidency. Throughout the flight I kept thinking of his daughter and praying they would survive the next few months. Bottom line: human kindness is always the most dependable safety net.

When I returned weeks later, they had vanished, the Olympic pool had been destroyed by a bunker buster bomb and the beautiful city the mayor had wanted to save was a ruin.

ASSESSMENT of THREAT

I got this email in Pula, Croatia, after getting Naomi out of jail.

FROM: HELLEN ROSE
DATE: TUESDAY, 16 SEPTEMBER 2014
SUBJECT: URGENT TO: GEORGE GITTOES

Hi darling,

Sorry to have to tell you this but the Aus Emb called me an hour or so ago and apparently we have been clearly named in a kidnapping threat. The Taliban have authorised a kidnapping of George Gittoes & Hellen Rose.

It's not sounding serious but the local intel guy may be able to tell us more if this is real.

H xxxxx

FROM: GEORGE GITTOES
DATE: TUESDAY, 23 SEPTEMBER 2014
SUBJECT: RE: MESSAGE FROM THE EMBASSY [SEC=UNCLASSIFIED]
TO: '[DELETED]'

Hi [Deleted],

This is George Gittoes emailing.

We had an uneventful night at the Yellow House Jalalabad last night. I have interviewed many people since arriving back re our security situation. My professional estimate is that we are safe. The general opinion of the police, security service in Jalalabad and our neighbours is that a mistake was made in not letting the local malik (authority figure for where we live) and Mosque Mullah know that we were doing the women's workshops. This was the job of Zwandoon (the co workshop person with Hellen) but he did not do it and did not tell us he had not done it. We assumed it had been done.

The malik has now been to the workshops and totally approved of the way they are being done. From the beginning we have known how culturally sensitive it is to have groups of unrelated women coming to an address. The malik thought we have arranged everything perfectly and he has given his total support. We are now going to the mosque and paying a donation to

the mosque. This is not a bribe but something that should have been done but has been neglected, again, against our orders. The system here is for everyone in each neighbourhood to pay a fee to help maintain the mosque and pay its staff. We have not been doing it over the last months. I have always made sure it was being done, in the past.

The Taliban chief, Maulana Haqqani, has also been here three times and given us his blessing and protection. I will try to make contact with him today. I am certain nothing has changed.

I am also requesting meetings with police, intelligence and security officials to get their reassurances about our safety.

We have been assured by everyone that the threat has come from some local without influence in the Taliban. I was thinking it could be Pakistani Taliban with links to ISI (Pak Intel) but no-one agrees with this. They don't think it's anything more than some local radical being offended by the workshops. The malik has promised to put everyone in the know about the good work we are doing and sincerely believes this will mean no more problems.

We have been told by police etc that they are 99% certain we are okay.

Hellen spent one night at the Spinghar Hotel. We are both back at the Yellow House now.

We have a lot of people here protecting us and all are heavily armed. Hellen and I are also armed. But we are all confident there is no need for the guns.

For your peace of mind I suggest you send someone to the YHJ who knows all the intelligence details of the report and we will create a meeting with police, Jal intelligence officers and security plus other relevant individuals. They can see for themselves the security arrangements we have made.

At this stage Hellen and I intend to continue to stay here and continue our valuable work.

Please do not judge us irresponsible with this – it is actually the opposite.

I can understand how people in Canberra who are unfamiliar with this kind of thing would be wanting us out of here, but this would be a cowardly reaction and we are Australians and proud of our ANZAC tradition of courage in the face of threat. We can celebrate the courage of our diggers in the First World War but need to be reminded this tradition is as much a reality in the present day as it was one hundred years ago.

Best regards,
George

2015

Celebrating Eid

There are two Eids – Eid al-Fitr, which is the feast marking the end of Ramadan, and Eid al-Adha, the festival marking the culmination of the annual pilgrimage to Mecca and the sacrifice of Abraham.

Trying to explain to even the most educated people in Australia and the US about Islamic culture and history is always an up-hill battle. Very few people know the difference between Sunni and Shia or basics about the Koran, such as the fact it recognises Jesus as a prophet and incorporates much of the Old Testament.

Neha is the only person in her family who's presently in work, so it's her obligation to get back soon and buy goats and sheep to be slaughtered in the halal way for their family dinner. We have two rabbits destroying our garden and she asked if she could serve them as part of

this feast. I got a dark look from Zabi who is a total animal lover to the point of being mainly vegetarian. He said, 'I already have three rabbits as pets but I would also love to have these two as well. If they breed I can sell them as pets to other children'. Zabi is getting the rabbits and they will survive Eid.

A few years back I was living in Peshawar and there was the constant bleating and bellowing of animals as people walked them to their homes from the markets. Most had been painted in happy holiday colours and designs. Someone who knew nothing about Eid would think these were much-loved pets and had

been decorated out of affection. As people slaughtered their animals the gutters literally flowed with blood, like rainwater after a torrential downpour.

This morning, while getting a shave and haircut at a street barber, I had two turkeys gobbling away next to my feet while I was on the barber's chair. I decided I would purchase the turkeys for the boys as an Eid gift. They all smiled from ear to ear and said their mothers would love it.

We have a beaten-up yellow and white taxi with a completely cracked windscreen and broken door handles. It means we're under the radar getting around Jalalabad. Once at the poultry market, we couldn't find any turkeys. The demand of Eid had taken them off the scene, leaving only chickens and roosters. Finally we spotted a man with just two poor-looking specimens of turkeys. Their legs were bound and they were squashed down onto the road.

Making films has a strange steam-train kind of momentum where it's difficult to put on the brakes, even when circumstance disagrees. I decided one of the two was large enough to be a reasonable Eid gift. This would be Zabi's turkey. We moved the turkey seller to a more picturesque location in the market, where life was as busy and as colourful as a coral reef. He'd been sitting in the gutter next to the intense traffic. I gave $30, the going price for a large Eid turkey, to Zabi and directed him to bargain for the bird on camera with Irfan and Saladin supporting him. The problem was the huge crowd. Waqar and Amir Shah kept doing retake after retake as the throng of people would overwhelm the action every time.

Each time the turkey looked more and more overcome by the heat and tension of its starring role in all this.

From this busy corner I recognised the bullies, standover men, pickpockets, hustlers and honest sellers trying to make a few bucks for Eid. A few fights broke out. Just as

Western families often have their worst fights over Christmas, these hot Jalalabad streets breed anger.

The boys came and showed me that the turkey's neck had gone very limp and some kind of green slime was issuing from its widely opened beak. The bird was stressing out and, within minutes, was dead.

The seller wouldn't refund our money but was prepared to cut, quarter and pluck it. I sent Zabi home with this early Eid gift for his mother, no longer alive but dismembered in a black plastic bag.

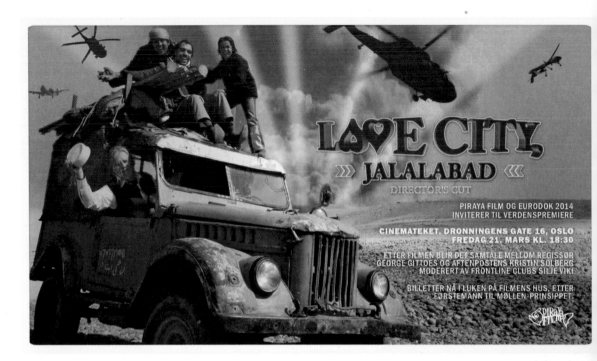

TORA BORA

The snow-capped mountains of Tora Bora, where bin Laden fled after 9/11, loom in the distance above the walls of the Yellow House – part of the history of the war on terror.

A couple of years back I purchased a wedding tent which we converted into a circus tent. The interior is lined with silk cloth dyed with beautiful patterns predominantly in gold. It a was new enterprise then, and, similar to my idea to use the ice-cream boys to sell our movies, I thought of a circus tent as a way to reach villagers outside the city. The fact was that if we only relied on urban sales we could not sell enough to justify the cost of production and needed to open new markets.

We decided to take our main stars, Ashid for the children and the action heroes Amir Shah and Marshook Shedab for the men and older boys, and our clowns like Amad Zia to make everyone laugh. I was the ringmaster with my little monkey, Dali. This worked and enabled the villagers to connect what they were seeing on screen and over a few hours they became movie lovers.

As with everything we do at the Yellow House which involves local communities on the outside we had to find a safe way.

Usually I go out with Marshook and Amir Shah to visit the village elders about a week before we would arrive with our tent and get permission. I am good at spotting injured people who need hospital attention and would always collect a few suffering individuals and take them back to Jalalabad with us to get hospital treatment. Many would have simple things like crushed fingers which could be easily fixed by doctors but if left to nature could mean amputation or lack of function for the remainder of the person's life. Most were teenagers and when we would return they would be the first to welcome us and would show off the progress made with healing their injury.

In every village, however, there were Taliban representatives, narrow-minded religious mullahs and basic dour conservatives who would oppose the erection of our tent, even with the permission of their council of elders.

The solution was our brave monkey, Dali.

We would arrive in our ancient, cerulean-blue, Russian-made jeep owned and driven by my friend the famous Mujahideen hero, Asam. Asam would have shotguns hidden in the back in case of real trouble but we never needed to use or even display them.

My trick was to walk a few hundred metres ahead with Dali on a leash, attached to a harness. Children would spot us and since none of them had ever seen a monkey, become overexcited with wonder and joy.

Dali never disappointed them with his impressive repertoire of amazing tricks.

With my long hair and beard I looked like a wizard from a fairy story – a Gandalf character – and the kids immediately accepted me without timidity.

Once the truck arrived at the village the crew would begin putting up the tent in a spot that the elders had approved.

This was always the moment where the enterprise was likely to come unstuck and where Dali would save the day. Kids would come from everywhere to see his tricks but this would attract dark looks of disapproval from the black turbans. Almost sensing the moment when the heavies were about to close us down, Dali would dash towards the tent and, like the Pied Piper, the kids would all follow him in. He has his own little flap in the canvas he would disappear through and, seeing his audience settle, he would climb the high centre pole and slide back down again like a fireman. We had an ancient whistle which would accompany his slide with funny sounds and everyone would laugh. Dali would do this three or four times to give our human performers time to take the stage and then I would announce the beginning of the show.

Our films would project through the performances and the audience would be drawn in to perform with the professionals, getting the whole community on side.

Meanwhile, the bad guys in the black turbans would watch everything with critical eyes, yet by the end they'd be laughing and would realise no-one in the community would support violent actions against us.

Once outside we would give the children in our audiences balloons and sweet candies. I always have a chuckle when I see the men with the black turbans queueing up to get treats for their own grandchildren.

None of the kids had seen balloons before and thought they were something they could pull back and flick their friends with. They needed blowing demonstrations. It was always fun to see how something as simple as a balloon could bring so much pleasure.

Most of these kids have never had any schooling, and possess only one set of cotton clothing to see them through arctic winters. Modern medicine is unknown to them. In the past there had been a tradition of storytelling and even travelling puppet shows but the Taliban put an end to all of this. When we told some of the ancient stories such as that of the magical flying creature, the *Simorgh*, old men would cry and castigate themselves for being convinced by the Taliban these ancient stories were evil.

When packing up our tent and getting ready to leave, as is the tradition, a small *jurga* would be called to discuss the event. The general discussion would always be in our favour and quite a lot of anger would be expressed that these Saudi-influenced Taliban had taken away the folk culture and traditions they had all enjoyed in their own childhoods. This really is the triumph of art over oppression and we would leave knowing we had ignited a mini cultural revolution against the fundamentalists.

When Obama set a date for the withdrawal of forces, our contacts in the mountains told us it had become too dangerous to take our travelling circus back.

We had never taken our tent all the way to the top of the Tora Bora mountains and this had been our symbolic goal from the beginning. To prove we could take art where even the most elite American Forces were unwilling to go. Amir Shah felt that, as an Afghan, it would be safe for him but may not

be for me, a foreigner. He proposed that he go to Tora Bora with our Yellow House carpenter, who is an amateur actor and from a village high in the Tora Bora mountains, and Zia, our clown. Against my better judgement Ashid, our small person, decided to go as well. The idea was to perform some community acting workshops and pave the way for the full circus.

They returned the following night in a state of total shock with the vehicle seriously damaged.

Things had gone so well, at first, that Amir Shah had gotten carried away and fired AK-47 machine guns into the sky. While Amir Shah is an action movie star and often uses guns in his roles, the bullets are blanks. But he could not resist the offer to try shooting real ammunition. They even fired at a passing American drone. In their misguided and euphoric state this seemed like a great joke. But the local Taliban fighters assumed that they were American spies who had fired at the drone to give away their position.

Taliban fighters came to arrest them. The villagers were able to group around them long enough for them to get into their car, but the whole way back Taliban vehicles were in hot pursuit. Zia kept the camera rolling through all this and their total fear and panic is captured in full. Poor little Ashid was screaming and sure he was going to die. Fortunately, the car I had hired for them was a new one and although they damaged it terribly on the rough unpaved roads it kept them ahead of their executioners.

The four of them returned to the Yellow House with pale faces and shaking hands. It is rare to see Afghans so afraid. For days they did not want to open our gates for anyone, sure that the Taliban would find them even in Jalalabad.

I did not want the bad guys to win so spent hours in the edit room studying the footage. There was one very talented young villager, Mir Zaman, who had shown real acting ability during the workshops. He had told Amir Shah he wanted a chance to get out of the village and work in film. He had a damaged eye from when a splinter had punctured it as he was chopping down a tree. My solution was simple, we would use the one and only mobile phone owned by the village and I would offer to get him to an eye doctor for treatment. He could then go back to the village and try to convince both the moderate Taliban and his community that it would be a wonderfully good thing if they would allow our circus to visit.

Marshook suggested that I go with him to talk to the elders in the Tora Bora village. He felt we could convince them of the truth. I was happy to do this as it did not put anyone at risk besides myself and Marshook. Naturally we were very tense. Hellen thought I was totally mad but waved me off with a kiss.

As we approached the village women came from everywhere, wailing. Women normally stay inside, hidden away, and we started to question our judgement.

To our relief the wailing had nothing to do with us. The village did not possess a vehicle of their own and one of the most important elders had experienced a stroke. All feared he would die if he did not get urgent medical attention – our arrival was a godsend.

Without hesitating I told them they could take our vehicle. Since he needed to sit in the back with his wife and sisters there was no room for me. Even if there had been, I couldn't, as a non-family member, share the same space as these women. I agreed to stay behind.

The people were astonished by our generosity.

I was invited back to the home of the Malik. I told him about what we were doing with the Yellow House. He already knew the young villager was receiving treatment for his eye and promised they would recieve and protect our circus and that neither the Taliban nor kidnapping bandits would be able to touch us.

Finally, the day came when we were on the way to Tora Bora with our circus tent on top of our famous blue jeep and we were stopped by patrolling insurgents. Our worst nightmare seemed about to begin but they had been told in advance we were coming and had waited to warn us that an American Special Forces team with helicopters had attacked a village near where we were taking the circus and people were in mourning for the dead. Then they invited us to share tea with them, but we elected to keep going with a grateful wave to the guys with the guns.

The children of the village had spotters on hilltops who called out the news of our approach. I walked in front of the truck with Dali, my circus monkey, on a lead and harness. Soon I had hundreds of children dancing and squealing with delight as we made our way to the village centre, making constant stops for Dali to perform his amazing tricks. Once we got the tent up, all children of every age removed hundreds of round river stones and rocks so we could put our mats down where the audience would be seated. This was the most excited bunch of children I have ever seen.

Of all the achievements of my life, taking our cinema circus to Tora Bora has to be at the top of the list. The joy it brought to the children was immeasurable.

MONKEY BUSINESS

About six months ago, Dali was stolen by Kuchis. Kuchi are much like some European gypsies and hustle for money in busy city and market streets. A monkey like Dali is valuable to them as a good earner. I offered a reward for Dali's safe return and since then the Yellow House has become a refuge for monkeys. The replacement for Dali has become Tim Tam, a young baby boy monkey who's easy for me to train with the kind of tricks children love to watch.

The boys take Tim Tam out on their carts when selling ice-creams and DVDs, the way I used to take Dali out when we took our circus to outlying villages. He is an amazing draw and a fantastic selling tool, especially when one

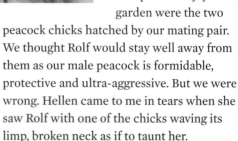

of the boys hands him a popsicle to eat. He holds it by the stick and eats it like a human – snarling at anyone who comes near his treat. Seeing Tim Tam lick the flavoured ice, everyone wants one.

One day Itchy turned up with a big gruff male monkey, which we called Salvador because Dali's partner, Gala, was named after the wife of Surrealist Salvador Dali. Gala took an immediate dislike to Salvador and would not let him near Tim Tam, whom she had adopted and treats as her own child. When we were away in Norway and London we got the very sad news that Gala had been killed. Everyone assumed it was the very large leopard-like native cats that live on our roof and usually content themselves killing rats.

Then the rabbits were killed, followed by our much loved Kuchi pup, Ezmarai.

I had always felt the leopard cats were harmless and had begun feeding them food scraps, to the point where they would take it from my hand. I began to suspect the male monkey.

With Gala out of the way, I would come into the garden to find this monkey holding Tim Tam down and raping him. I told Itchy to find another home for him and changed his name from Salvador to Rolf. Rolf, however, was also an expert at freeing himself from the night cage and any rope or chain put on him, and had become uncatchable and psychopathic. The pride and joy of our garden were the two peacock chicks hatched by our mating pair. We thought Rolf would stay well away from them as our male peacock is formidable, protective and ultra-aggressive. But we were wrong. Hellen came to me in tears when she saw Rolf with one of the chicks waving its limp, broken neck as if to taunt her.

Itchy could not find a home for Rolf so I brought a fisherman to try to net him, thinking I would give him to the army, who prefer monkeys to guard dogs. But the fisherman couldn't catch him with his lead-weighted nets. We then tried to drug Rolf with sleeping tablets mashed into his bananas but he picked the pieces out defiantly.

When Hellen began doing her women's media workshops, Rolf would swoop down from a tree and hit passing students on the head and sometimes scratch their face with his claws. The already timid women were terrified by him, the neighbours were outraged by his raids on their crops and constant scaring of their children.

The problem escalated into a very serious situation that could end our work at the Yellow House when Rolf tried to kill our next-door neighbours' newborn baby. He was caught in the infant's crib with his hands around its throat.

Hellen had finally had enough and told me to shoot him. I told her it would be bad luck and bad karma to kill a monkey – that it's like killing another human being.

But we had tried every kind of trap and professional monkey-catcher and Rolf had outsmarted everyone. Finally, Amir Shah borrowed an air rifle. He shot Rolf about eight times but the small lead slugs haven't slowed him down or frightened him away from his reign of terror around the Yellow House.

I have to face the fact that this afternoon I will need to get Hellen's revolver and shoot Rolf. I am the only member of the Yellow House who can shoot accurately enough to make sure it is a clean shot. This is not something I would ever have thought I would do. I have painted these monkeys, including Rolf, in about a dozen small oils and am genuinely a monkey lover. But I have learnt that monkeys are as individually different from one another as humans and they have their psychopaths and paedophiles as the human species does.

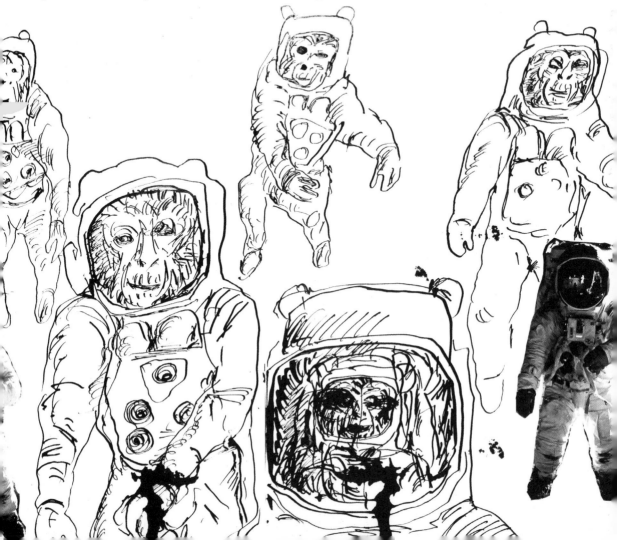

Sermon on the Hill

If I was given the chance to time travel to one time and place in history I would choose to go to the foot of the hill as Jesus delivers his Sermon on the Mount. The only thing that differentiates present-day Jalalabad from a biblical setting is the cars. But with no cars able to move on the hill today, I was cast back 2,100 years or further, to Abraham's time.

Rural people come from everywhere to sell their one or three or six cows, sheep or goats. Animals are decorated with coloured dyes – psychedelic pink, cerulean blue and mauve, or with patterns in ginger henna. The giant white and black spotted Brahman bulls do not need much more decoration but they have brightly coloured plastic flowers attached to the bridles around their heads. There was a long-haired goat dyed orange with curly horns – it looked like an hallucination from Mars.

I look up onto this mount full of the mist from small fires with thousands of silhouettes of men in ancient-looking garb with their beasts and it is like a digitally created scene out of a modern blockbuster like *Gladiator* – it is real, on a stupendous scale and I am in it.

I have a long white beard like a biblical character, and wear Pashtun clothes with the long tunic shirt and baggy cotton pants tied around my waist with a cord. I have sandals and a shepherd's black and white cotton woven scarf. No-one realises this old man was ever a boy born in Rockdale, Sydney, Australia.

It is as hot as on Mars, and fights begin over food and water for livestock. Everywhere there are opportunist farmers hawking from huge bundles of post-harvest corn and wheat crops.

I meet the boys near a small herd of long-haired goats that have been sprayed with loopy abstract patterns in blue, using some kind of aerosol can. Animal graffiti. I put my arms around the three of them and a crowd forms. I lose my anonymity. It is time to split. I sense my feet below me and realise I am on holy soil – meaning I have once again gotten myself to the surface of the moon and can hear Christ's words, 'The meek shall inherit the earth'.

I get to the summit of the mount and have become so attached to so many of these beautiful animals that I feel depressed by humanity's cruelty – that we must celebrate God by killing his most beautiful creatures. That these wonderful, living, visionary creatures will be reduced to chopped meat and consumed by hungry apes in a feast to appease a God.

At this moment a small goat catches my eye. Its eye is like the eye of God penetrating my soul like a needle. I feel a shiver go through me. A very old, fragile man has it held by a loose piece of string. It is beautifully patterned in black and white but the seller has added bold dots of henna. I have never seen something so beautiful in my life. It is a living work of art.

The thought of it being quartered and eaten in just two days is too cruel to believe. It seems to be talking to me with its soft white lips, like in one of those Disney movies where animators make the animals' mouths move to human speech. It is saying, 'Save me from this'. I can. I can do something. I negotiate with the old man and get the goat for $65.

Hellen has named him Aladdin. This goat is a living metaphor for what we are doing here. I cannot save all the animals from their fate and I cannot save all the street kids of Jalalabad from poverty and illiteracy, but I can make a small difference.

THE DARK ROOM

Irfan lives in an unpaved street in the inner city with putrid open drains and children forever outside in torn and holey clothes. It is desperation alley. As he carried his prized fat turkey home for Eid he was grinning from ear to ear with such infectious joy all the other little urchins began following him, skipping with the euphoria of the moment.

He slid through a crack in the gate patched together from different materials and the street kids all struggled to peep in but a dirty brown sheet hanging between the gate and his yard gave a second layer of privacy. My arm brushed the coarse brown curtain aside and I entered absolute pov-ertyville. It was a relief Irfan's father was out – probably scoring drugs or alcohol for his addict's Eid. But his sisters were there – four and six years old with beautiful green eyes like gemstones and the youngest is blonde. Irfan has fourteen brothers and sisters and their mudbrick hovel is only about ten by twelve feet square, maximum. No glass windows, just some bricks broken away at the top of one wall to let out smoke and a hole in the front side covered by internal rags. The door has a crude but beautiful abstract pattern on it brushed in white. I could hear what sounded like a newborn baby inside, crying incessantly this dark, dark room. I know Irfan's mother was sick from the home birth and visited a hospital yesterday.

There is a small open fire with some cooking pots. It's the kind of fire made with a few stones that I've improvised on camping trips and I wonder how this can work as a kitchen for a family of at least sixteen. An even bigger worry of the moment is how she is ever going to cook the turkey. There's a big wooden box where food is prepared, it's covered in the slime of decaying food and flies. There's only one street pump to provide water for about two hundred houses.

When we got back to the Yellow House Hellen had prepared Eid gifts for everyone – luxury foods of various nuts and sweets. But knowing Irfan's mother had been in hospital Hellen included in his Eid bag some sealed delights specifically for her, to brighten her life, for a moment.

A few hours later I found Irfan hiding in our *hoojrah*. He'd opened the packets marked for his mother and gorged on them. It wasn't that he was hungry – he'd had a huge Yellow House lunch for Eid. I wonder if his mother will get the half-consumed remains in the torn packaging or if they will never reach her. I haven't got the heart to tell Hellen her kind gesture to this other woman in her dark room was sabotaged.

Neighbourhood Girls

Until girls reach the age of ten they have a good life playing with the boys. Older women and girls look at these young ones with envy. It's as if they have a short window of freedom and are aware of it, so they soak up every free moment before it goes. They don't have to wear scarves over their hair. Good mothers dress the little girls in something equivalent to party clothes and enjoy knowing the girls are having such a good time.

We have started our own school at the Yellow House for the ice-cream boys, with the help of Inam, the son of the local police chief. Inam is studying engineering and has been a frequent visitor as we can give him access to our Yellow House computers and printers to assist with his assignments. Like his father he believes the best way to stop boys from becoming gangsters or being susceptible to the brainwashing of radical groups is education. Here in Jalalabad there is a blackboard exam for older children from poor homes and it filters a lot out, making it too difficult to enter state schools. Older boys who are totally illiterate are too disruptive in class when placed with younger kids learning the basics. Our street vendors are in this excluded group because, although bright, they can't read or write well enough to pass the tests.

When Inam can't make it, he has organised tutors from the school who are teaching the boys. We have set up the Secret Garden Café area like a formal school with the whiteboard etc. The teacher is a big heavy-set guy and is head of discipline at the school. Unfortunately, he doesn't speak English, but he is recommended by the headmaster and it seems this is the go. He's a tough guy and what the boys need.

I got them new textbooks and exercise books and they are happy as punch. Saladin and Zabi never stop smiling with delight. Irfan is trying hard to keep his mind on the ball but wanders off into a dream world. I told the teacher that he's an artist and should be treated as gifted, talented, so he needs extra attention.

WHITE MAGIC

I was sitting on the step looking at my dirty sandals and feeling the knee replacements under my skin and suddenly my legs transformed into the chubby little legs of a two-year-old. I was transported to our backyard in Rockdale and I could see and smell the white and yellow spiral flowers of the frangipani trees. I wore little shiny, black, button-over patent-leather shoes with short white socks and grey flannel shorts my mother had made. Where I am now would be as suddenly strange to the boy in the garden as walking on the moon was to Neil Armstrong.

It is a perfect day. Everyone at the Yellow House, including the three ice-cream boys, who are now full-time employees running the film distribution business, is virtually dancing with joy. The Yellow House garden is beautiful – I can hear our monkey, Tim Tam, calling for his breakfast banana. He always knows when I'm awake. A few weeks ago we put in lawns because winter is approaching and the ground turns to mud. It will be great for people to sit on when we do our shows on the open-air stage. Hellen contacted the Sufi gardener from the ancient garden at the Spinghar Hotel and he has agreed to come in once a week to look after it.

He has planted all kinds of yellow flowers around the edges. This has created a conflict for me because I have to herd the peacocks into the second block and close the gate on them. They would eat all the flowers in minutes. These totally vain birds cannot stand any competition in the beauty department and spend all their time searching for mirrors in which they can admire themselves.

Hellen and Neha met with a Pashtun singer whose old bearded father was willing to support her career in music. This is like a minor miracle because even the *thought* of a woman singer is totally banned here and could lead to death. The old wizened self inside me shivered with a sense of foreboding – the Yellow House has almost become too good.

When we set up the Yellow House I made a list of all the things we would like to achieve here, and now everything on the list has been ticked off. The Yellow House is realising so many utopian ideals I worry that forces of darkness will want to come and destroy it. I've seen so much darkness in my life it's hard to accept that all the light the Yellow House is shining out into Jalalabad will not become a beacon to lead destructive forces towards us. Please think of us and send white magic.

There is growing apprehension among the journalists. We are surrounded by AWB paramilitary, many masked with balaclavas, all heavily armed.

There are no South African government police or military present to protect the journalists. The AWB (Afrikaner Weerstandsbeweging or Afrikaner Resistance Movement) hate the international press; they could see a massacre of journalists as a dramatically original terrorist initiative.

I have been told I am 'marked' and have been personally threatened several times. I have been poked and jabbed with nightsticks. The fact that I am also drawing has made me a different kind of target.

The boy in this drawing is about fifteen years old, and positioned to the left of where Eugène Terre'Blanche (AWB leader) stands at the rostrum. He is like a theatrical prop – the obvious reference is to the Hitler youth.

This ploy has probably been more successful than its AWB orchestrators anticipated. From the moment he came onto the stage with his black and red flag, there has been a group of photographers snapping away at him. Flashlights are creating a continuous strobe effect across his face.

I feel sympathy for the boy. He is too young to understand the political incorrectness of the AWB and is clearly being used. He is a trapped animal.

They seem to be hoping – like all torturers – that he will crack. He is a victim of both AWB propagandists and the international press. Both see him as a symbol. The only escape for this living, human, fifteen-year-old boy is to close his eyes and try to wait out the ordeal.

But he cannot close his ears to the venom of Terre'Blanche's racist hate-speech. Behind him, an AWB sniper is a counterpoint to his innocence: beauty and the beast. In the AWB crowd there are much younger children than this boy – some are only kindergarten age. What must they think seeing their fathers with these masks and so many bristling with deadly weapons?

Terre'Blanche's brother, Andries, had been observing me from the podium. With his bodyguards he came up to me swearing abuse in the vilest language and demanding I hand over my film. When I refused he took out his and gun and hammered the camera from my hands and it was smashed.

When I saw his neck bending to head-butt me my Rockdale training kicked in. I got in first, crunching his nose across his face with the tip of my forehead and sending blood spurting down his chin.

His goons laid into me for injuring their leader but the world's TV media filmed it all and screened it on SABC that night. Later I heard Mandela himself had seen the footage and remarked that seeing blood on the face of these facists would help reduce the fear people had of the AWB terrorists.

When Mandela won the election I gave him my painting Long Awaited Kiss Of Freedom. *He was pleased in turn to remind me of that bloody nose.*

THE EXECUTIONER'S ART

I was weeding the garden when a bullet whizzed past. It hit Rolf, our rogue monkey, in the hip and he went cartwheeling to the other side of the garden. From behind the curtains and flywire of our bedroom windows, Hellen had taken aim with her Mauser handgun and hit him: a brilliant sniper shot. Rolf had not been able to see her take aim and that enabled her to achieve what no-one else had.

It was one thing, however, for Hellen to shoot Rolf, but something else to finish him off point blank and look into his eyes as the trigger was pulled. That task fell to me.

As I lifted the gun, Rolf looked up at me with an expression of total derision on his face as if to say, 'Fuck you – do it now, you piece-of-shit human,' then he spat at me.

I put a bullet in his heart from about six feet away then carried his limp body to the back block to bury. Bodies go heavy when death releases the inner energy of muscle and the living electricity that animates us. Rolf swung from my grip like a bag of wet cement.

The ground was hard and with a lot of effort I was able to dig him a shallow grave. As I swung the shovel during this miserable chore my mind went back to Abu Ghraib in Iraq.

In the days before the American forces entered and secured Baghdad there was total chaos.

I heard that the gates of Abu Ghraib prison had been smashed and many prisoners escaped captivity. This was the biggest sign yet of Saddam losing his grip on power.

I arrived as scavengers were pulling out whatever they could steal. Smoke was coming from buildings and sporadic rifle fire had bullets pinging off the walls, but this was a moment I needed to record.

In the main quadrangle I passed heroic murals of Saddam on horseback leading the nation to a victorious future. I walked past cells where the corridor walls illustrated an alternate history with prisoners' depictions of Saddam wearing horns in scenes like Hieronymus Bosch's vision of Hell. The same painters probably did both. The cell doors hung open and I felt very alone and vulnerable until a teenage boy beckoned to me to follow him.

We approached the gallows building. A group of men were comforting a woman and I asked them why she was in such hysterics. They told me she had found the names of her husband and son on a list of names of those executed earlier that morning. The man said, 'Why would Saddam order this? No-one believes he's still in Baghdad and they say the American tanks will be here tomorrow. How could he be so cruel?'

I asked to be shown where the gallows were. It was a clinically white industrial kind of room. The gallows were made from welded steel with hinged trapdoors and a handle to release them. There was rancid burning under the structure filling the air with smoke.

I entered alone. Perhaps I was the only person prepared to pass through that door of death.

The nooses were still there – thick white fibre with tissue delicately wrapped around the front of the noose. On all of them the tissue was yellowed, obviously from the throats of the condemned. Later I asked my assistant, Mohammad, what he thought. He answered, 'It's part of the executioner's art, to cushion the roughness of the rope when it's placed around the neck.'

The executioner's art!

Small groups of people, seeing I'd managed to enter without being shot or killed by a booby trap, began to enter. They were the relatives. They would examine the lists attached to the entry wall to search for their loved ones' names, then burst into tears when they found them.

A man came up to me with one of the nooses and said, 'We cannot find their bodies and we need to bury something of them. Do you think we could take the nooses so we have something for the coffin?' I thought of the tissues, yellow with sweat and particles of skin and said, 'Yes, take them.'

They knew I was a foreigner but they needed someone to authorise the taking of the nooses. I interviewed them and photographed them with the nooses and let them go.

Perhaps I should've told them I'd guessed where their relatives' bodies were but I didn't have the heart to. Earlier I had seen a pack of dogs tearing at the soil in a flat field in the outer area of the jail.

I'd walked over to the dogs and a large mastiff sauntered over and dropped a bloody skull at my feet like a dog wanting to play with a ball. Some people saw the direction I'd walked and followed. The bodies were in very shallow mass graves and the dogs had torn flesh and limbs from the top layer of bodies.

There's always someone ready to exploit any situation. One of the scavengers came over with a piece of flat metal and offered to dig for a fee, with the hope of uncovering loved ones. The only way of identifying them was for him to fish in their pockets for IDs. I began filming this grotesque circus. A camera lens gets more detail than a naked eye – I could focus on the wings of the swarming flies and the tiniest gory detail of dogs pulling away intestines.

The scavenger would get very vocal and excited when he discovered an ID tag, calling out the name in the hope a relative was there who would pay for possession of the corpse. I was so absorbed in capturing all of this that I was shocked when the scavenger suddenly began to spew vomit in arcing projectile bursts. I couldn't help laughing and later when I viewed the tapes the camera shakes at this moment and my irrepressible laughter is recorded on the soundtrack.

The GHOSTBUSTERS

We were filming in the city when a crippled man hobbled towards me on crutches followed by the tiniest-of-tiny shoeshine boys. His name was Majid. I could hardly believe my eyes. He was so small that the sack of shoeshine gear he had over his shoulder seemed almost as large as he was. I told Waqar to follow us with his camera to some steps where I would let him clean my very muddy shoes while I told him a story my mother had told me about Tom the chimney-sweep.

When I was a kid every adult seemed to need to tell us how lucky we were that we had not been born into Dickensian London where nine-year-old children worked deep in coal mines and their younger brothers and sisters swung the ventilation doors. But the stories that horrified me most were those of young chimney-sweeps like Tom, who got stuck in the dark of chimney stacks and suffocated.

In another story, Tom is accused of stealing and is chased into a river where he drowns but this is told as a transformation. He becomes a water baby and ventures into an underwater kingdom. I still choke up when remembering this story. It is so beautiful and so sad. In my story for Majid, Tom sails a boat to Australia where he learns to swim and surf and becomes a marine biologist looking after all the colourful creatures of the Great Barrier Reef.

I took Majid back to the Yellow House in time to attend one of the classes being given to the ice-cream boys and share a lunch with them prepared by Itchy. The sight of the food made his eyes huge and I told him he can come to the Yellow House whenever he likes and attend class and share a meal.

After Majid left I brought our Yellow House crew together and explained how we needed to film as many small child workers as possible and repeated what I had told Majid about Tom and the water babies.

All the years I have been coming to Afghanistan I have been fascinated by the ghostbusters. I have never failed to make donations into their outstretched hands, feeling instinctively it would be very bad luck not to.

They are dirty and tough and make the ice-cream boys look almost middle-class by comparison. They work on busy roads with small smoking cans with wire handles and they spin them to make them smoke then waft the vapours inside open car windows. The ghost-busters are Kuchi, a form of Afghan gypsy.

Majid had made me realise I needed to enfold the ghostbusters in both the Yellow House and our film. It turned out that one of the ice-cream boys, Saludin, is friends with a gang of them and often joins them on the road, selling magic and exorcism.

Saludin suggested he bring them to the famous ice-cream parlour, 'Like us, they would never have been there and they would love to be allowed inside to taste everything.' The ghostbusters entered, very wide-eyed. Their leader is Dilbal and there are three others: Hazrat Ali is soft-looking, with long hair; Farouk is tough and nuggetty; Faisal is impish.

The boys play a non-stop pinch-punch-and-slap game. Their physical humour reminds me of the Marx Brothers and the Three Stooges. It's a way of entertaining themselves and is a joy to watch. The whole nose-pulling and ear-tweaking and slapping routine is in fast motion and would be fantastic for our film.

Once they finished their ice-cream, the ghostbusters took me to the market and showed me the combination of green herb leaves they buy and mix with special seeds – both are burnt on coals which they get from the barbeque fires of friendly shish kebab vendors. They could probably get away with using simple smoke and people wouldn't know the difference but they are true to the tradi-

tional mix of shaman exorcists, going back thousands of years. The Taliban have either killed or forced into exile all the old Sufi shaman who taught these magic arts – condemning them as demonic and un-Islamic. Getting rid of demons, ghosts and bad luck with smoke goes back to the original religion of Afghanistan which was Zoroastrian and included the worship of fire.

Those inside the cars have to decide whether to pay for this unsolicited service or roll up their windows. The seeds and leaves are expensive so it's a bit like creating art or a documentary film and hoping people will appreciate and buy it. For the people in the cars it's hard to refuse as the smoke is to get rid of bad luck and bad spirits. Not to pay them could bring the opposite.

When the ghostbusters steal stuff on the streets they move like the wind and I'm reminded of my favourite film as a kid, *The Thief of Bagdad*, which ignited my whole appreciation of Islamic culture.

ATTACK
ON POLICE STATION

This morning there was a giant explosion and the walls shook and I could hear glass shatter in all the windows of the Yellow House. Everyone rushed outside thinking we were being attacked but that wasn't the case. There was a lot of smoke a few blocks away near the police station and adjoining TV studios.

There was a bang on the gates and Ashad ran to check but it was just the three ice-cream boys. They'd been on their way here and passed heavy fighting between radicals and the police. People they spoke to were confused if this was the Taliban or the first feared attack of ISIL, or Daesh, as they are called here. The boys thought their teacher Inam's father, the police chief Asan, could be one of the combatants.

As the day progressed we heard that the TV station had been blown up by a huge truck bomb and that fighters and suicide bombers had then attacked the police station. We tried to get our cameras close to the action but all the roads were blocked. This is part of the film story now, so we'll have to rely on local cameramen who may have gotten in there before the blockades were formed.

It is now 9pm and the sound of heavy gunfire has silenced. With this has come the very bad and sad news that Inam's father has been killed while bravely trying to fight off the attackers.

A Merry Old Soul

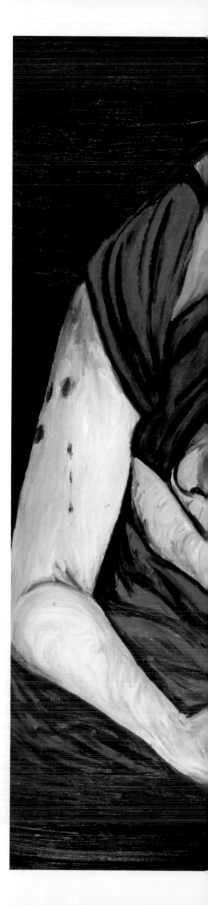

What is an old soul?

There certainly is a difference between people born with a level of self-awareness and innate wisdom and those born clueless. Is this proof of reincarnation, or genetic transference?

I had the chance to meet and draw a portrait of His Holiness the fourteenth Dalai Lama in Sydney in 1996. His ambassador called me out of nowhere and politely asked if I could visit His Holiness at his hotel room in the city. As I sat and sketched, the Dalai Lama talked. He confessed that he finds life and all of creation so beautiful he hopes he can keep being reborn while ever there is sentience in the universe.
He said he would love to remain self-aware from rebirth to rebirth. I felt uplifted by this and totally agreed. I love life and cannot imagine any Paradisial state after death to be any better than inhabiting flesh and blood on a never-ending road to greater self-awareness.

As I was leaving I asked him why he wanted me to do his portrait. He told me he had been shown a book of my art, adding: 'Your art is about compassion and so am I.' As simple as that. Then he gave me some magical items which he said I could put under my pillow or mattress to protect me from nightmares.

for 3 days. I thought the loss of Josep
the father - would probably be the wor
thing to happen to the family - but he was
with stress and I agreed to go - because I
knew this meant walking the needle park -
a safe place, even for a home kid like RF
're u walked the park for hours, questioning
addicts if they had seen your father. At
point I turned to catch a guy about to slas
my back or throat or face with a box cutter
We were getting surrounded by small dang

was a relief where we crossed the road
could see my old friend the gypsy Jann
musings. Infact I heard must have leapt
it was only to offer us tea - no news. As
us sipping the ar by tea I began to hea
harmonium. No one risks performing mu
dance in public places - only protected and
hidden by high wall - RF was asked the
o who was playing if he had seen his

Sufi in the Needle Park

The ghostbuster boys have told me where to find the Jalalabad underworld: the needle park. It's a large park which straddles both sides of the highway near the Spinghar Hotel. They tell me the most desperate section of the needle park is a lemon orchard where addicts camp between the trees.

When we arrived with our cameras, a good-looking young man of about twenty called us over. He was in tears as he showed us cuts he had given himself to fight the pain of the addiction. He said he had a couple of kids and more tears rolled down his face.

I looked over to Irfan. How long had it been like this for him – how often had he found his addict father in the park with shit in his pants and a used needle next to his arm?

Then we came upon two theatrically out-of-it junkies who performed crazily for the cameras. One of them looked into the lens and said, 'What is this new president, Ashraf Ghani, doing for us?!'

I looked around and saw a man holding a box-cutter in his hand. I stared him down and he put it away but, as I turned, a giant of a man was holding up his clenched fists like one of the figures in Goya's darkest painting of combatants, towering over the landscape.

We quickly moved on. As we walked, I heard a harmonium and a song of spiritual longing. I looked for the source: an ancient Sufi mystic. Irfan walked over and sat beside him and the old Sufi immediately sang about a boy seeking his lost father. Sufis have the gift of fortune-telling, as the song ended I noticed tears in the old man's eyes.

Since first arriving in Afghanistan five or more years ago, I have been interested in the plight of the Sufis. Jalalabad was once a Sufi centre and it was the Sufis who brought Islam to this region, but the Fundamentalists hate them because Sufism teaches that not all wisdom and truth is found in the Koran. The Taliban have killed many Sufis, but some have sought sanctuary in Pakistan.

Some of the excited guys grouped around him were recording him on their mobile phones; they told me that this Sufi has been in hiding with the Kuchi nomads and only now felt impelled to share his songs with the world again. They knew him when they were children and say he is one hundred years old.

With Daesh (ISIL) infiltrating the city more each day I didn't like his chances in the needle park, so asked Waqar to see if he could persuade the Sufi to come to the Yellow House.

I learnt a long time ago that Afghanistan is a place where people still believe in miracles.

THE YELLOW ROOM

I had been drawing handicapped mine victims as they experimented with their newly made limbs at the ICRC (International Committee of the Red Cross) Centre when someone suggested I visit a badly injured twelve-year-old boy. The sunny garden courtyard which led to his room did not prepare me for the complete change of reality I felt as I passed through the door.

Abdul Qadir stretched out on an iron bed like a living skeleton, seeming to emit a light (to me it was yellow) which charged the room with his presence. I had not seen anyone as emaciated as Abdul since Somalia, but those people had been only moments from dying. Abdul was very much alive, with clear penetrating eyes. He had horrific scars from a stomach wound and was paralysed. Why he wasn't on a nutrient drip I do not know. His mother, Sarah, tended him, so silent a presence it took a moment to realise she was there.

Two months ago, Abdul and his older brother were leading a donkey loaded with wheat when it trod on an anti-tank mine. His brother and the donkey exploded into small pieces. Abdul was blown through the air before crumpling to earth with his intestines spilling out.

Sarah is a widow with three other children to care for but refuses to leave her son's side. She moves him when he whimpers from the pain, caused by any part of his anatomy remaining inert for too long. When he cries she gently lifts him to reposition the cushions.

Never before had I felt the drawing of a subject to be so totally inadequate in communicating their presence. In that yellow room the door between life and death was wide open, his bed above an abyss. Abdul clung to life, his spirit floating above his body unable to draw away, while his mother's prayers keep him suspended between realities.

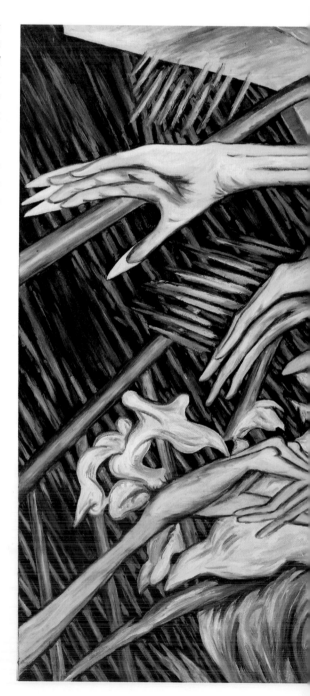

NON-EXISTENCE/ SELF-AWARENESS

After meeting the old Sufi I am finally able to understand a line by the Persian thirteenth-century poet Rumi, that has stayed with me since I first read it as a teenager: *Oh, let me not exist! For Non-existence proclaims in organ tones, 'To Him we shall return'*. I think I've spent my life waiting for the time when I knew what this meant.

That state of non-existence that Rumi writes of would seem to reject self-awareness – there's no room left for it. But perhaps non-existence is actually the ultimate state of self-awareness. It's a return to what existed before time and the universe.

I think what Rumi believed is what the Dalai Lama told me when I painted his portrait: there's a choice. It's possible to enter a state of non-existence and not return; but it's also possible to have a return ticket from oblivion in your back pocket.

Perhaps this is the meaning of all the Sufi poems about the moth and the flame. There's nothing that makes the world appear more beautiful than returning to it after being consumed by the flame. Possibly there are religious techniques for achieving that state, but for me it has needed faith merely to stumble around in the dark hoping I will find it.

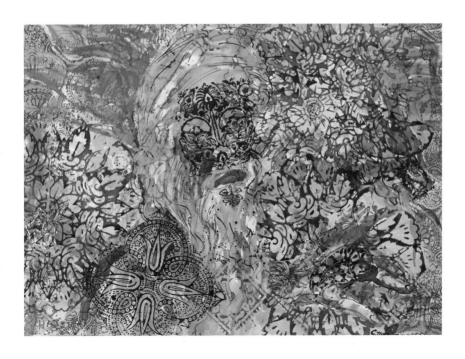

Jalllallabad Sufi

JALALABAD SUFI

Seating the old Sufi on the lawn of the Yellow House was like a circle closing. The Yellow House was now as complete as it was ever going to be. I asked him to rest, but he began to play his harmonium and sing.

As Hellen entered through the blue gate of the Yellow House, she theatrically threw off her burqa. The Sufi laughed at her audacity, there was an instant rapport between them. She joined us on the rugs laid on the lawn, and they started singing together, creating a strange harmony, merging their two voices to make a third – auditory magic. The Sufi said, 'We have brought God down to earth'. I've rarely seen Hellen so happy.

George met a very old Sufi playing his harmonium and singing in the junkies' park surrounded by 'middle-class' followers, the educated and other musicians. The Sufis are still secretly revered by the Pashtuns. Neha and Amir Shah are in a flurry over him. Neha rushes past me with a drink from the water cooler for him, her pretty little eyes shinning. 'It is very, very good luck to have Ba Ba Sufi here, very good luck!' she says, and she rushes on trying not to spill the icy water in her jubilance. George has set up a large blanket in the garden with cushions and soft pillows for the Sufi. He looks like a picture from a children's fairytale of genies on flying carpets. He's sitting quite astounded, smiling and looking all around him, nodding to George and stroking his magical long white curlicued beard, every now and then laughing and saying, 'Very good, very good', in his broken English. His presence fills everyone's hearts and seems to complete the true picture of our Jalalabad garden. There's an atmosphere of incredible peace and stillness somehow surrounding him. He calls me over, waving, his hand cupped in a full arm gesture that's slow and delicate. I sit next to him even though in this society that's forbidden, but nobody in the garden cares, they are just excited to hear us sing together. He starts to play his old harmonium that has travelled with him for many, many years. I watch as his old black fingers fit into the little worn grooves on the keys and the droning sound mingles with his voice in the afternoon sun. I am unsure of the words so I start to sing just simple, sustained, single notes that blend into a harmonic with the notes on the harmonium. It's as if my voice enters the harmonium and is emitted through its wooden speaker, making a third note that fills the air in the golden light. The marigolds become more orange-gold and the lawn a lusher green, the faces of the children glow with smiles and the other musicians, there to witness the spectacle, gleam as they put their hands to their hearts in joy, their eyes rolled towards the shimmering bluer-than-blue skies. The peacocks and monkeys are quiet and watching. Our song fills the air in a way that encapsulates the walled garden in an intense 'opposite to the outside world' way. We are in a new world, a meditative group trance.

He gestures to me, his eyes glittering like black diamonds. He speaks, and I somehow understand his words. He says, 'We have brought heaven down to earth, heaven down to earth.' He repeats his words, laughing, his arm outstretched towards the skies, hundreds of green beads and ta'wiz (magic words in tiny silver scroll pendants) sparkling around his neck, his laughing toothless and ancient face totally beautiful in the ever-golden afternoon light.

I invite him to come down to my Magic Room, a space where I can sing and be free to do what I like away from the eyes and ears of all, in the bomb shelter right beneath the men's hoojrah. I've had it clad out as a traditional cushion room, walls and ceiling in red and black velvet and bunting with beads dripping in the velvety subterranean womblike haven.

The Sufi loves my room and blesses me.

When he emerged from Hellen's room, the Sufi had a serious look to him. He said, 'I must leave, I must go and feed my wife and son.' He told us he lives a long way out from Jalalabad, in a Kuchi camp. His home is a poor tent. His wife is ill and his son is mentally handicapped. Hellen gave him a saucepan full of cooked food still warm from the Yellow House kitchen and Amir Shah drove him out to the camp.

He returned two days later. I took him to the back of the house and we set up our circus tent so that he could give a class to the ghostbuster boys. The boys have a chant they perform while exorcising, but no-one has ever taught them the right words. It starts, 'Bungadah, bungadah.' They wanted to learn it and the old Sufi could teach them. The boys were jumping out of their skins with excitement to learn ancient magic songs. The Sufi laughed with delight. He loved having a class of keen little boys; he told me he had been a teacher, before the Taliban outlawed Sufism.

Two journalists were visiting the house, and were entranced by his singing. One of them commented, 'You do realise you have two women, one using a camera, one without a head scarf, and a Sufi teaching children. Everything the people of this city oppose! Aren't you frightened?' He's right. The Yellow House challenges everything here – if we survive, the city will have passed an important test and left its dark past behind. As if to prove him right, our neighbour's head appeared above the wall, complaining about the music.

During the class I had been painting. When he had finished his teaching, the old Sufi came over to look at my work, and I decided to paint his portrait.

As I brushed in the colours of his face, we chatted much as I had with His Holiness the Dalai Lama. He said that his voice had come to him as a gift from an angel in a dream. In the dream, the angel had offered him a cup. His sleeping self drank and when he awoke he found he had this divine singing voice.

But then he spoke of darker things – of how the Taliban rounded up his Sufi friends. How they gathered the coins that people had thrown them for their singing and said, 'This is money for doing the work of the devil – it is tainted so you keep it.' Then they pushed the coins up the Sufi's asses. Finally, they cut off the Sufi's heads and threw their bodies into the Kabul River.

Later I went for a walk along that same river. It called to mind the early days of the war in Baghdad when the Tigris River was almost blocked with charred and bloated corpses.

He said life is too short not to enjoy.

The old sufi has used the money we have paid him for recording his harmonium music & songs (for soundtrack) to take his wife to hospital in Kabul. He has been here again today & I did my first interview with him while I painted his portrait. Under the Taliban he needed to escape to Quetta in Pakistan but other Sufi had ...ds on ... ...ly now he safe to ... again ... his Harmoni... of its hiding ... . He ...tes ... himself ... being as much a Shaman as a Sufi. All he prayers...

NO EXIT

What is unusual about this war is the way the bodies have been left to rot – in cars, on the strips between lanes on highways, in rubbish piles and even, as I found this morning, in the garden of the national art gallery. I've only seen a few bodies covered with a sheet of plastic or debris by people embarrassed by the nakedness. These dead are very dead, awfully dead, decaying like uncollected garbage no authority will accept the responsibility for.

Talk of souls or transcendental spirits could not sound more empty or ridiculous in this context. They are so grotesque I have shied away from photographing or drawing them. My instinct for mental self-preservation tells me to avoid putting them into full focus – their decay seems infectious. Too often I have walked on them by accident and needed to wash the soles of my shoes, hoping this will flush them away. When I first arrived in Baghdad I went to the old city and bought a book of Jalaluddin Rumi's Sufi poems from the Mathnawi – this great thirteenth-century set of ramblings has kept bringing me back since I was in high school. Rumi is the original Whirling Dervish. I hoped he could kickstart my mind into being able to see Baghdad at a higher cultural level – rising above the fires and violence. But reading him at night over the sound of howling dogs and exploding rounds has made his ecstatic revelations hard to digest.

This place has taught me I can only connect with Rumi when insulated from serious human suffering. The bodies are so inanimate they evoke nothing but revulsion and the reflex of inhaling through the mouth when approaching them. Yet everywhere there are the semblances of ghosts – not near the bodies but concentrated in places where the aftermath of extreme violence lingers like smoke. Yesterday, possibly because I've become accustomed to finding roasted skeletons in cars and tanks, I thought I saw a crouching gunman taking cover behind a twisted chassis. There were rapid bursts of gunfire sounding nearby so I wondered if I should take cover, but as I walked closer I realised the figure was something I had created with my own mind from the melted metal and upholstery and the vehicle's reconfigured interior. No bodies remained from the street battle yet the metamorphosis appeared more alive than any corpse.

I tried to analyse how an inanimate construction had appeared so actively human – it had the same grimy colours of putrefaction as the dead – but its eyes weren't hollow. It looked back at me in a moment of courageous resistance – frozen in a last quixotic stand against American armour. It wanted me to recognise it – permanentise its existence before

a bulldozer pushed it off the road. Perhaps the non-existence Rumi and the Buddhists extol really is as hard to achieve as they make out.

This city is so overcrowded by those who've been killed it's as if all the doorways out of existence have been closed to them. The sign above Baghdad reads *Exit To Non-Existence Closed*. While thousands of looters are smashing storefronts, palace gates and doors everywhere, the ghosts of Baghdad crowd together in panic, shut out.

Writing this gave me the creeps, so I washed my shoes again and scrubbed the soles. Out in the darkness beyond the lobby the dogs growled and barked in angry packs as they fought over corpses. Like the citizens of Baghdad, I've been unnerved by the constant gunfire and smell of death. I can hear Rumi saying, 'What you should fear is not death but never being able to leave existence.'

A few days after writing this I was filming interviews with American soldiers and I needed to talk to a sergeant in a tank on a nearby corner. Soldiers were not permitted to talk to the media and I felt I would be in a lot of trouble. When I was only a couple of steps from the tank a wolf-dog shot out from underneath and took hold of my leg above the ankle. I could feel my bone crushing inside its massive jaw but if I'd tried to pull away my flesh would've been torn open by its fangs.

There was a whistle from inside the tank and it let go. The sergeant emerged from the hatch in the turret and tried to claim the wolf didn't belong to him and he had no responsibility for it, but when I pointed to the food and water bowls next to the treads he had to admit they'd been feeding it. As I limped away he called out to me and there was laughter in his voice, 'Wolves are the best early warning system ever devised!'

The receptionist at the Andalus where I have my apartment claims these wolf-dogs have escaped from Saddam's palace across the river. I was lucky it was only my leg mauled – these animals are now so used to human flesh it could have been much worse.

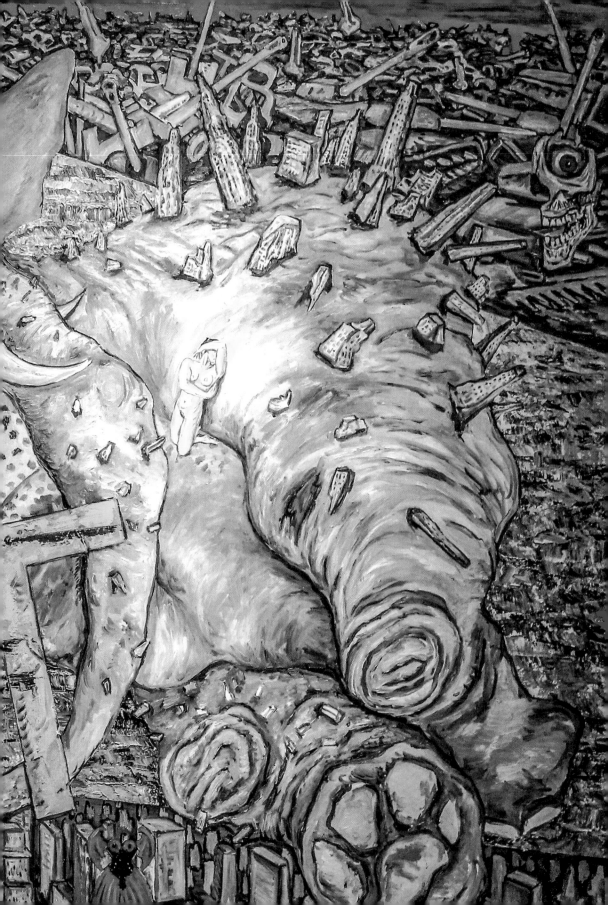

TRANSITORY STATES

The hardest thing to understand and accept about mystical states is that they are always transitory. The Sufi doesn't have to carry his moments of union with God with him into his tent while he spoons food into the mouths of his two disabled loved ones. I can gain profound understanding while sitting with him and then spend the night worrying about the out-of-control finances on this film. While we are alive, human worries will always flood in to drown the deepest discoveries of our souls. That's what it is to be human.

Everyone who follows a path to find truth thinks the point where true wisdom and knowledge are achieved will be stable, firm and irrevocable; this is deluded thinking. All great moments, all ecstatic epiphanies, are unsustainable if we choose to continue to live in the family of mankind. All we can do as mystics is to help others to get there.

Bottom line is: if you can reach IT, you can begin to enjoy the certainty of knowing it gets easier and easier to get back to that state again. As does the old Sufi, after he has played his harmonium and sung and by those means achieved that sought-after union, we must all return to our tent and the needs of our loved ones.

Mystical union is the end of searching but this truth is a salve and not a cure for the discomforts, suffering and worries of life. Only death can bring life without pain.

DEATH AND the BOY

This killing fields monument is one of those erected by the victorious Vietnamese, as both a way of justifying their invasion and a propaganda reminder of the evil of the Pol Pot era.

Unlike the impressive concrete, stone and glass structure on the outskirts of Phnom Penh, this one is very humble and in bad repair. The rows of skulls are behind wooden lattice – not glass – and there is a full human skeleton wired to the lattice in front of the shelves – bones are stacked beneath.

Though long dead, there is still an overpowering smell of death coming from the bones and skulls. The young boy of my drawing immediately met me as I approached and offered to be my guide. I had a cool can of Coca-Cola which I shared with him, and some peppermint candies. His name seems to be Wotne – but since he can't write I can only go on the sound.

He has been taught a few English phrases to use with visitors like myself. I can make out 'killing fields' – 'Vietnamese' – then he says – 'Family – brother– sisters– father' and points to the rows of skulls. He isn't trying to make me think that his families' skulls and bones are in this structure, but that they mostly have been killed. He is an orphan and his home is with the dead.

A brightly coloured temple is in the field next to this grim monument. Since Wotne patiently stood for my drawing for well over an hour I gave him five one-dollar notes. This was obviously a lot of money to him. I have stayed on, drawing the detail in the background structure of skulls etc. behind his portrait. A few minutes ago, some irregularly uniformed soldiers (wearing red and white checked scarves of Khmer Rouge) came and led Wotne around to the side of the building where they thought they were out of my sight.

Concerned for him, I moved to where I could see what was happening. They grabbed him by the shirt and yelled at him until he gave them the five dollars, and the remaining candies.

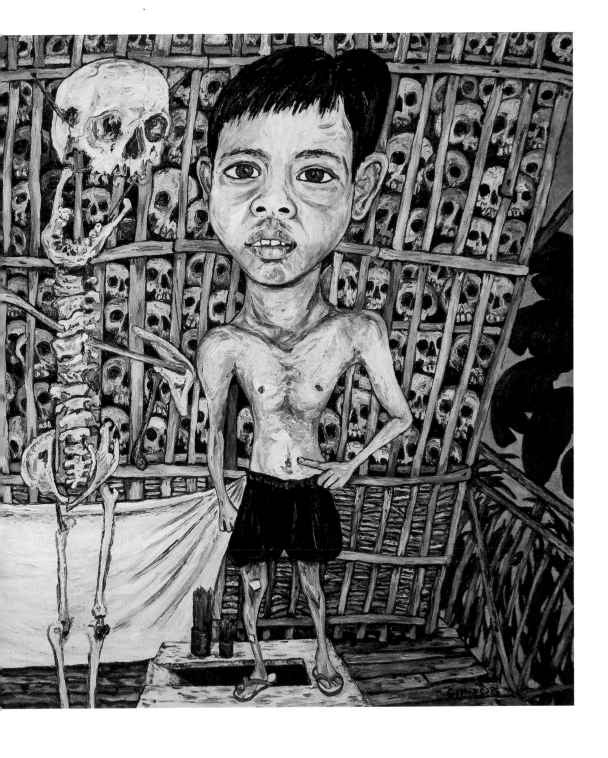

Rose Petals

It's 7 December, my sixty-fifth birthday.

I try to make my birthdays non-events – I never was comfortable with parties – but something incredibly beautiful happened today. The four ghostbuster boys came up to me, their pockets filled with rose petals that they threw over me like red and pink snowflakes. Then they decorated me, putting roses in my buttonholes and behind my ears. Somehow they'd found out it was my birthday. They'd probably stolen the roses from a shop or a hotel garden on their way over from the Kuchi camp. I gave them a big hug.

The boys love coming to the Yellow House for all the creative reasons but most of all for the clean lawn, which is free from human excrement and vile garbage. Here they can wash and use a toilet that flushes. I ask them if they would like to use one of our washrooms. This will give us the chance to give them some anti-fungal cream for their skin. Dilbal has been bitten on the leg by a dog; we'll be able to clean that wound up before it gets infected. You can understand why they are so frightened of animals. In the unhygienic conditions of their camp, an animal bite could mean the loss of a limb or worse. Their culture doesn't consider doctors an option.

We haven't been able to get permission to film at their camps, so I gather up the boys and take them to visit the old Sufi.

There's nothing picturesque about this gypsy camp. It's on the outskirts of the city, wedged between the walls of various industrial areas. The tents are made from old rags, there's no sanitation, running water or electricity. The Sufi's tent is absolutely empty, except for some mats covered in dirt. It's too low to stand in and food is scattered over the unswept floor.

Most of the men here are as dark brown as the Sufi. Women come out with their faces and hair uncovered; by the way they flaunt themselves I think they might do a bit of prostitution on the side. Everyone is polite and helpful. One man who seems more African-black than the others, with red stubble on his chin, competes with the old Sufi to recite the magic words of the exorcism the boys are learning.

Next we take the Sufi to the greenest of green fields and he plays until the sun goes down. The landscape is a vista befitting his green Sufi soul. I think it is rare for him to get away from crowded tents and screaming babies.

The ghostbuster boys add their sweet young voices to his, looking like little angels gathered around him, absorbing shamanic knowledge from his ancient songs.

'Ecstasy' was once one of the most beautiful words in the English language, describing the state attained by revered mystics and saints. Now it's a word for a party pill. Back in the days of the original Yellow House, the 'spiritual quest' was a central topic of conversation. Now people are embarrassed to talk about ecstasy, or their attempt to find their road on a spiritual journey. How much this is due to rational modern science, and how much due to materialistic consumerism is hard to say. The world seems to be in the business of packaging ecstasy – as a blockbuster movie, a luxury holiday, or a new car.

The ecstasy of mystics is free. It is a form of liberation. If someone can gain ecstasy by singing like the old Sufi, then they don't need more than the basics to be fulfilled.

STEEL

I've heard that criminal gangs run beggars in Kabul and decide to ask the boys about it. It turns out that many beggars in Jalalabad are controlled by these gangs, but not our four ghostbusters or our ice-cream boys. All the boys volunteer stories of their tangles with the gangs. Irfan says he has been beaten to a pulp for telling a relative in the police about them, and Dilbal has been tortured for hiding his profits from them. Their base is the needle park. The boys have all been threatened by the gangs with the (possibly infected) needles discarded by the junkies who shoot-up there.

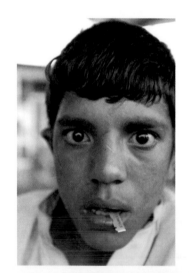

The gang I met there today are aged between eight and fourteen years old. They are run by a much worse older gang that arranges murders and kidnappings. Since first coming to Jalalabad I've been warned about these kidnapping gangs – most recently by the Australian Embassy.

The gang leader looks no more than ten years old and is called Steel because he's so hard. He claims to be thirteen but I doubt it. Steel is famous for having beaten a cop almost to death. He shows me how he keeps a razor blade in his mouth, between his teeth or gums and lip, or on the inside of his cheek. He is never without a means of doing harm.

When I ask this gang why they extort from younger kids like the ghostbusters, they say they have to pay an older gang. It's shark eats shark eats shark.

I am excited that I've found them, but also pretty frightened I've opened Pandora's box. If I go ahead and include the gang in the documentary, the odds are that something bad will happen to me or someone close to me. During the filming of my documentary *Rampage* in Miami, a brilliant young man, Marcus Lovett, was murdered by a rival gang. Like Marcus, Steel is incredibly charismatic. The camera loves him, but he is a psychopath, controlling everyone around him through intimidation. He didn't unnerve me on a face-to-face basis but I don't want him banging on the Yellow House gate at night or climbing our walls.

We will be introducing ourselves to kidnappers and murderers at the top of this gangster food chain – people who will see Hellen and me as prime targets.

I must be nuts.

MARCUS

DENZELL

ELLIOT

Little Marc

When I was young, I wanted to be a poet and was encouraged by the rebellious genius of the youthful Keats and Rimbaud. They didn't live long but they had the wisdom.

Like painting, poetry is an embattled medium in the twenty-first century. And just as graffiti artists have kept visual art alive outside the galleries, rap is the new voice of youth culture. I discovered the true power of rap in Iraq while making *Soundtrack to War,* and also working with Eminem in Detroit while he was making his *Encore* album and the anti-Bush song 'Mosh'. It made me feel I was in the creative centre of the universe, much as a visit to Picasso might have done when he was painting *Guernica.*

I met Elliot Lovett while filming *Soundtrack to War* in Baghdad. Elliot was the greatest freestyle rapper I had ever heard but he had always said his younger brother, Marcus, was the true genius of the family. In fact, it was Elliot's idea that I should film a sequel to *Soundtrack* in his hood, the Flat Top projects of Brown Sub, Miami.

When I arrived to shoot *Rampage*, Marcus and his small gang were making a meagre living selling drugs. None of them even owned a car and all were still living at home with their mothers. Still, they saw themselves as street soldiers and proudly pulled up their shirts to show scars from bullet and stab wounds. Every one of them had lost brothers or friends.

Elliot had told me it was more dangerous in Brown Sub than Baghdad; he hadn't been exaggerating. The poverty made it hard to believe I was in America. Teresa, their mother, provided for all six of her grown children and some homeless 'cousins'. Their project house belonged in the townships of South Africa or Mogadishu, not Miami. They owned nothing and ate off paper plates because they had no crockery.

My video camera was connected to a hand-held wireless microphone, like those used by stage performers. Marcus and his posse loved this. They immediately grabbed the mike and launched into battle, spitting rhymes machine-gun fast. At the end Marcus tilted his head sideways, eyes like saucers, and warned my camera, 'If you mess with Little Marc I will kill you.' Marcus was on fire with creativity and the fire had spread to his life.

White and Australian, I was alien as hell to his culture, but I had been absorbed into the pack. It was like being surrounded by Shakespearean characters, all with heightened verbal powers and all wanting their turn on my mike.

The plan was to get Marcus into a studio – his raps were more real than anything I had heard released in commercial music since 2Pac and Biggie Smalls. Gangster rap was dominating the charts – and Marcus was a gangster's gangster, with street cred and star-quality charisma. As I followed Marcus with the camera, mean-looking cars would slow down while the occupants shouted abuse and turned up the volume on their stereos, booming out amateur recordings of rival gang rappers. A gun would appear from the back seat and point in our direction, followed by laughter and burning rubber as the vehicle screamed off. I quickly learned rap is an element of gang warfare. Words often precede bullets. And if Elliot was the scariest soldier I interviewed in Iraq ('APPROACH WITH CAUTION' was practically tattooed on his forehead), his brother Marcus, the street soldier, was infinitely scarier.

My cameras gave Marcus the kind of attention his rivals wanted for themselves. If I helped him win a record deal, this would put him at the top of the heap, but it could also place him in great danger. Elliot would have known this but was willing to gamble on the dream of rap stardom as a way out of poverty for the whole family. And he couldn't have been happier as my cameras captured Marcus outperforming all the others, inventing new rap songs, literally in the street – the beat was in his head, he needed no accompaniment. His powers were phenomenal.

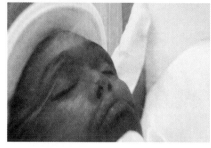

The sooner I got Marcus out of Brown Sub the better. I flew to Atlanta to arrange a studio, so that we could produce a professional demo that could be pitched to record companies. Veteran producer Terry Clarkson was excited by my early recordings and agreed to collaborate. I rang Elliot with the good news. After his first 'hello' the phone went silent. I heard sobbing; then, in a broken voice, Elliot said, 'Marcus is dead'.

Marcus's gang held the Flat Top single-storey housing projects. The two- and three-storey 'High Tops' were a few blocks away.

The day after I left, there had been a drive-by; automatic weapons were fired into the house. Marcus felt responsible for putting his mother and sisters in danger and decided to end it one way or the other.

Those responsible were throwing a party at the High Tops. Marcus went, carrying heat (a semi-automatic handgun) with only one of his posse as backup.

A rival gang member, a kid of only fifteen, pulled his weapon faster.

At the funeral home, Marcus was laid out in an open coffin. When I arrived, Teresa was screaming and sobbing. Elliot was standing at military attention, a ticking time-bomb of revenge. His youngest brother, Denzell, swayed from side to side, staring at Marcus's face. Alton, the second-youngest, was hugging and trying to console Teresa.

As we left, Denzell ran into the middle of the freeway, wanting to die rather than live in a world without Marcus. Miraculously, traffic stopped. He was dragged back to safety.

I rolled my camera through it all.

When we got back to the house I asked if I could see and film where Marcus had been shot. Elliot looked at me strangely. As I got into the car with my camera I realised why – guns were being passed in through the windows to the others squeezed in around me. There was a good chance my naive suggestion had precipitated a revenge-fuelled gunfight.

The concrete blocks of the High Tops were deserted: it felt like Tombstone at high noon. We walked over to the patch of grass where Marcus had died and the friend who'd been with him told his story. I just wanted out of there while our luck held, but Elliot and the others wanted to speak their minds about the killers, probably knowing they were behind the nearby closed doors and windows, listening. Still, nothing happened and I got them back into my hire car. For some insane reason, I decided to walk back and film on my own. The gang members came out. I'd been told they were older ex-crims with a reputation for taking in homeless boys, abusing them, and then forcing them to commit assassinations; because they were minors they would only spend a few months in juvenile before being released.

I wasn't stupid enough to lift my camera and film their faces but was glad I made myself meet them.

Within a couple of days, I had the three remaining Lovett brothers, Denzell, Alton and Elliot, on a plane to Atlanta. Once in the recording booth, Elliot's frustration, grief and anger erupted in a powerful rap eulogy, 'For My Brother'. Fourteen-year-old Denzell's raw raps were also charged with the memory of Marcus. I hoped a cooling-off period might steer them away from revenge and into art.

The Lovetts are still family to me. Denzell is now in his twenties and has five kids. He has been shot twice. Post-traumatic stress has caught up with Elliot. They all still live under the same roof with Teresa. For the people of Brown Sub, nothing got better under Obama.

LITTLE HITLER

teel's gang are a ten on the 'scary' scale. They have no morality – like the kids recruited by Pol Pot in Cambodia, only self-programmed.

Most people want to be good, but if an easily led individual comes under the spell of a true psychopath/sociopath, then they will compete for their favour by doing bad. The same individuals go the other way under a Gandhi. We have met good boys from very poor backgrounds, like the ice-cream boys and the ghostbusters, who only want to do good. And then there are the boys controlled by Steel, who make life hell for them.

We meet the gangsters at a row of pool tables that run along the raised concrete embankment of the Kabul River near Najib's. This is Jalalabad's Sunset Strip. The pool tables are dilapidated and often the smooth slabs of marble show through the worn green baize. The balls are missing and the cues are warped and bent. A structure of thick bamboo and stretched grey felt covers the tables, but its torn sections flap in the breeze like bat wings. It's a scene out of *Mad Max Beyond Thunderdome* and you'd have to be mad to step into it.

I booked two tables with a carney who was clearly terrified by memories of previous encounters with the gang. As he took the money, he let me see he was carrying a sharp knife. The gangsters have a quota of booty they must meet each day and whenever they pocket something, they flash it around at one another so that they can all see what they have. Later, Steel smiled up at me – he had stolen the guy's knife.

We film Steel and Bulldog playing on the bottom table. Bulldog is Steel's big brother, his chief henchman and enforcer. There is also a full-time sycophant in the gang who sings praise and claps every shot they make with comments like, 'Bravo!', 'Excellent shot', even if the white ball is sent jumping off the table or missed entirely. Kings and dictators all need their entourage and these brothers have theirs. Equally, we all have to find a way to survive in this world – the kid doing all the clapping had found his.

A schoolboy walked past on the other side of the road. Steel crossed to him and demanded money. The kid had guts and resisted, but not for long; Steel thumped him into the ground. He knows all the moves George Halpin taught me to put people down. It's uncanny. I felt complicit, but no weapon was pulled, so I didn't make a move to stop it.

When Steel returned, Bulldog patted him on the head saying, 'Well done'. If anyone needs to know how a madman like Hitler could take control, they need only spend time with this gang. Steel is a little Hitler and just as ruthless with human life, yet he made sure everyone in the gang got an equal share of the takeaway I ordered and, when finished, he and Bulldog got plastic bags and filled them with leftovers for gang members who missed out. Steel is the smallest in the gang but the undisputed leader. Psychopaths who are also politicians are much more dangerous than lone wolves.

As we walked to Najib's restaurant, Steel lifted my hand to check out my George Halpin-forged knuckles. They passed his test.

NAJIB

I've realised there is a safer way to film the child gang world. I need to involve the biggest shark of all – Najib.

Najib's restaurant and base overlooks the Kabul River. He is a kingpin gangster, but this is only part of his complex personality. He also likes to act in films. We have a kind of magnetic bond. A couple of years ago he gave me a friendship ring that had cost him a few thousand dollars.

The only good food in Jalalabad is at Najib's restaurant. He keeps quail in cages and cooks them seconds after they've been killed. The fish comes direct from the river, the chickens from his farm, and the goats and lambs are slaughtered a few hundred metres away; their carcasses hang on hooks at the entrance.

There are always plenty of AK-47-toting guys hanging around the restaurant: Najib's personal army. Najib himself always wears a two-gun holster under his coat. His cars and bikes are all custom-made in California. Najib doesn't belong in Jalalabad – he's a gangster with universal style who would fit better in Miami, Chicago or New York.

Last year, Najib's own brother was kidnapped. He retaliated by kidnapping the brothers of the four kidnappers and arranging an exchange – their four brothers for his one. It cost him $40,000 on informants and beefing up his army, but still that was a lot less than the $400,000 the kidnappers were asking.

Najib approved of my idea to use his restaurant as a base for filming the young gangsters and, as I expected, he is happy to extend us the umbrella of his protection. He will co-direct and play himself as the king of the gangsters. Najib knows all the child gangsters and assures us they are all terrified of him. I believe him.

The plan is never to bring the child gangsters to the Yellow House and to ask all our good kids, the ice-cream boys and ghostbusters, not to reveal our location.

Amir Shah, Waqar and I will shoot the *Snow Monkey* drama within a few hundred metres of Najib's base and restaurant.

I'm back in the gutter and feeling comfortable.

Relja
Sarajevo, BOSNIA, 9 MAY 1996

When Harley was six years old he loved to play with toy guns,
but when anyone from the intellectual/artistic community came
to our home they acted shocked that we allowed these toy weapons
and the games that went with them. Today I visited the BOSNIAN
artist Nusret Pasic in his apartment in ~~Sarajev~~ Sarajevo. Every
window had been shattered by bullets and shrapnel marks
scarred every wall. As we talked about Nusret's powerful
'Sarajevo Library' series of war works - featuring aged
claustophobic figures with burnt faces inside burnt books and
other damaged spaces - I saw his son Relja complete a drawing
in which heroic BiH troops, tanks and jets destroy a Chetnik
army. When I showed interest in Relja's drawing he decided to
show me his play costume. He fitted his bulletproof vest (cardboard
and cloth), put hand grenades (plastic) and a knife in his front pocket,
then his home made paper helmet with camouflage, then picked
up his toy machine gun and faced me as a soldier.

SACHSENHAUSEN

When Harley was fourteen, I took him with me to Geneva to put up my Minefields exhibition at the UN to coincide with an International Landmine Conference.

Young mine victims – usually missing one leg – had been brought along to try to gain support for a worldwide ban on landmines. The organisers were happy to leave them in hotel rooms with no money and reel them out for display when needed. Since they were around Harley's age, he took charge and organised to take them to a big European circus and other attractions. The fad at that time was small fold-up scooters with wheels

like skateboards. These teenagers loved using Harley's – most of them could put their prosthetic leg on the base and propel themselves along at speed with their good leg. So Harley started asking the charitable organisations responsible for these kids to purchase scooters for them. There was resistance, but Harley was persistent and they all got scooters to take back to their home countries. Harley said, 'You know, Dad, this is the first time they can go as fast as if they could run.'

From there we travelled up to Berlin to visit Sachsenhausen, the concentration camp thirty kilometres outside the city. Built in 1935, it was the first concentration camp and so became the training camp for all the others. Like the brain of a spider, it was the administrative headquarters for genocide. SS officers trained at Sachsenhausen before applying what they had learnt at Bergen-Belsen and Auschwitz.

When we got there, we were confronted with two white, ceramic-tiled operating tables, each with a lip to catch the draining blood. On the walls were enlarged photographs of ghastly experiments: electric wires planted in brain tissue. There were cabinets full of instruments and chemicals. We could feel the walls screaming. Harley was pale. Even the ovens outside hadn't shocked him like this.

I will always worry about the effect that my work and life has had on my kids. Sachsenhausen had a profound effect on me. It took weeks for Harley to get over the experience. We had stumbled into the heart of modern evil.

My painting WHI
between tiled
those that inm
I remember the t
at Klheho. Abo
it's T-shaped ent
never and ano
fields of Cambo
moved into Ber
Abu Ghraib, the
working condit
invidious colo
If I were told all

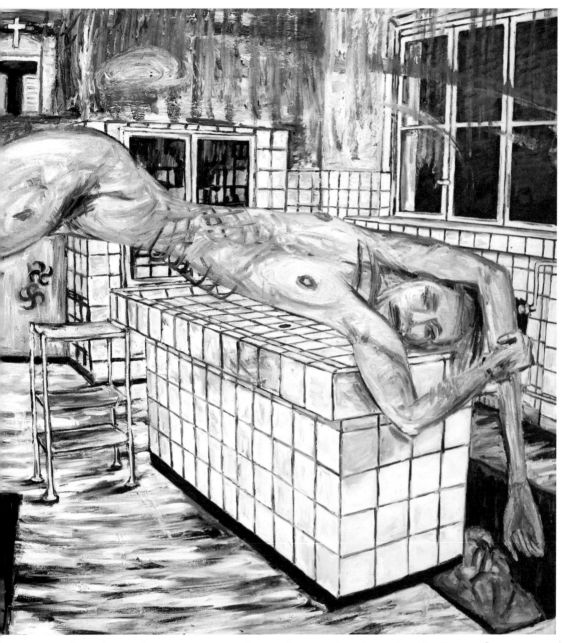

tures a female victim, a tortured reminder bridging the space
on are of blood and flesh. Pits full of human parts, like
o dig before the ovens were installed, are positioned below.
UN dug with front-end loaders, as mass graves for the dead
nan and the table I painted in the little virgin Mary chapel with
longed there, hovering. The UN was created to make sure there was
ide on the scale of the Holocaust, but I have walked the killing
a and Rwanda. When will it ever stop? When Russian forces
idn't destroy Sachsenhausen, but, like the Americans with
d to use the facility. They kept the tiled operating tables in good
further developed the research conducted there in their own
cts. The US still runs Guantanamo.
were to be destroyed but one, I would choose WHITE ROOM.

I was proud of Steel and more than once I thought of Old George Halpin and how he would set me up to fight opponents who were taller, older and had longer reach. He said "if you want to survive in this game you have to know how to take down big guys - remember the bigger they are the harder they fall"

FIGHT CLUB

Steel is famous for fighting full-grown men. So I sent him out to find someone we could film him 'fighting'. I would pay whoever he found. He came back with an older teenager, a tough street thug but not a serious challenge for Steel. But there were some big men in the nearby café and eventually a thick-set guy agreed to spar with Steel, for a fee. A large audience immediately appeared out of nowhere.

I had decided that we wouldn't film anything in the needle park – it's full of Daesh (ISIL). Now, here I was, a mad wizard ring-master shouting instructions to Waqar and Amir Shah over a noisy crowd in my poor Pashto.

The fight was to be five rounds so we could get all the footage we needed. It was supposed to be for show, with punches pulled and neither combatant hurt.

Steel's opponent was a man named Fathi Shah. Fathi went into wrestling mode – picking Steel up and spinning him around and not giving him a chance to kick. At one point he had him upside down in a bear grip and looked like he was going to pile drive him into the ground, but in the last fraction of a second he pulled up. I told him no wrestling, but Fathi got really heavy-handed and began to make real contact. I told Fathi to tone it down, Steel needed to be able to show his stuff. With this, the last two rounds belonged to Steel. Once he stopped mauling and wrestling and really fought, Fathi had the shit kicked out of him from every angle and with such speed he didn't know where he was. The crowd was very satisfied and there was a lot of laughter whenever Steel got a good kick to Fathi's neck or gut. Fathi was sweating and panting, but he was thrilled to be the focus of all this attention. Steel remained nonchalant and cool. I was relieved neither of them was seriously hurt.

By then we had a really large crowd and they were excited in a dangerous way. I suggested we head for our car, but the crowd came with us. Steel was so wound up by adrenaline and the crowd's reaction that he began doing spontaneous circus somersaults on the lawn. The somersaults were so unusual I can't describe them except that I'm sure any other athlete would need a trampoline to manage them. He told me he had done some circus work and loved the limelight. He had suddenly morphed into a satyr-like creature. He then repeated the move three times for our cameras. The crowd now felt they had a travelling show and weren't going to leave us.

I can forget any chance Daesh (ISIL) doesn't know Bubba Gittoes is back in Jalalabad.

GOLD GRILL

In 2006 my son Harley was twenty, loved the rap music of Eminem, 50 Cent and 2Pac, and wanted to be a cameraman like his dad. I knew it was risky bringing a white kid to Brown Sub, but he wanted to join me on the *Rampage* shoot and, in my mind, the advantages outweighed the danger. The culture of the Sub is all about family, and Harley was accepted instantly: having my son there to watch my back meant everything. Plus, Harley is a head taller than me and solid. I've taught him to fight the George Halpin way: never back down.

Harley arrived after Marcus's shooting. I needed to put a face to the kind of heavyweight gangsters in the drug trade who'd taken Marcus out, and I couldn't do this with the Lovetts beside me, not without risking getting another of them killed. I didn't want any harm to come to my own son either, but the task fell to us. Elliot had told me where to find them and where the deals were likely getting done.

The whole of Brown Sub knew me as the man who'd filmed Elliot rapping in Iraq, in a rap battle where he'd clearly smoked the others. This had gotten him seen nationally throughout the US on VH1. It was the first time anyone from their community had 'made it', and they wanted to meet Elliot's war buddy, George Gittoes, the dude that made it happen. Every rapper on every block hoped I would do the same for them.

We cruised up to a freeway underpass near a few blocks of dilapidated shops and got out with our cameras. As soon as I lifted my camera, my lens captured guys exchanging money for drugs. Suddenly the guys were swinging handguns at their hips and running towards us at speed. The dealers had spotters out watching for undercover cops.

We made like the movies and slipped into the nearest doorway. It was a gaming parlour. I found myself looking into the face of gangster Willie T, a broad smile exposing his full golden grill, one hand resting on a silver-plated magnum on the counter. The guys chasing us burst through the door panting and surrounded us.

Thank God Willie T had seen *Soundtrack to War* on VH1. Once I'd proven I was George Gittoes, Willie started pitching himself as a rapper superior to Elliot, asking the inevitable question, 'Why don't you make a movie about me?' The rest of his squad of 'soldiers' were all rappers as well. Within minutes I'd won over my own private ghetto army in the hood.

Willie pulled up his shirt and showed me a recent shotgun wound to his chest and shoulder. He said, 'Point blank! But a man's gotta do what a man's gotta do'. He was twenty-one with the maturity of a forty-year-old. His wife brought over his toddler son and I got a classic shot of Willie passing his chrome-plated gun to his boy. Willie's wife was one of the most exotic creatures I've ever had in front of my camera. As Elliot would later say of her, 'She looks like she walked off the set of *Star Trek*!' After we'd agreed he would feature in *Rampage,* they headed back for their home at North Beach, Willie opening the door of his white Mercedes for her like a true gentleman.

Within two days Willie called me. His place had been hit by mercenaries with machine guns paid by a rival gang. There were bullet holes everywhere, but it was the mercenaries who'd taken casualties and not Willie's squad. The guys were 'gee'd' to the max and I suggested Harley and I take them to their favourite restaurant for lunch. When we got there, Willie looked down and said, 'They won't let us in with heat,' then on second thought he said, 'but if you and Harley carry for us, we could.' Security on the restaurant door obviously knew Willie and the squad, and I could see real fear in their eyes as they frisked them. I felt the cold steel of Willie's handgun against my spine where it was pushed behind my belt and hidden by my shirt – Harley would be sharing the sensation. Over lunch Willie suggested I set up a rap battle between him and Elliot, saying 'he may have been to Iraq but he's a pussy'.

Harley was having the time of his life and Willie offered to keep an eye on him while I took Denzell, Elliot's brother, to LA for an interview with a major record company. I'd taught the middle Lovett brother, Alton, how to shoot second camera, so he could cover Harley's role.

Two nights later I got an excited call from Harley. He'd been chillin' outside Willie's house at North Beach when a customised car with a raised chassis and high wheels did a drive-by. The bullets missed Harley by inches, tearing holes in the door of Willie's garage. My first question was, 'Did you film it?' He said he'd got it all. He told me he'd worried

his whole life he would be a coward. Now he knew he could be cool when his life was in danger. I asked him if he showed fear and he proudly answered, 'No!'

Steel is like Willie – I imagine if I could bring them together to share street smarts and compare scars from their self-defined wars, they would be instant comrades. Street soldiers.

SHAKEDOWN

I woke to hear Zabi, Saludin and Irfan banging on the Yellow House gate and in tears because their ice-cream carts have been stolen. Steel was demanding one hundred dollars for the return of each cart, their suppliers were asking the same in compensation.

Steel and his gang stole the carts to get our attention. It wasn't random. Up to this point I had managed to keep the ice-cream boys and ghostbusters away from them. But with the stealing of the carts, the worlds of snow monkeys and gangsters have merged. Now Steel could bring us to him on his turf and on his terms.

One of the gang's favourite hangouts is near a slaughter yard for goats where broken fairground sculptures have been abandoned. As we arrived I saw the carts, one on its side, near a giant, pinkish-red fibreglass swan.

They saw us coming but didn't run. Steel's eyes were fixed on mine from a hundred metres away. This was going to be interesting.

Again, Steel demanded a hundred dollars per cart. I could see he could go either way; he and his gang might suddenly lash out at us with their razor blades. But then he recognised one of the guys behind our cameras, Amir Shah, the movie star. A sudden change came over him, a golden moment. His face lit up, and he admitted that he had always wanted to be in the movies. We shook on a deal to return the carts in exchange for a part in our movie.

Steel has no idea what a documentary is – he only knows the low-budget Pashto action dramas like those Amir Shah makes. But this is okay, the boys can make a separate drama with Amir Shah. Steel will play the bad guy.

I just want to be sure I can protect the ghostbusters and the ice-cream boys. Steel may yet scare off the rest of the cast to ensure he is the star.

THUG THEATRE

My plan to use my friendship with Najib as a way of out-gangstering these little gangsters has worked well. The only authority they will defer to in Jalalabad is Najib, so while we may have a special relationship, he's obviously the king of the city's underbelly. Still, I would go to him before the police if I were in real trouble.

The gangster kids see everyone as a soft target. I wanted to take them to lunch at Najib's, but first I taught them a few useful fighting and acrobatic tricks. They loved it. They also needed to know I'm not a soft target. On the walk over we played a game of 'most evil laugh'. I'm pretty good at an evil laugh but they were on a roll, scaring passers-by and restaurant workers.

This will be the first time the gang has been allowed inside Najib's restaurant. I walked them past the carcasses of skinned and headless sheep. Najib met us at the approach, hugged me and then lectured the boys on their various misdemeanours in gangland. Then the Don took us up to the private entertaining level on the roof. It overlooks the Kabul River and the scene wouldn't be out of place in Santa Monica. I have enjoyed many meals here with Najib, but he was unwilling to eat with me while I was with the boys. Obviously it would hurt his status to sit with them.

I have a perverse streak and while we waited for someone to come and take our order, my inner imp saw an opportunity. Amir Shah has a black belt in karate and takes his combat prowess very seriously. In his latest movie, he takes down an unbelievably large gang of fighters single-handed, to the point where it's funny. I suggested Amir Shah show the gang some of his karate moves. He did so, to 'wows' and applause. Then I suggested the gang show me how well they could play a gang who were up against Amir Shah. To my surprise they acted out Amir Shah's fantasy and all obediently went down on cue. Then I suggested he do it just with Steel. Steel is half Amir's height. He's never studied karate or boxing, but his moves were spectacular and put a shocked Amir Shah on the defensive. With a hard kick to the stomach, Amir Shah went down. As he slowly eased himself up from the ground he smiled and pretended not to be hurt. From then on, Steel held back his punches and kicks with real discipline, but everyone on the roof knew who would have won in a real fight. My grandfather always said, 'In the ring you can be pretty like a dancer but on the street there are three rules: give no warning, move fast and leave them too fucked-up to strike back.'

When we first met him, I found it almost impossible to accept the local legend that Steel had beaten a policeman almost to death, but I believe it now. He's maybe the height of an average seven-year-old, but has phenomenal, almost demonic, strength.

While we were waiting for the meal, our brave little team of four ghostbusters saw us and I invited them to join us on the roof.

Filming RAMPAGE in Brown Sub, Miami, I was impresse
worked out a non violent and creative form of con
contests full of insults, put downs and slurs but wit
Here in Jalalabad they 'have dance battles. My id
to contest with the gangsters in a dance battle to the
To make it more colourful I took a box of our workshop
transformed into zombies, werewolves and weider crea
one another's dancers with more and more innovative p
excelled and to my surprise the gangsters graciously
stole our attention back when he began smoking
mask. As he exhaled the smoke issued from the ey
it gets. I knew instantly that would become the

I'd previously learnt that Steel and Bulldog's older brother had tortured Dilbal, but he still dared to come up. I told the gangsters they were not to harm the ghostbusters, they were under both my protection and the protection of Najib. It was interesting to watch the interaction. I admired Dilbal for his courage. I'm not sure I would've been able to face this gang when I was his age. At one point I got him over next to Steel and asked about the torture. Steel showed no remorse or regret. It was like the Mafia; it's not personal, it's business.

When their lunch was slow in coming they began a chant, 'lamb, lamb, lamb'. They may be gangsters but they're all still hungry little boys who rarely get a good meal.

When we got back to the Yellow House after lunch, Amir Shah said to me, 'Steel is a real fighter!' That's a huge admission for Amir Shah; he has the biggest ego I've ever encountered.

The truth is that people can learn the moves in a gym, or in the ring with referees, but there's no substitute for life-and-death experience. The authorities here know this too. Whenever these gang members are arrested they're out again the same or the following day. The police are ordered to let them go – the anti-terrorist wing has discovered that they're the best early warning system for insurgents in town with ill-intent. These kids see and know everything, they have ears and eyes everywhere on the streets.

But empowering a thug can have terrible consequences.

e way young men had
sing improvised rap
ins, knives or punches.
o get the ghostbusters
nsic of the laqman players.
s along and the boys
s they attempted to trash
nces. The ghostbusters
ed defeat. But Steel
till wearing a full latex
reepy and sinister as
first image of the film.

Blinding Lesson

BAIDOA, SOMALIA, 27 MARCH 1993

At the entrance to the Baidoa Airport perimeter, where 1RAR Battalion [1st Battalion, Royal Australian Regiment] are based, there are two war-damaged statues. One is a soldier holding a gun, the other a demonic lion. Yesterday morning, as I sketched these pre-civil war relics, symbolising Somalia's failed military ambitions, I became friends with a boy, ten-year-old Mohamad. The Australian guards at the gate had nicknamed him Mohamad Ali: they had seen him fist-fighting and were impressed by his style. He was clearly a war orphan and lived near the gates, trading and getting gifts from the truckloads of soldiers as they stopped. (Sinister men lurk in the shadows and strictly control the gangs of youths and their commerce.)

I noticed Mohamad had a chunk of flesh out of his shin from a bullet or piece of shrapnel. It was badly infected. I thought that if it wasn't treated he could lose his whole leg. So I walked back to the medical clinic at headquarters and collected antiseptic ointment and bandages to treat Mohamad's wound. After it was dressed I gave him a US dollar and some ration packs.

Today I was sitting with my drawing on my lap about twenty feet from another young boy. Mohamad approached him with something clutched in his fist. It was the tin opener out of the ration pack I had given him. As the other boy looked up at Mohamad, Mohamad jabbed the tin opener into the boy's eye. Mohamad turned and stared for a moment at me, then ran off, his clean bandage still on his leg. The other boy was left weeping – blood streaming down his hands from his eye. I started carrying him towards the guard post – he weighed almost nothing in my arms. An aid vehicle saw us and stopped. They took him from me and promised to rush him to a doctor.

Mohamad had vanished from sight.

FAROUK CUT UP

tchy was down in the vegetable market when Dilbal came running up to him for help. Little Farouk had been injured. Itchy bundled them both into his rickshaw and rushed them back to the Yellow House. Farouk is only about ten but nuggety and tougher than the other ghost-busters. When I got to them, he was in the back of Itchy's rickshaw, heaving with emotion, and couldn't get out words to describe what had happened. But the razor blade cut down the bridge of his nose told me it was Steel. Hellen ran over and calmed him down. Steel had stood over him for his meagre earnings. When he found there wasn't much, he suspected Farouk was withholding and started torturing him. There are already huge bruises on his arm where Steel twisted it and on his legs where he was hit with an iron bar. Unable to squeeze any more money out of him, Steel kicked him into the gutter for his brothers to find. Before leaving he asked him why he cried, saying he wouldn't have hurt him as much if he hadn't cried. Then he spat on him, called him a cry-baby and left.

I told Steel to leave these kids alone, that they're part of the film and under Najib's protection, so this is just straight-out perverse.

I see the potential of all these Jalalabad street kids and want to help them to a brighter future but, as with Denzell, all I can really do is help them on their way. What they do with the opportunities I create is up to them. There is also a danger that by spending time with Steel and the gang we are encouraging a monster, or that we could become entrapped and end up in jail ourselves. It would be easy to become so carried away shooting this documentary that we lose the sense of crossing the line. Being Australian doesn't place me outside Afghan law.

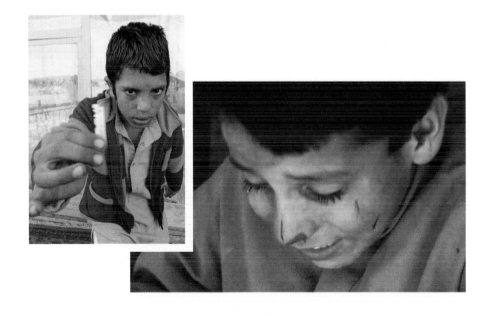

THE BUST

Filming in Miami, I wrongly assumed that our Australian nationality and movie cameras gave us a sort of immunity from American law enforcement and surveillance.

One day I left a radio mike hooked under Willie's t-shirt; I forgot to take it off him when we finished shooting. Back at our hotel I realised it was missing so rang Willie, only to be surprised by a voice I didn't recognise.

Willie had been doing a drug deal when his suppliers lifted his shirt and found the transmitter. Naturally, they assumed he was wearing a wire for the cops and threatened to shoot him. It took a lot of talking on my end before they put the guns down. To this day I have never forgotten to remove a mike from anyone.

That same day, Elliot was driving our red Dodge Durango hire car and Trigger, a rapper friend, was in the back seat with Harley. Trigger asked if we could stop the car to get some chewing tobacco. Trigger was underage so he asked Harley to go with him.

Elliot and I sat in the car listening to the radio, not realising we were parked near the territory of a rival gang. As Harley and Trigger came back, cop cars came from every direction, encircling us.

Gun-toting detectives from the FBI and Narcotics division held Harley and Trigger with their hands on the side of the vehicle. Elliot was told to pop the boot and they searched it, finding nothing. By this time a crowd had formed around us. It was a black neighbourhood and these people obviously hated the cops. They shouted a wonderful chorus of abuse in our support.

Finally, the officer in charge asked me what I was doing with 'these blacks'. He seemed to have taken me for a Russian mobster carving up a new territory, in cahoots with Willie's gang and the Lovetts. As I explained the situation to them, disbelief gave way to confusion, then frustration and finally cold anger. 'If this kid is a rapper as you claim, then show me some of his CDs – we need evidence.' I said, 'We haven't got any CDs but he can rap something.' Elliot let go of a rap so stella', and so authentic, there was no doubting his talent.

Bush + Kerry fight it
out on TV while Brown
sub + hope burns

I'm in Brown Sub + not much
has changed since 1968 + Joe Delaney
still working on the street but
with a movie camera.

SNAKE EYES
The Goat Rustler

One of Steel's gang is a goat rustler. His nickname is Snake Eyes because he has two tiny points of yellow in his eyes, even when he's in the shadows. Those eyes are unnatural and he uses them to both win people over and intimidate them. I mentioned it to Waqar and he said that both he and Amir Shah had been unnerved by his eyes. It's one of those things beyond reason. Two yellow laser dots of light.

Our male goat, Aladdin, is lonely and oversexed, he's even tried to mount the male peacock. I've been wanting to get Aladdin a mate but there hasn't been time. It inspired a plan to get the gang to stage a goat theft for the film.

Snake Eyes tells me he usually steals goats from the shantytown that surrounds the US air base. I imagined we would go to the base area and I would negotiate to buy a goat on the condition the seller was happy to cooperate with our scene. This idea was a bit dicey, since the boys have already stolen a lot of goats from these people.

Najib keeps some goats in a shed near the restaurant. So we decided a better solution was to buy one of these. Then, after her film debut, she could come back to the Yellow House to meet Aladdin.

When we arrived, Steel wasn't there. This was the second time in two days he'd stood us up. Bulldog was there with Snake Eyes, but we still needed a goat driver.

There's a Kuchi camp at the back of the empty fairground where the gang hang out. The camp is set against a reed swamp, it looks amazing. A good-looking gypsy kid named Sami was prepared to pretend to be the goat-herder who loses his goat to the gang. Sami seemed as tough as any gang member, although his shaven head and dirty orange clothes made him look a bit like a young Buddhist monk. The gypsies were all smiles, but I was reminded of my favourite Guy Ritchie film, *Snatch* (Brad Pitt plays a member of a gypsy family that brings everyone they come in contact with unstuck). I wondered if it was going to be harder to get out of this than getting in.

Fortunately, our executive producer, Najib, came over to assist with the selection of the

goat. He took us all over to the pen so that everyone was involved in selecting my goat. I think I got a good one – she's white with small horns, some decorative black patches and a kind of ballet skirt of long hair that falls from her hips. She's bigger than Aladdin, so there will have to be a lot of ritualised foreplay. I'm sure Aladdin will go for quick sex, but I can imagine her butting him off effectively. Hellen has suggested we name her Juliet.

On closer inspection, the picturesque area where the reeds meet the tents – where I had planned to shoot the goat-rustling scene – turned out to be a goat slaughter yard. Nooses hung from a bar on a pole for hanging and skinning carcasses. The ground was covered in dry blood, tufts of fur and a billion flies. A smell emanated from the yard that would make anyone gag.

A little way off I saw a square patch of ground in the middle of the very green swamp of reeds. It had a trail leading down to it and some bamboo buildings nearby, so I led my small army of gang members, gypsies and film crew down to it.

I got Sami to tie the now very frightened Juliet to one of the poles. She would have been able to smell the death all around. Sami started cutting reeds and feeding them to the goat for the camera. On camera it would still look wonderful because all the blood would be out of frame.

Bulldog was wearing an oversized black velvet coat which any nineteenth-century dandy would have been happy with, although it was scruffy and way too big for him. I showed him how to put down Sami in the scene by demonstrating a street-fghting move, an old Rockdale classic, and then asked him to practice it with Sami. He didn't get it right, so I put Sami down again. The third time he got it down pat.

I then asked Bulldog to show us his most violent side. I talked to him about one of his gang members with a disfigured face. I said, 'you had him held down while Steel burnt his cheek', which he seemed proud to admit on camera. I directed him to channel that brutality, but to remember that this was just drama and not to hurt Sami.

I'd noticed a small ginger-haired man come up while this was going on. A couple of goats were brought over and he started sharpening his knives and pulled on an oversized pair of blood-spattered pants which ballooned out, making him look like a grotesque circus clown. I realised this guy must be the goat butcher. He tied them firmly below his hips, looking uncomfortably at our cameras. He didn't initially want to, but he eventually let us film as he beheaded two goats. He then hung them and began to skin them. This really set the mood. There was blood everywhere. But during the tangential filming of the slaughter, our donkey and cart had vanished, along with the man who hired it to us. I asked Amir Shah where he'd gone and he shrugged, 'He's Kuchi'.

If I thought too much about setting up things like this in foreign and dangerous places I would never do it.

Protecting Angels

When George Bush Senior lost his attempt at re-election after the first Gulf War, Saddam Hussein took it as a personal victory. He came out onto a public platform and fired a rifle into the air to commemorate it. He had many statues made of that moment and placed them all over the city, believing the power of art would distract from the failures of his dictatorship. In the build-up to the first Gulf War, he had his tailors sew form-fitting cloth covers for all of them. The result looked like the work of the conceptual artist Christo.

His image was everywhere in Iraq, including the birthing wards of every maternity wing of every hospital. The first thing a newborn would see was the smiling face of the father of the Iraqi nation, towering in front of their mother's bed.

During the Iraq War, someone high up in the propaganda department of US forces ordered that steel ropes be used to drag down the statue of Saddam Hussain outside the Palestinian Hotel where CNN and other world media had stationed themselves. They didn't have Saddam himself, so the leaning statue became the symbol of the end of his dictatorship.

But this wasn't the only one. Teams were sent out and statues of Saddam fell all over the city simultaneously and countless murals of him were vandalised. To George W. Bush and his Secretary of Defense, Robert Gates, the perception of the war was as important as actual battlefield gains. Little of this erasure and ridicule of Saddam's images was an Iraqi outpouring of hatred for their former leader, as was reported by the Western media. These symbols of a glorious and powerful Saddam which had taken decades to create were all thoroughly messed up or torn down within a few days.

I knew it would be no time before scavengers carted off the Saddam statues to be melted down for their metal. I had taken plenty of photographs but it was possible that nothing tangible would remain of this historic reversal of fortune. So I made it my mission to see if I could save the head of one of these statues for posterity.

Not far from the original Palestine Hotel statue the world had seen fall, I found another equally large statue lying face down in the gutter. I sourced a metal worker and we lugged an oxy-acetylene torch down to it, only to find the statue was filled with concrete. It wasn't a genuine hollow bronze sculpture, just a layer of metal over the concrete – our torch was useless. I found a blacksmith who had a circular grinder and abrasive disc, with a generator to run it on, and organised for him to bring his truck to my apartment early the following morning. I didn't sleep well – I was overexcited by my plan – and was ready an hour before the appointed time. Then there was a call from reception: the driver of the Aramaic Archbishop for Baghdad was waiting for me downstairs.

عالم صدا

التحقيق، بينما يرتدي ثيابه في زاوية معتمة تفوح برائحة براز وعان، قال متمسماً كأنه يكلم الحيطان أو ثيابه: أبناء الكتابة لو انتظروا ساعة أخرى لكان جائعاً طوال الشهور الستة في السجن كان يتلقى زيارة كل أسبوع. هذه الزيارات تحولت إلى روتينانيه حبسه. كانت ساجدة تأتيه بتمور وخبز طيب وسكر وشاي. أخبرها أنه توقف عن شرب الشاي.. منذ الزيارة السابعة باتت تجلب له حبوب بن محمصة. لم يأت من كان ذلك خطراً. في الزيارة ساجدة وحدها، أمامها مشى لاحظ منذ النظرة الأولى بياضاً سأله خاله عن أحوال م حسين: كنت محبوس في

بحقه أخيراً أبرم التآمر قوم الشتاء أ اعتاد بمرور الأيام أن عد الثالثة والنصف به لكن مع قدوم موسم ال النزهة. بات سجين عة ليلاً نهاراً، التمارين ال ستمرت تحمي جسم بالتعفن والصدأ.

في الزيارة العشر الحرب دائرة في المو على نفسه. قسم مع ال وقسم ما زال في قب رأسه، من دون أن يطو بعد لحظة صمت: شبح كان وجهه أبيض في ظلمة ما تحت الأ الفطر والطحالب. رأ أصابعه ومعصمه.. ألكم الحيطان.. رياضة حين أن فصل الر رغم عواصف الرمل ب نزهة كل يوم متاحاً.. ونور الفضاء. تضاءل المسجن. سمع مجمو للهرب. غم أن الموصـ ومجاور. الرئيس قاس الشيوعيين، مجموعة على نبض مئات القوم وجوارها. القوات الجو على مقر الرئيس قاس المؤامرة بساعة واحد الموصل بالمدفعية الث الوهاب الشواف أصـ في المستشفى. بينما طبيب شاب خريج مو العقيد خمس رصاصات

بينما ينظف الموس بالماء سمع ساجدة تناديه من المطبخ، تسأله كيف بحت الشاي؟ قبل أي يجيب انهالت الطرقات على باب البيت لم يسمحوا له لبس ثيابه، جروه إلى المغفر بملابس النوم، حافياً، ساجدة أرسلت لأحد صبيان المسلخ خلفه، حاملاً ثيابه وصيابه، عجزوا عن إثبات التهمة عليه. حكم سنة شهور فقط. أثناء التحقيق، حسين تلقى اللطمة الأولى على فمه، كاد ينتسم، أغمض عينه فلجأت رطوبة سائلة دماغه بعد

وراء الجدار قرع باب البيت الثالث بعد الجامع ذي المئذنة الخشب.

مساءه صوت من وراء الباب الموصد: من؟

لجاب: لغة عربية ولهجة ذات رسالة خالدة.

فتح الباب، نور أصفر واهن بان لحظة

الليلة الثالثة عشرة على انقلاب ١٩٥٨ اجتمع في مركز البعث سافة ٤٣ عضواً بحضور ثلاثة من القيادة القطرية. العقيد أحمد يكر كان غائباً، أحد أعضاء القيادة حاً ومحللاً سياسة الحزب المرحلة. قال إن الحزب يدعم عبد عارف، ومعه معظم الأحـزاب الأخرى، وقسم من الجيش. لكن يبعض الضباط الأحرار، يون مشكلة أيضاً وعبد الكريم هو المشكلة الكبرى. قال عضو القطرية إن العقيد عبد السلام قال للرئيس جمال عبد الناصر الجمهورية العربية المتحدة، حين دمشق، إن العراق يريد أن يكون م جزءاً من الجمهورية المتحدة ر وسورية. لكن المشكلة هي د السلام عارف قال لعبد الناصر الكريم قاسم هو محمد نجيب العراقي، عضو القيادة القطرية تمه وعاد إلى الجلوس. صدام في المقاعد الخلفية وجد الكلام عن عارف مزعجاً. قال في سر يص هو لن يؤثر قبل أن يمسك السلطة، وحدثه قلبه أن عبد الكريم الحزب من قبل أن يخوضها.

ذلك الصيف الملتهب أصيبت امرأة ره الله طلقاح بفالج نصفي،

I'm good friends with the Archbishop and knew his driver well. He was sitting there all tense and anxious; he had bad news. He told me the Archbishop had seen me being killed in a dream and angels had warned him that he must send for me, or else the dream would become reality. I told the driver I had a tradesman organised and he took my arm as if to drag me to the car. He was insistent. I wrote a note for the guy with the grinder, apologising, and went outside to where the Archbishop's Mercedes was waiting. At the church, the Archbishop had breakfast prepared. We were halfway through it when a call came in for the Archbishop. He nodded gravely, then looked up and told me there had been a savage firefight at the intersection where the statue lay; dozens of people had been killed and wounded. Had I been there with the blacksmith, we would certainly have been among the casualties.

I'm constantly asked if I feel protected. I have too many stories like this not to.

I went back a day or two later. The disc spun and spat dust particles as it cut through Saddam's throat. An angry crowd formed. Despite what was going out via the world's media, they weren't happy to see such disrespect for their leader. Mohammad, my brave translator, was with me and it took all his charm and savvy to convince them not to mob us. Eventually we got the head onto the back of the truck and made our getaway. I had to get some boys to spend a few days chipping out the concrete from inside to leave the metal skin.

When it was time for me to depart Baghdad, I squeezed this huge metal head into the back of our hired GMC and headed for Jordan. I could already imagine my piece of salvaged, Saddam Hussain-era art sitting in the collection of the Australian War Memorial. But when we got to the border, the Jordanian military guards peeked in the back of the vehicle and laughed at my audacity. There was no way they could let me take it into Jordan.

As I watched them carry it off I realised they would probably sell it to a scrap metal dealer. All that risk had been in vain.

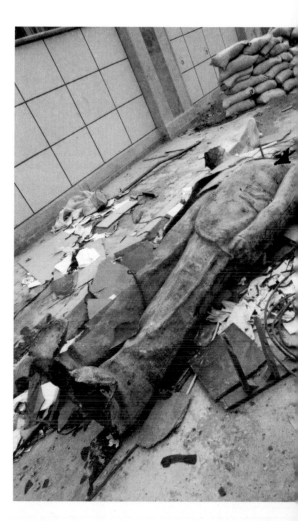

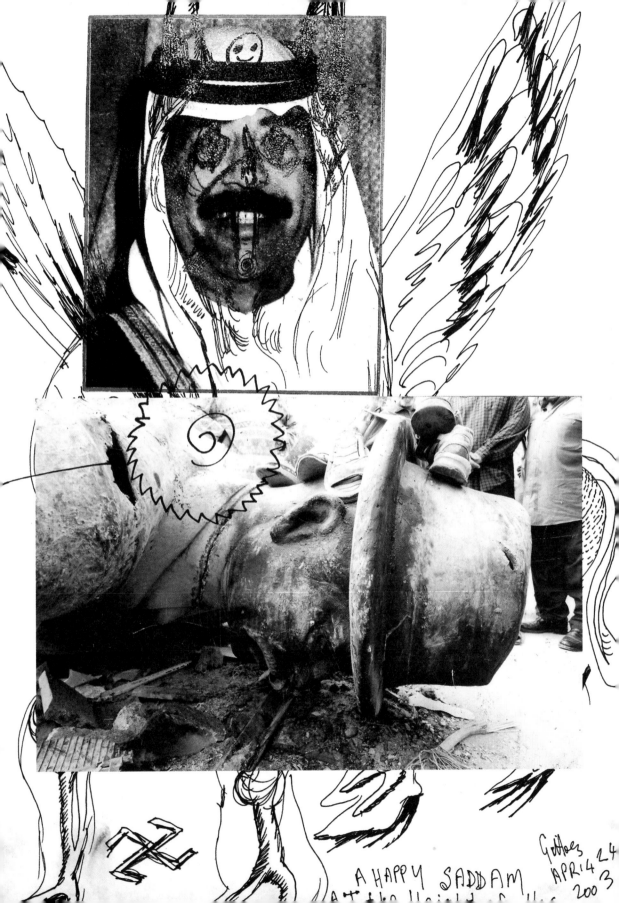

A HAPPY SADDAM

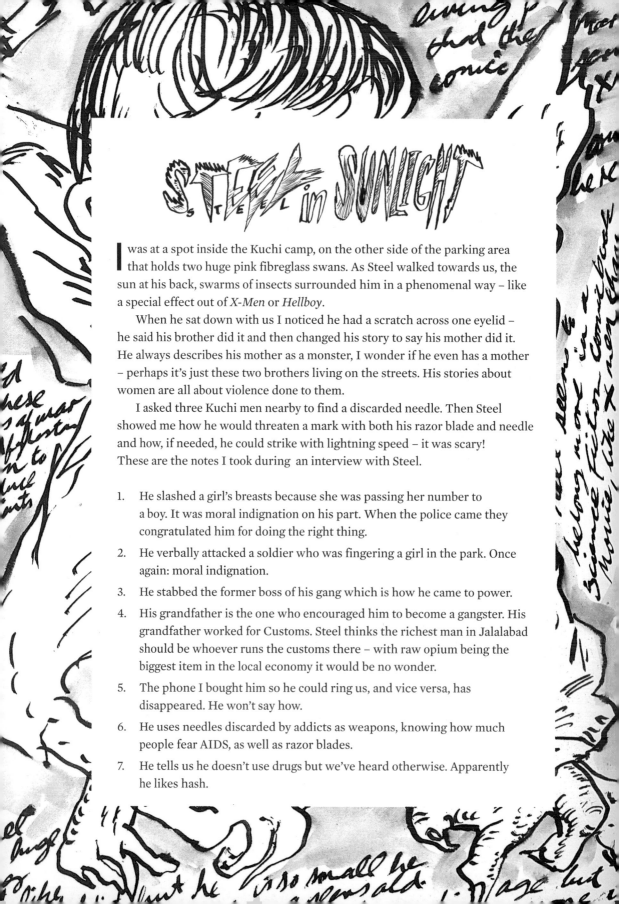

STEEL in SUNLIGHT

I was at a spot inside the Kuchi camp, on the other side of the parking area that holds two huge pink fibreglass swans. As Steel walked towards us, the sun at his back, swarms of insects surrounded him in a phenomenal way – like a special effect out of *X-Men* or *Hellboy*.

When he sat down with us I noticed he had a scratch across one eyelid – he said his brother did it and then changed his story to say his mother did it. He always describes his mother as a monster, I wonder if he even has a mother – perhaps it's just these two brothers living on the streets. His stories about women are all about violence done to them.

I asked three Kuchi men nearby to find a discarded needle. Then Steel showed me how he would threaten a mark with both his razor blade and needle and how, if needed, he could strike with lightning speed – it was scary! These are the notes I took during an interview with Steel.

1. He slashed a girl's breasts because she was passing her number to a boy. It was moral indignation on his part. When the police came they congratulated him for doing the right thing.

2. He verbally attacked a soldier who was fingering a girl in the park. Once again: moral indignation.

3. He stabbed the former boss of his gang which is how he came to power.

4. His grandfather is the one who encouraged him to become a gangster. His grandfather worked for Customs. Steel thinks the richest man in Jalalabad should be whoever runs the customs there – with raw opium being the biggest item in the local economy it would be no wonder.

5. The phone I bought him so he could ring us, and vice versa, has disappeared. He won't say how.

6. He uses needles discarded by addicts as weapons, knowing how much people fear AIDS, as well as razor blades.

7. He tells us he doesn't use drugs but we've heard otherwise. Apparently he likes hash.

MEETING the GANGSTER KINGS

When I first contemplated working with the gangsters my plan was to stay clear of the older guys, but then I changed my mind. I asked Steel to take me directly to the gangster king – Gulab – and also to introduce me to the guy who extorts money from his gang (also named Gulab).

Gulab, the king of the park gangsters, didn't disappoint. With his cloak thrown toga-like over his shoulders and his thinning hair combed to one side, he reminded me of Julius Caesar. When he sat for the interview, he made the chair look like a throne. Steel

proudly leant an elbow on his shoulder and it was soon obvious Gulab viewed him as his prodigy. From Gulab, we heard about Jena, a great gangster who was killed by a hidden bomb in a gang war. Gulab said, with great humility, that he doesn't feel that he can ever replace Jena, but thinks Steel has a chance.

I asked Gulab about the knife scars on his face and he related a bloody night when his enemies attempted to assassinate him – he killed them, but not before they slashed his face. He said he'd also received other, *more serious,* wounds. When I suggested he reveal these scars for our camera he angrily said, 'I liked my nuts'. Obviously he wasn't going to reveal this injury to his manhood.

Meanwhile, Amir Shah had found the other Gulab who answered their questions unaware the camera was rolling. I arrived at the moment he became angry about this.

He grabbed his bike and began doing wheelies and stunts very aggressively . . . seeming not to care if he hit people in the crowd with the bike. People cheered and clapped his stunts anyway. When he slowed for a moment, I went over and put my arm around him and things changed for the better. From that point on he performed for the cameras.

By now we had a huge crowd around us. Bulldog was shooting stills with my camera and Steel was holding my hand at the front. When a kid tried to outpace us, Steel spun around and kicked him. Steel wanted every gangster, murderer, thief, conman, drug dealer and kidnapper in the park to know we had made him the star of our movie. Here he was, tiny, yet elevated by the cameras and attention, to the giant he feels he is. Steel, the child gang leader, the young Scarface of Jalalabad, being filmed by Amir Shah, famous action hero, and promoted by me, Bubba Gittoes, his producer and sponsor.

Sensing the exhilaration of the crowd, I lifted my camera and shouted, 'Gangsters of Jalalabad!' A hundred fists were raised and the whole crowd repeated 'Gangsters of Jalalabad!' It was a euphoric moment.

I couldn't imagine a special forces op in Afghanistan being more dangerous than what I'd just done in the park. The Jalalabad park is a lawless place where anything can happen. As it is, I'm the only foreigner who walks the streets of Jalalabad unarmed and often alone, but the park is a no-go zone for most locals, who see it as too dangerous. There are no visible police or security forces. The all-male groups who frequent it include various tiers of gangsters, general tough guys, addicts, homeless madmen, and religious terrorists and fanatics. The kids I'm filming are like a school of piranhas, particularly with those razor blades in their mouths. For a foreigner to come here is reckless, but to come here and create a spectacle while shouting in English seems suicidal.

I'm not naive, of course Steel was manipulating me to the fullest. But it's a two-way puppet string: I was in showman-mode creating cinema magic and Steel was building his legend.

SARAJEVO COLLEGE AND ORPHANAGE FOR MENTALLY
DISADVANTAGED CHILDREN, SARAJEVO, BOSNIA, 8 MAY 1996

Today I drew the kids from the Sarajevo College and Orphanage for Mentally Disadvantaged Children. One drawing is of a twenty-one-year-old man called Sasa and the other is of a ten-year-old girl – Nerima. Now I'm attempting to combine their two faces. Sasa was born with a serious mental illness. He was receiving treatment and occupational training at the college. His father was a Muslim and mother a Serb. During the war both of his parents were killed. He could no longer get into Sarajevo for treatment, so became the responsibility of his Serb aunt. She didn't want to look after him, so turned him, as a Muslim, over to a Serb Concentration Camp. Sasa tells terrible stories of torture and starvation in the camp. His Serb captors, it is said, enjoyed tormenting him as a way of forcing lunatic behaviour which they found entertaining.

Somehow he was freed and made his own way back to Sarajevo. Now he is driven by a powerful need for revenge which has no focus. When he is at peace his pale green eyes and blond hair make him look like an angel, but when he is angry he transforms into something vicious and wolf-like. When Sasa appeared this morning he was angry, as he assumed I wouldn't show him the same amount of attention I had shown the others by drawing them. But when I made him the centre of attention, his face transformed, so much so it was impossible to reimagine the monstrous look it held only seconds before.

Watching Sasa transform in and out of his two extreme selves, I felt I had come closest to understanding the 'HOW?' of war.

Sarajevo has been transformed from a beautiful, civilized European city into an apocalyptic ruin of broken glass, rubble and rocket scars. What has happened in Bosnia in the last four years is like an ultra-slow-motion retake of what happens in Sasa's face when he changes from angel to demon.

Nerima Smajic is another war orphan. She is classified as emotionally and intellectually damaged by the war. Every aspect of her life story reads as tragic. However, Nerima bubbles with happiness. With her twinkling eyes and pixie face she resembles a fantasy character created by Disney studios.

Leaving the college, the extremes of Sasa's and Nerima's faces haunted me and merged into this single insane image – a face of war.

Shatter Chatter

When I was in Sarajevo towards the end of the Bosnian War, the long seige had shattered the minds of many children. I helped out at a mental asylum and orphanage for mentally damaged children.

The kids here in Jalalabad have experienced war all their lives, unlike the Bosnian kids who had experienced most of their early pre-war lives in safe, nurturing homes, going to school and living with the kind of security enjoyed in other European countries like Poland and Germany. Afghan kids seem superficially tougher, but the pain they have suffered is still very visible in their eyes.

LOVE STORY STEEL and SHAZIA

A few girls always hang around Steel's gang. I have noticed Steel passing out counterfeit money to them. Most girls only receive a few notes but when Steel got to one girl, he pulled out a thick roll, put a band around it, and handed it all to her. I asked her name – it's Shazia and she is his girlfriend.

So now we have a love story for the film – *West Side Story* or *Romeo and Juliet* meets Bonnie and Clyde. I've been trying to persuade Shazia to do an interview, but she refused, 'You could offer me a million dollars and I wouldn't do it. I wouldn't do it for anything.' I wasn't surprised, it's virtually wired into the DNA of Pashtun girls never to let themselves be photographed or filmed.

So I was shocked when I heard the rumour yesterday that Shazia had changed her mind. I sent Amir Shah out to check whether this miracle could be true and he when he came back he said, 'It's your lucky day. Shazia has decided to do it. We have to do it now before she changes her mind.'

My plan was to film her and Steel on the rooftop of Burger Chief, away from onlookers, so they could talk freely about their relationship.

Shazia is incredibly beautiful; she looks like a young Sophia Loren. She is also very articulate. At one point, she picked up a sharp piece of wood to demonstrate to us what she would do if she saw Steel getting hurt in a fight. Steel said his ambition is to become rich so he can buy her a beautiful house on the other side of the river. I asked him if he had something particular in mind and he nodded. He took us to the river and pointed out a lavish mansion to Shazia and told her that he intended to buy it for her some day. (It belonged to the head of the Department of Customs.) He said he wouldn't have let any of his gang or his family live there, it would be just the two of them, living in luxury and peace.

I was just taking my last snap of Shazia when, out of the corner of my eye, I saw Steel bite through the stems of some bright pink flowers and form them into a bunch. He crouched down and handed them to her and I was able to capture the moment.

We spent a long afternoon filming with Shazia. Like Steel, she is a natural in front of the camera and when she got over her shyness she loved working with us. I can't help hoping that she will gradually become more comfortable with us. As we left, the sun was going down and they were both illuminated in golden light – it was heart-throbbingly romantic.

THE BOYS GO TO SCHOOL

After months of preparation at the Yellow House, today the boys took the test to get into school.

We have bought them all new pale blue uniforms, exercise books, pencils and pens. We were almost late because Itchy and Neha fussed over them, brushing and combing their hair and ensuring they were spick and span.

At the school, the headmaster was dubious about their chances. Inam calmly gave him a list of what they had learnt under him and the other tutors at the Yellow House. When I looked over at the boys, their faces were pinched and worried.

There are no desks or chairs in the classrooms – just a large blackboard and chalk. All the students are from better-off families and have been told by their parents to shun the street kids because they carry lice and diseases.

A space was made, and our group of ice-cream boys and ghostbusters sat down among the other students. The atmosphere in the room was sceptical and I sensed a desire for our boys to fail. The first up to the board

was Irfan, who astonished the examiner by answering his question in perfect written Arabic. Everyone in the room clapped. Saludin was next, but took his time thinking about the question. He looked up to Inam and across to me and said 'this isn't something we have learnt'. But Inam told him he could do it, and he did. None of the boys were as confident as Irfan, but all passed. For the first time since his father's murder, Inam was beaming with joy. The boys had defeated class, poverty and the expectations of the school principal – it was like a rainbow on the horizon, a sign of hope for a better future for Afghanistan.

We had planned to film our boys triumphantly exiting the school gate but it was impossible. Hundreds of kids formed an excited mob around the cameras. It got dangerous and Irfan got crushed into a gutter by the hysterical crowd. Waqar pulled him to his feet and we had to take refuge in a roadside shop. Even then the crowd of faces were pressed to the windows waiting for us to come out. It was the kind of experiences the Beatles had with fans. I thought, *this won't hurt our boys when they go back to school!*

I got a call today from the Headmaster. It did not sound friendly so I walked immediatly to the school. I could see the boys in class and wondered what they could have done. But the Headmaster wanted to personally surprise me with the good news – the boys are being moved up two classes. They have excelled!!!!!

LYNCH MOB

Yesterday we were out filming the old Sufi and the ghostbuster boys in the countryside when I was hit hard by something in the back. I couldn't identify the culprit, but it was a warning.

This is an area where we have filmed many times with the full permission of the elders and community. They know us and would never normally object. The difference this time was that we had brought a Sufi and he had played music in their fields. They are superstitious enough to think this devil-music could blight their crops.

These people live near many beautiful ancient Buddhist monuments. Over the last twenty years they have not only destroyed all the statues of Buddha, but also almost completely erased the structures which contained them. The Taliban told them that Buddhists were snake worshippers, hence the *Nagas* (cobras) which often surround the seated Buddha figures.

When the crowd grouped together and began chanting abuse, I bundled the old Sufi into my car. Stones hit the windows and doors as we rolled out and away from this lynch mob.

The only face I have painted as many times as the old Sufi is that of Immacule, whom I made a drawing of at the site of the Kibeho massacre in Rwanda. I called this drawing *Eyewitness*. The accusation in Immacule's eyes has made that drawing the symbol of my life's work. With the portraits of the old Sufi, I want to open the inner eye to what it is to live in this world and see into the other side.

EYE WITNESS

I know I only have a few hours for sleep – but sleeping is impossible tonight. I have seen thousands of people hacked, shot, blown up – the faces will haunt me forever ... The day began with Captain Carol Vaughan-Evans (unit doctor) leading us to where hundreds of wounded had gathered – most had horrible machete wounds. This young woman, Immacule, sat patiently in a state of shock – a friend of hers had stitched up two major machete wounds in her head but the slash across her face still hung open. I lost track of her when the RPA Tutsi commander told us to get out because they 'were going to finish the rest off'.

Carol defied this order and led her brave Australian unit back to collect more wounded. After this I spent many exhausting hours helping the wounded and documenting slaughter, always aware that, if we survived, my photographs could be used to bring these merciless killers to some kind of justice as the war criminals they are.

Late in the afternoon I saw Immacule sitting alone. I asked Carol if I could help her and she explained that when the brain has been exposed amid such filthy conditions there is little that can be done. She must have sensed my exhaustion and suggested I 'sit with her so that she isn't alone'.

It's hard to justify taking the time to make a drawing when there are lives to be saved. But I took a sheet of paper from my drawing satchel and began to sketch. Immacule asked me why I was drawing her and I replied, 'I want the world to see what has been done to you.'

She understood this and became determined to remain conscious long enough for me to finish. This intimate collaboration bonded us. It was like I was tattooing her onto my heart. I could see her drifting – her spirit flickered in and out of life. After a few minutes, she asked me to show her what I had done and was shocked to see what she had become, saying, 'You have made me look ugly – I'm beautiful.' As I continued to work, her eyes never left mine – clinging to life until I had finished.

Too soon, she was gone. All that remains is this drawing and these eyewitness notes.

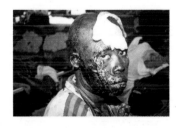

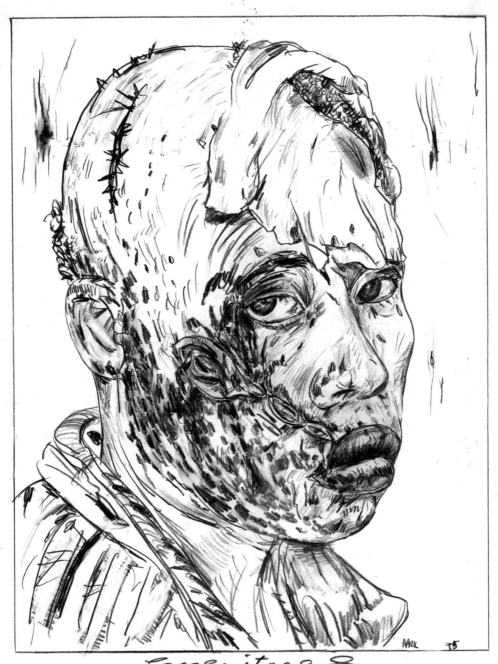

Eyewitness

I know I have only a few hours for sleep — but sleeping is impossible tonight.
I have seen thousands of people hacked, shot, blown up — the faces will haunt me
forever .... the Day started with Captain Carol Vaughn Evans (unit Doctor) leading us to
where hundreds of wounded had gathered — most had horrendous machete wounds.
This woman sat patiently in a state of shock — a girlfriend of hers had stitched up
two major machete wounds in her head but the slash across her face still hung open.
I only had 15 minutes to do this before the RPA Tutsi commander told me to get out because they were
going to finish the rest off." I hope she is one of the ones we helped out — people were
being killed on either side of us — I had to focus completely on getting a pregnant
woman who had been shot through the arm, chest and hand — out.
The medical unit stretched out around me all twist + turn — everyone in has
pushed themselves to the limit to save lives but the memories of those left behind will never go away

April 95

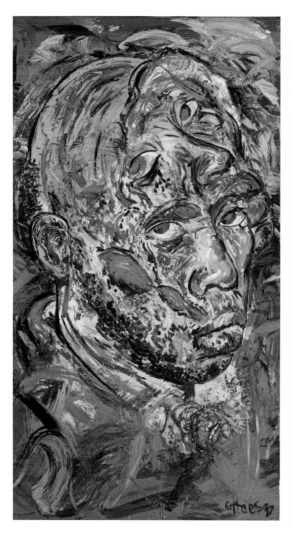

Shetani Night Vision

I allow nothing to enter my peripheral vision — focusing solely on the woman. I pull her body up against mine and use a plastic bag to block air from entering her punctured lung. I remove dressings and tourniquets from my kit. Together there is a chance we can get away. My need to save her is not selfless, she is a shield to help fend off my monsters. She is taller than me and heavy boned but I am able to lift her to my shoulder and carry her across my back, her leg dragging, Dead from the bullet wound. From the corner of my eye I glimpse another Shetani — it has a double face resembling two aspects of a woman I have seen die earlier in the night. It is a paler green-blue with a fluorescent glow — the face and scull have been slashed open with machete wounds — the red of blood making an optical flicker against the black. The fake wounds it has decorated itself with become more numerous — nails, shards of glass and metal blades appear in them. It is now a walking voodoo fetish. As it passes a spear emerges from it, protruding from one side and out the other — changing to a red tipped elephant tusk as it pales to white. I look away as I feel its eyes connecting to mine. My retinas feel singed and I am temporarily blinded.

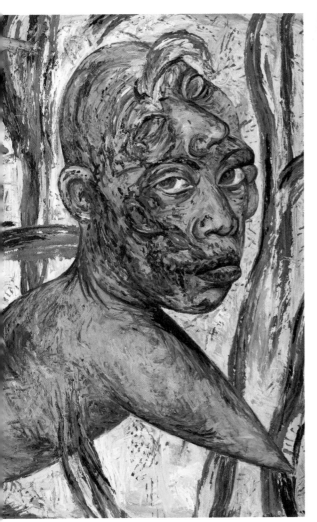
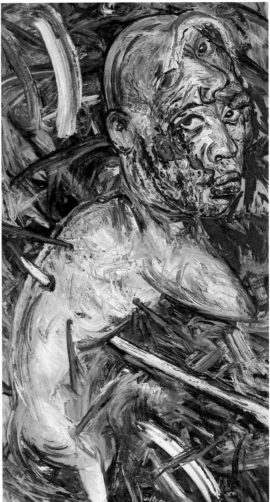

CHRISTMAS EVE on BUDDHIST HILL

t's dark, windy and freezing cold outside. My plan had been to shoot our final scenes on three rooftops today, separating the different groups of boys between them, but this suddenly seemed overcomplicated. Instead I got all seven ghostbusters and ice-cream boys into a taxi and told Waqar and Amir Shah to meet me at the Buddhist hill. Steel's gang appeared at the car windows and they climbed in too. Steel squeezed into the front seat, between me and the driver. I had Tim Tam on my knee. Steel might be a tough gangster, but he was frightened of the monkey. He bunched himself up, not wanting to lose face, and I tried to keep Tim Tam interested in the world outside the window.

We now had twelve kids in the small car plus myself, my monkey, the driver and Ashid. We pulled up near the graveyard at the base of the Buddhist hill.

I have made friends with an extraordinary balloon salesman. His name is Billal and he's nineteen and already married with a small son. He smiles a lot and tells me it is because he got to be with the girl he loves in a rare love marriage. Billal sees himself as a showman – a kind of circus carney – and is excited by the idea of learning to act and make films with us at the Yellow House.

We are going to experiment to see how many of Billal's lighter-than-air balloons it takes to carry a GoPro camera through Jalalabad as he hawks his wares. Most of the balloons are silver and white and are inflatable passenger jets or dolphins. They are totally surreal and beautiful, floating through the streets of this medieval city like a school of fish. They're like an installation piece by Christo, the way they transform drab reality into something magical and exotic.

As we piled out at Buddhist Hill we were hit by the freezing wind. Half the boys, led by Steel, shot up the hill without consulting me. There was no alternative but for me and Tim Tam to go after them.

As I stood there with Ashid and the monkey, I noticed that two of the boys – Saludin and Snake Eyes – were shivering, so I opened my coat, put a boy under each arm and tried to hold the coat around them. As I did so, a group of armed men came up the hill behind us. They looked mean and carried antiquated RPGs and AK-47s. There was no insignia on their clothing to indicate they were army, so they were probably Taliban, or bandits posing as Taliban. Either way, it wasn't good for us.

Fortunately, they were quickly enchanted by Ashid. They hadn't ever seen an adult as small as him and he soon had them chatting away. The sight of me, an old man, sheltering two boys from the cold must have seemed a bit pathetic; they left me alone. I was hoping they wouldn't notice the camera slung over

my shoulder. I was thinking, *Eventually they'll move over to me and this could turn very bad.*

Through all this, a huge herd of goats and sheep were moving over the hill. As they got closer, their tall, ragged shepherd suddenly spread his arms and began climbing towards me. I thought it had to be a case of mistaken identity, but it wasn't. It was Asam, the same man who got us through that tense meeting with Haqqani. As a former Mujahideen hero, Asam's the type of guy any soldier instantly respects. He had his cousin with him, who I also greeted warmly. After watching all this hugging and greeting, the armed men must have decided we were just part of the community and continued on to wherever they were going.

I will never know how close this was. I certainly didn't fit the profile of a foreign spy, not with twelve ragged boys, a monkey, a tiny person and some shepherds. Still I'd thought, *This could be it – I could die here, on Christmas Eve, on a cold mountain a long, long way from home.*

It was so cold Tim Tam had begun to sneeze – most of the mucus hitting me in the face. I imagined myself catching some exotic form of monkey flu.

We'd arranged for Billal to bring up some of his balloons, and the wind was now playing havoc with them. Somehow, the balloons, boys, a disgruntled musician with harpsichord, Waqar with the cameras and tripod, Ashid, me and the monkey all made it to the top through sliding pebbles. I felt one-hundred-and-five, rather than sixty-five, my knee replacements made every step awkward.

When Amir Shah finally made it to the top, there were about forty village children following him. I'd bunched the kids together,

with the monkey and the balloons, behind Mutazar, the musician. This would have to be it – contained and simple.

We sat a laptop on a rock beside a small set of speakers. Mutazar had decided it wasn't necessary for him to sing and was just miming to a recording. I told him this looked lame, which got him singing. After about four takes the boys had learnt most of the words and were singing along. This was starting to work. We took close-ups of their faces and I could see how this scene would cut together well with the previous scenes in the movie. The song was written for them, for this movie, and the boys started to realise this and take ownership of it. It's hard to read Mutazar, but perhaps this inspired him – he looked genuinely 'into it', enough for the take, so I made the call for everyone to leave the mountain for the warmth of the taxis below.

On the drive back I savoured this moment. This stretch of road is as picturesque as New Zealand. Everything and everyone seemed to glow – old men with turbans and sacks on their backs, farmers harvesting cauliflowers, a small child pushing a tyre along the road using a stick, it was like something out of Brueghel.

The monkey had been sneezing over me for the whole trip, so when we got back I headed for the bathroom to scrub my face and hands. Then I then put my pyjamas on, got under the blankets and into the foetal position.

NIGHT DRIVE WITH HAQQANI

One of my plans for *Snow Monkey* was to go out to Haqqani's village and film young Taliban. The police and intelligence forces, even Najib, all told me this was madness, but I've left it up to Haqqani to decide. Regardless of the advice, I'm up for it. Not a week has passed where we haven't been in touch about a way to do it, but there's been constant violence on the road to his village, from IEDs to kidnappings.

Early this evening, one of his Landcruisers pulled up. Haqqani was driving, but his usual smile was absent. Something was very wrong. In the passenger seat was a mean-looking maulvi, a high-level Taliban leader. Haqqani told me we were going to his other home, on the outskirts of Jalalabad. Waqar gave me a 'this could be trouble' look, but grabbed the cameras, knowing I would want him to try to capture this whatever happened. Waqar would never think of backing out and leaving me without his support, even in a situation like this, from which there may be no way back.

His frightening passenger refused to shake my hand when offered, he looked at me as if I were vermin. Two of Haqqani's sons, his bodyguards, had AK-47s. Normally they'd be grinning and hugging, and shaking my hand –

but they were they stiff and unreadable.

We all squeezed into Haqqani's Landcruiser. I was told the maulvi wasn't to be filmed. It was clear this was a test. While Haqqani likes me and regards me as a friend, the maulvi was dangerous. In situations like this I become hyper-alert to the tiny details of body-language and conversation. It's how I've survived so many bad situations.

My reading of this one was that the maulvi planned to make an example of Haqqani, that he wanted to demonstrate how foolish he had been to trust me. I thought, *this could be the end; by morning, my decapitated body could be on the news*. I thought, *I should have told Waqar to stay behind*.

As we gathered in Haqqani's *hoojrah*, the maulvi led the prayer. The atmosphere was tense. He'd spent an inordinate amount of time meticulously washing his hands, arms and feet. I hoped this wasn't some kind of purification ablution like that performed by halal butchers before they slaughter a beast.

Waqar, Haqqani and his sons laid out prayer mats and joined him. I knew it might be smart to do the same, but I also felt this would be hypocritical. I felt like an insect, pinned to the cushions I leant on.

Their prayers were interwoven with sermons and sutras from the Koran, all sung by the maulvi in a discordant, artless tone. When they finished I said lamely that, in my own way, I prayed with them. Haqqani's sons began bringing in tea and sweet cookies. These boys all knew me and we exchanged tense smiles under the intense scrutiny of the maulvi.

I said to Haqqani, 'You are a very rich man, I envy you all these beautiful and talented sons – I have always wanted to film you with your sons gathered around you.' Haqqani loved the idea and all fourteen of his sons were brought in, including the youngest baby.

Seeing this, the maulvi smiled for the first time, saying to Haqqani, 'You make me wish I had two wives as well!' Haqqani said, 'I have six daughters too.'

After the cakes and tea I did a long interview with Haqqani, with his fourteen sons sitting tightly around him. The imp in me couldn't resist asking the boys controversial questions about how the Taliban can justify using children as suicide bombers.

I looked to the maulvi, he was taking in every word.

The main meal arrived. I began to stand, saying Waqar and I would find a way home on our own. Haqqani wouldn't hear of it. I should've kept quiet and just socialised with the older boys during the meal, but I got into a discussion of politics with Haqqani – although I stuck to subjects like corruption where I knew we had common ground – and soon the maulvi joined in. As the boys brought in a range of desserts and fruit, I recalled that the Incas used to allow those who were about to be sacrificed to eat whatever they wished.

As the food was cleared away, the maulvi stood, becoming stern again. We stood to attention before him – thinking the worst could still be on the cards. His face was set in a deadly serious frown. I thought this could be it. But to my relief, he apologised for his rudeness earlier. Then he admitted, 'I had bad thoughts about you and even nastier intentions.'

He went on to explain that I had changed his opinion of me: whatever the test was, I'd passed. Mainly, he said, it was because he could see the children loved me. He asked if I would join him at some later date when he and his fellow maulvis can teach me some finer points of Islam. Of course I agreed.

It had been a long six hours.

As we stepped into the cool air of the courtyard, Waqar turned to me with a relieved smile that said, *we shall live to see another day*.

I will never know what the 'nasty intentions' were, but when I felt the breeze on my face as we walked out of the *hoojrah*, I felt lucky my head was still attached to my body. We all crammed into the car and drove back to the Yellow House. It was dark and there were several military checkpoints to negotiate. Haqqani's car was full of automatic weapons but the soldiers, who searched all the other cars, never questioned Haqqani or dared to look inside. They know who Haqqani is.

At the gate of the Yellow House, the maulvi got out of the car. I hugged him and he said, 'I will tell the other leaders your work is to be supported. I am sure you will join us in our struggle,' and added, 'and we'll teach you how to pray.'

SHIT

This morning I wandered among the dead – after three days of slaughter the refugee camp had been flattened. This place is hell. People caught between the Rwandan RPA soldiers and the Interhamwe machetes – their corpses covered in mud by the battering rain, partially hidden in the shroud of discarded possessions. I was steadying myself to take a photograph when a man sat up, shaking his head, slowly regaining consciousness – a deep head wound exposed skull above his eye. I helped him to his feet as he took in the horror of the scene before his eyes. He could barely talk – fluent in French but little English. His name was Joseph.

At this point I was called away by Medical Sergeant Major Rod Scott who was leading a section detailed to body count. My cameras were needed to make documentary evidence. I hardly raised them from my chest on that walk however, because we were being so closely watched by resentful and suspicious RPA. At one point we found a row of dead children – graded by size and stacked like sandbags. One of our troop had a simple 'bean counter' – a device like a stop watch which was clicked once for each body sighted. Our progress was slow and frequently challenged.

I saw Joseph in the distance – he had gotten ahead of us in his search for his family. I called to him. There was obviously something wrong – something terribly wrong. He was holding something like a muddy football – the whole frame of his body heaving with deep sobs. Coming closer I saw he was holding a bloody head, the head of his young daughter – all he could find of his family.

He was paralysed by shock and indecision – ignoring the extreme personal danger of being alone in this 'no man's land'. I offered to help him bury her. He refused, saying she needed a proper church burial.

The tension was rising. RPA began pointing guns at us, insisting the body count stop. As Sergeant Major Scott argued with some officers, I looked into the small building we had used a few days earlier as a temporary field hospital. It was now stacked to the rafters with bodies. All along the sides of the road we had seen drag marks with blood stains – proof that the RPA had worked hard through the night to conceal the actual number killed.

I realised Joseph would probably never know the full fate of his family.

Near a quadrangle of former classrooms, there is a patch of ground where people go to shit. There are also dead bodies scattered in this place, including a mother, her baby attached to her back by a length of cloth and her son curled up next to her.

At about 4pm this afternoon I saw Joseph squatting down, shitting. He was still holding the head of his daughter while trying to keep the flies away.

Shit, war is SHIT!

Few people in our society have witnessed decapitations. The TV and newspaper images of recent decapitations by Daesh (ISIL) like the one where the son of an Australian volunteer fighter holds up a human head are designed to shock. But I have been where heads rolled like corn cobs in a harvest. At Kibeho, thousands of people were decapitated by machete - many of them women and children. To have seen men weilding blades on that scale makes these guys with their turbans and hunting knives less Intimidating. It isn't a sight that one can become detached from, but no images in the media or on YouTube can equal the horror of Kibeho x

SOFT POWER

When outside in Jalalabad, men and women cannot show affection publically, not even hold hands. To be seen kissing is unthinkable.

Hellen was heading to the airport on her own, her protection entrusted to Mohammad, one of our most reliable drivers. As we walked towards the vehicle the eyes of the military guards and pedestrians on the busy street were on us . . . but I could not resist. I put my arm around Hellen's waist and we locked lips – a long passionate kiss. It was our Bogart and Bacall moment – high romance in a city that wants to deny any expression of love.

I was on my way back down the mountain road when Hellen called from the airport. She'd had her passport taken from her at immigration. I got Mohammad to pull over so I could call some people who could help us if necessary – as I waited for an update, Mohammad started the car.

As we rounded the next bend we saw trouble ahead. Vehicles were queued in the road and there was the sound of heavy gunfire in the distance. One of the many battles between the army and the Taliban. If it hadn't been for Hellen's call and the waiting, we would have been caught between the crossfire. Fortunately, there was room enough on the narrow road to turn and head back to Kabul. Indirectly, Hellen had saved my life.

As we drove, I had to ask myself, *What has America created here?* The soldiers and police, especially in Kabul, now have uniforms and lots of GI Joe gear. But they all wear black balaclavas covering their faces, exactly like the ISIL fighters in Iraq and Syria. This way they can behave like monsters with impunity – their own mothers wouldn't recognise them. These generic soldiers have nothing that distinguishes them as Afghan save a small black, red and green flag patched on to their uniform. They could be robots. If these guys were placed at a roadblock in Washington or New York City, nothing about them would look foreign or incongruous. It's an unashamedly intimidating look, somewhere between *Star Wars* and the Gestapo.

At least a third of the vehicles on the roads are police, army or private security forces, all kitted out in expensive equipment. Most of the rest of the population is unemployed or working below the poverty line. My film documents parents who can't afford to send their children to school and little ones who are out collecting rubbish from dawn until after dark to survive. Yet behind high walls and razor wire, the elite live in lavish houses. Is this a model for the future here? In Europe and America, the working class is increasingly jobless. Globalisation has made it so that countries with workers' rights can't compete with cheap unregulated labour available abroad, where people must work for three dollars a day, without holiday time or sickness benefits. Everywhere, the protests of the unemployed are suppressed. The barons of industry hate nothing more than unions.

In 2011, I saw the brutality of New York cops towards the Occupy Wall Street protesters in Zucotti Park. I told the protest organisers they should put out a poster, like the one Bush put out in Iraq showing the 'most wanted' of Saddam's regime, featuring the richest one per cent. No-one had the nerve to accept my suggestion. The real targets of the anti-one per cent campaign are always so protected: comfortable, anonymous and out of sight.

I can easily imagine a future where both middle and working classes are mostly unemployed, or forced to work in extreme austerity measures, where unions are banned and all protest is suppressed by the only people with jobs outside the super-rich – the police, military and private security. This is the future we are moving towards.

Afghanistan is already that dystopia out of science-fiction – a largely unemployed population is held down by a vast, state-run, military fist. And I wonder to what extent the Americans are using it as a grand experiment in people control? Afghans are famous for their courage and independence of spirit. If they can be successfully repressed then it's possible anywhere. And America has been trialling drones and lots of other advanced military hardware here – equipment which is passed on to civilian police forces back home.

In my film *Miscreants of Taliwood*, I talked about the blindfolded leading the blindfolded. Can the super-rich who run the corporations really think they can enjoy a future, holed up Scrooge-like with their piles of money, in an oppressed world? America talks about human rights abuses, but won't reform its own penal system where the majority of prisoners are black and/or poor. And it's in those prisons that military contractors get cheap labour to make the helmets and uniforms of the army and police. Many of the soldiers I interviewed in Iraq for *Soundtrack to War*, like Janel and Josh Revac, told me they'd been offered the army or jail. Of course they jumped at the relative freedom of the army, 'serving their country'. America had to appear to support the Arab Spring and the toppling of Mubarak's military dictatorship in Egypt, but we can be certain the same kind of people who authorised torture at Guantanamo Bay and other rendition venues were asked to ensure that an even more severe dictatorship was re-established after this short flirtation with democracy. Nothing is more worrying for the elite corporations that run America than to see people protest power.

History has so many examples of elites ignoring the suffering of the masses, from the Roman Caesars to the Czars of Russia. But are America's actions in Afghanistan an experiment, a strategic move to exploit its vast mineral wealth, or just folly, like in Iraq?

The Perfect

THE PERFECT MOMENT AND
A BULLET PROOF MIND
Sunday Nov 10 - 2002 New York.

New York's recently opened Museum of Sex
features Robert Mapplethorpe's self portrait
with a bull whip up his arse. Robert shares
the space with a pickled head — its nose eaten
out by syphilis, the story of a sausage maker
who took pig intestines home and invented the
first condoms and the video of a gang bang
which the black porn star explains any more
than 8 men is excessive — one for each orifice (8)
one for each hand (2), one for each arm pit (2)
and one in case the others get tired. Robert's
whip becomes a tail and in this context his worry
look is that of a zoo exhibit, in this expensive peep show.
Today & tommorrow (10-11 Nov) Remembrance is observed for U.S.
Veterans. The TV shows Vietnam Vets assembling at the
Washington Memorial while names are slowly read.
When Robert died of AIDS in 1989 it was the height of the AIDS
era — his solo exhibitions had opened around the world to serious
critical acclaim but 4 months after his death the Corcoran Gallery
of art in Washington cancelled his retrospective "The Perfect
Moment" citing political considerations. When "The Perfect Moment" opened
at the Contemporary Arts Centre in Cincinnati on April 7, 1990 it was
closed by police and its Director indicted on obscenity charges.
As I see President Bush on television commemorating Veterans day I
wonder what has happened to the acres of quilts of the AIDS era.
The UN has voted through new tough measures for ARMS Inspectors to test
for biological weapons of mass destruction. American troops — a 200,000
commitment — are ready at battle stations — this is no Cuban Missile crisis
but the country waits on Saddam's reaction and the possibility of the
most lethal war since Vietnam. Commentators debate whether chemical
and biological weapon threats will require US forces to put on a "full body condom".
Presently they are getting Anthrax shots. The main concern, however, is whether
an attack on IRAQ will make America less vulnerable or more.
This weekends New York Times Magazine has a feature article with the headline —
'A Bulletproof mind' and in bold subtext 'Tens of thousands of American soldiers
engaged in close-up killing in Vietnam, and the psychological wreckage was enormous.
That's why today's Special Forces are being engineered not only for the traumas of
battle but also for its aftermath.'
'..... since 9/11 we have begun a war that may draw our soldiers into many battles
involving intimate killing. ..... The last time this kind of fighting occurred on
a grand scale, in Vietnam 50,000 Americans died and many survivors had injuries
that were not just physical but emotional — post traumatic stress disorder. Today
the military believe the U.S. is fighting an intimate war in the right way, because
soldiers have been prepared and equipped in a manner that increases the prospect of
their victory and decreases the prospect of their injury — whether physical or
psychological. ..... Dave Grossman, a former Army Ranger and West Point professor
of psychology refers to this phenomenon as "the bulletproof mind." New York Times Mag, Nov 10 2002

...nd a Bullet Proof Mind.

2002

KABUL BANK BOMB

Today has been the blackest of days. I was alone in the Yellow House when I heard a huge explosion. It didn't shatter any of our windows, but it was close. I had no way of knowing what was going on, but eventually Ishrad returned with the news. Kabul Bank had been attacked by terrorists, probably Daesh (ISIL), and many had been killed. I immediately thought of Steel and the gangsters. The bank is where they hang out, pickpocketing or selling holy pages of the Koran. But Ishrad quickly dispelled my fears – he'd already checked. All of our friends and the kids, including the gangsters, were okay. The only one missing was Steel's girlfriend, Shazia.

This is awful. This place is coming apart. We are targets more than ever and I can't see the people of Jalalabad recovering from this attack very soon.

Zabi and Saludin were near the bank – Zabi had actually shot footage of the carnage. It's horrific. I don't know whether we should use it in the documentary. I've never seen anything like it. Neha, watching it, observed, 'Zabi shoots it with an innocence that makes it more ghastly – the camera not only captures what is in front of it but also the shock he feels through his whole being.' What really got to both the boys was a man they saw with his face covered in blood and his mobile phone to his ear. He was telling his family he was okay. They saw him drop to his knees and die only minutes later.

Some time later, we hear that Zabi has been taken captive by ISIL.

I'm alive now thanks to the Holy Quran.

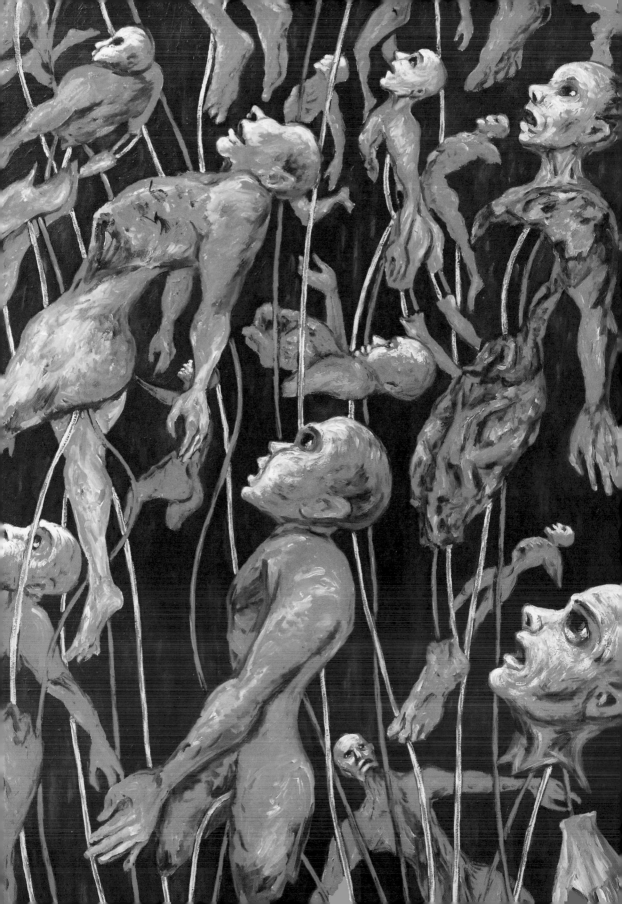

RETURN of ZABI

I'm always the first awake at the Yellow House. This morning I was sitting in the kitchen sketching when I saw a shadow pass the window. It was dawn and the sun was just breaking through the trees. I turned to the next window and saw a smiling face looking in. I couldn't believe my eyes – it was Zabi. He'd been missing for the past month.

I have never seen anyone as happy as Zabi was then. He was gasping in joy and couldn't speak. I called out to everyone and they came from everywhere to hug him, overjoyed to see him alive. He moved his mouth trying to form words but nothing came out, then he began to investigate every corner of the Yellow House and its garden as if he was trying to convince himself it was real, that he was really back. I finally got him to sit down and eat some breakfast (he looked very thin) and he managed to tell his story. His family had been forced to become refugees from their village by Taliban. It's a long way away in the mountains. When they returned, the original Taliban – who were Afghan – had been killed by a sect like ISIL. They threatened the villagers with death and destruction if they didn't make older boys like Zabi work for them. It was Zabi's job to carry their weapons up into the mountains or wherever they were planning attacks. The Daesh (ISIL) fighters didn't accompany them, so that if a predator drone, patrol or helicopter saw them and mistook the boys for insurgents, the actual insurgents would be safe. Zabi went on three dangerous missions like this, carrying guns into the mountains for them, before running away.

He said he experienced many bad things but when he tried to tell us, he choked up again. I went over and hugged him while Hellen got him a glass of water. Still finding

it difficult to speak he told us that he'd been present when a baby was born in the village. The villagers let off their guns in joy, a common practice at weddings and births here. In this case the mother had been thought barren so the baby was an answer to many prayers. The Daesh (ISIL) militants heard the gunfire and came to investigate. The villagers were happy to share their news of the birth with them. But the Daesh (ISIL) soldiers became very angry and asked to see the baby. When it was brought to them, one Daesh (ISIL) soldier held one leg and another soldier held the other and a third cut it down the middle as they *pulled it apart*. When the child's father tried to stop them, they killed him too, shouting at the villagers that there should be no celebration except the celebration of Allah, the only God.

Hellen said, 'As if these poor people haven't suffered enough already.'

Before escaping, Zabi heard that his mother and siblings had left the village for a refugee camp. He had no way to contact his father, but, knowing the Yellow House would give him sanctuary, he took the risk and fled. It was an epic journey back, on foot unless he could hitch a ride on donkey carts and motorbikes. Daesh (ISIL) is everywhere, and he worried he might be spotted by one of their numerous informants.

He then went around the building again, touching and checking everything. Electricity is still a marvel to him and he touched every plug and connection. Then he went out into the garden. He watered the plants and talked, as he has so often, to the peacocks.

Later, when he wandered into our editing room, he picked up one of the video cameras and held it like it was the most precious item on earth. He ran his hands over it, then flicked the ON switch and put the viewfinder to his eye. It was like he was checking himself, to see if he still knew how to use it. I said to him, 'You're a natural, like Waqar. You have real talent.'

Zabi replied, 'This can be my weapon to fight ISIL. They killed that baby, they send suicide bombers to the city – people need to see this evil. It can be stopped.'

Finding Shazia

I decided to throw the dice and drive around to look for Shazia. We'd heard that she was so traumatised by the bombing that she will no longer go near the centre of the city. Instead, she's working out near the US Army base. I don't think she realises that being so close to the Americans puts her at even greater risk.

We were almost at the perimeter of the US army base, where they have a big white spy blimp tethered. Driving slowly along the strip of sleazy places that cater for locals working on or around the base, I spotted a splash of colour – emerald green and magenta – in the distant dust. I was sure it must be Shazia. As the car pulled up next to her, Amir Shah said, 'George, you are so lucky – finding her is like one chance in a thousand thousand.' She beamed when she saw us. She had no shoes and had walked at least ten kilometres to get there.

Watching her over these many months on the editing screen had made Shazia much larger in my mind. But at that moment I saw her as she was – tiny and emaciated.

The men resting through the midday heat on couches outside their shopfronts were staring at us. What were they thinking? There are so many taboos about talking to women and girls in this society. Naturally Shazia was unwilling to be photographed with these men looking on, or even to get into our car for a lift back to the Yellow House where Hellen would have showered her with attention.

Despite her poverty, Shazia has natural nobility. She has the beauty and elegance of an aristocrat, even in hand-stitched clothes that are little more than rags. She was carrying a funny little square basket by a shoulder strap. It had what looked like children's books in it, she assured me they were religious texts for the study of Islam. They are the same as the pages the gangster boys sell to passersby. I'd expected to see her dirty with boot polish, since she usually shines shoes, but now she looked clean and stylish with her pretty little woven basket.

Shazia said she would ask her mother if we could film her. I asked her if she would like to come round tomorrow to see Hellen at the Yellow House and told her that Hellen will find her some new clothes. She seemed very happy at the idea.

Shazia told us that she had been outside the bank trying to sell phone cards when she decided to top up her supply of verses from the Holy Koran. She and the gangster boys sell these to the pious as they exit the mosque after prayers. She had just got some when she heard the first blast. I asked if she had been worried about Steel. She said, 'No, Steel is so tough he can withstand anything, even a bomb blast.' But whenever she goes near the site of the blast now, her hands begin to shake with fear . . . not because she fears another ISIL attack but because she believes the ghosts and spirits of the dead haunt it still.

The Children's Jail

There's a jail here for the rehabilitation of children who have been sent on failed suicide missions. This jail, and what they do there, is such a sensitive issue with the local authorities it has taken me months to arrange a visit. It looks like something built for a film adaptation of a Stephen King book – a mansion built in a style so weird we risk the viewer thinking we're trying to pass off special effects. If Walt Disney were alive, I can't imagine him envisioning anything more sinister as a place to keep captive children. Between the towers and lavish balconies there are sandbagged machine-gun posts, rusting metal stakes and razor wire. The mustard-coloured gates are covered in what looks like stars. Most of the walls are painted the colour of dried blood. There is a crudely cut peephole in the main gate – a metal flap opened and a single eye studied us before the door creaked open.

We were frisked, double-frisked, and frisked again, and our cameras were tested for disguised bombs. A motley group of uniformed officers and officials guided us upstairs. The cells were blocked from view with mattresses.

A huge guy who'd slipped in next to me said that he was the resident psychologist. His interview was one of the most fascinating of my career. He told me many things, including that the boys are not only brainwashed but drugged too. I can't understand the psychology of a suicide bomber. How they think they can earn a place in Paradise with Allah's blessing is beyond comprehension after witnessing carnage like the Kabul Bank. All the victims were other Muslims and most were poor people with no connection to the military or police.

Down at ground level, some of the prisoners were sitting facing the long cage while they spoke to visitors, probably family members. I got some shots of the exterior. Across the road was a *madrassa*, where young boys get religious education.

EAGLES

Last night I was uneasy. I have a real sense of impending danger. I'm planning to film an interview with Inam about Daesh (ISIL) at the bank bombsite. It's against all good judgement, but since we don't have to discuss the risk with anyone we can be as stupid as we want.

On the way out we passed a butcher who had fully skinned a bullock but hadn't yet quartered it. The carcass was on its knees, on a piece of sacking at the side of the road, like some strange pink and white Damien Hirst artwork – grotesquely beautiful in death. When we got to the the Kabul Bank, we found the road closed off, armed police guards defending it. They knew Amir Shah and let us through the cordon. Knowing the bloody scene the bomb had made with human limbs and ruptured bodies, the emptiness of this place was spooky. It felt like Sachsenhausen. The bodies had gone but death remained.

I was tensely wondering what was keeping Inam – we kept trying his phone and ringing his house, but no-one knew where he was. We watched shop owners roll up their security doors – they all would have lost friends and family in this blast.

As Inam still wasn't answering his phone and we were close to where Gul Minah brings her cans for cash and recycling, I decided to check to see if she was there. And there she was, in a red dress and a lot taller. She was glad to see us but refused to be photographed. She must have gotten into a lot of trouble by letting us film before. She led a proud little gang of kids up the road, their recycling bags over their shoulders and we waved at them as we drove past. Thank God she's still alive.

I felt restless and wired, every turn today seemed to be into frustration alley.

We saw Bulldog and stopped to talk to him. He had news: his mother was arranging a marriage for him, and Waqar and I were invited to the wedding. He'd been to Kabul to meet the family and seen the girl through a crack in a door. I asked him if she was beautiful and he said yes, smiling. Bulldog can't be more than fifteen but he suddenly looked a lot older. Their mother had decided she needed help around the house and this girl's family were indebted to theirs. Bulldog then confessed that the reason Steel had been avoiding him was that he was unhappy about the marriage. I asked him why and Bulldog said, 'I don't know – it's messing with his head. He has gone crazy mad about it and is threatening to kill me if I go ahead.'

A Kuchi woman in a faded red dress had been staring at me. To my surprise she came into the café where we were sitting and began talking to the owner and gesturing at the ground. Then she started pointing at me. Waqar listened to her and told me the old Sufi had been singing in a park when members of

Daesh (ISIL) attacked him. They smashed his harmonium, then they cut out his tongue before removing his head.

My vision went black – I had to steady myself against a pole and sit down.

Grieving, I made for Najib's restaurant. I needed something beyond words to understand this terrible news. I thought I would film the eagles that congregate on the river banks outside Najib's restaurant. The old Sufi loved the eagles and we had watched them together. I could imagine incredible close-up shots of these eagles in flight, my camera lens capturing the soul of the Sufi flying free. But when I arrived, for the first time ever, there were no eagles.

I searched the horizon for a sign of the beautiful birds. Instead, I saw hunters with guns. They had been shooting the eagles. A man with a rifle walked towards us followed by a begging urchin boy. I could see a small dead bird in his hands. The hunter had handed him the bird instead of money.

I wanted to be alone with my memories of the old Sufi, so I asked the boy to guide me down to a quiet spot where the river-rounded stones merged with and roiled the flowing waters.

I lay on the stones to get a shot of the twisting waters with the Tora Bora Mountains in the background. As I focussed my camera, a well-defined eye seemed to blink open and look back at me. The eye was one of the rocks. It was very unsettling and seemed to reflect my troubled thoughts. I decided it must be a natural phenomenon and clicked off my photographs, but when I lifted myself up I saw it was a piece of sculpture. A lone fragment of one of the Buddha sculptures which sat for two thousand years in the caves on the other side of the river until they were smashed and destroyed as idolatry by the Taliban.

The broken pieces of the sculptures must have been thrown into the river or pushed onto its banks. The caves were a destination for pilgrims for centuries and once held the relic of the Buddha's skull. They had been home to generations of monks.

I may have photographed the only surviving eye of Buddha.

Was this a sign from the old Sufi? I don't know, but I had found what I was searching for.

I tipped the kid with the dead bird and left with the Eye of God in my pocket.

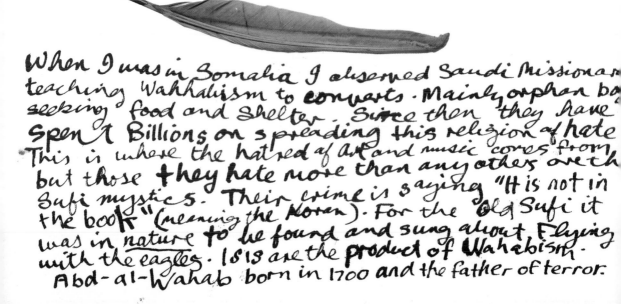

When I was in Somalia I observed Saudi Missionar
teaching Wahhabism to converts. Mainly orphan bo
seeking food and shelter. Since then they have
spent Billions on spreading this religion of hate
This is where the hatred of art and music comes from,
but those they hate more than any others are th
Sufi mystics. Their crime is saying "It is not in
the book" (meaning the Koran). For the old Sufi it
was in nature to be found and sung about. Flying
with the eagles. ISIS are the product of Wahabism.
Abd-al-Wahab born in 1700 and the father of terror.

LOSING MY Grip On REALITY

For most people the place where they were born is their reality; it's the setting of their childhood memories, where their family, workmates and friends live. I have built this Yellow House over four years and made it a home. Its reality has gradually solidified. The locals know me, the streets and shops of the bazaar are all familiar, as are their owners.

I now feel more connected to the world here than at 'home', particularly when out walking the streets. People here are always *doing things,* hand-cutting a field of cauliflower or hammering a piece of twisted metal into something useful, and I can buy that cauliflower, or help to hold the metal straight on the bench.

I feel an urge to hold onto all this a bit longer, even if a part of me yearns for the comforts of home. It's like the feeling of clinging to a dream before waking: even through the barking of dogs, crowing roosters, slamming doors, running water or muffled conversation, the vestiges of my dream linger. It doesn't matter if that dream is partially a nightmare, the urge to keep it from fading before opening my eyes persists. It's like that here – what I have, I want to cling to.

When I'm back home and want to reach into this world, the footage will be my record. But right now it's concrete – I'm touching it, eating its food and drinking its water, affecting the lives around me. Twenty-eight hours of travel is all that separates these two countries, but for me it's a world away.

My life of constant transit merges reality and dream; they become indistinguishable so that it all becomes transit, *samsara.* This merging is easier for wanderers between worlds. All I can say for certain is that I'm losing my grip on reality.

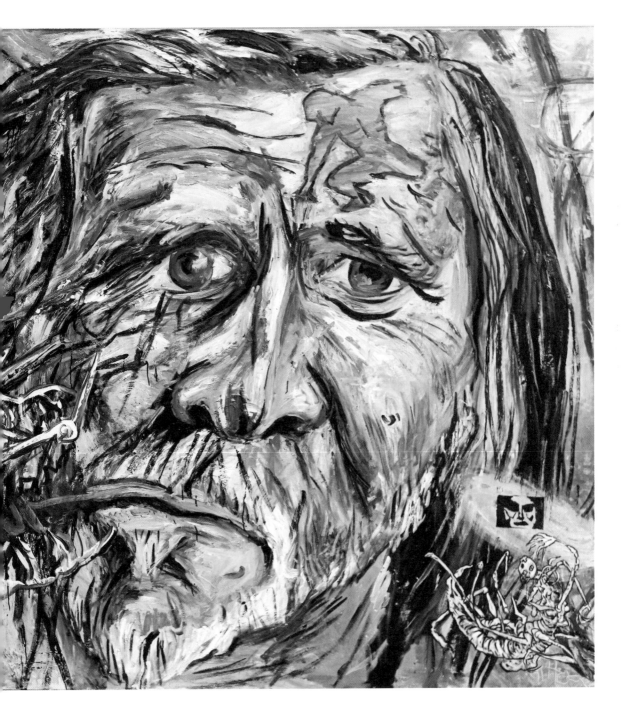

Farewell

'm preparing to leave. I have to go back to Sydney to collect the Peace Prize and also to finish the editing of *Snow Monkey*. Of course, the Yellow House will go on and we'll be back, but each of the children has come up to me, put his head on my chest and cried at our leaving. My cotton shirt is wet with tears.

The Yellow House has allowed these kids to experience childhood – something they would have otherwise missed. They've worked out ways to go to school after we leave and I've put safeguards in place to help them achieve this.

I've given my two goats to Zabi, the beginning of his own herd. Juliet is pregnant and Zabi thinks she'll have twins. I saw him off on the road, with the goats following on rope leads. Later, I dropped the peacocks in to Najib. They will join his existing peacocks and live in the garden in front of his restaurant until we return.

I went down to the park to say goodbye to Steel and the gangsters. A very small hand came out of the shadows as I passed. It was Majid, the tiny shoeshine boy. We lost contact with him months ago. He doesn't expect any charity and he started taking out his brushes to clean my shoes. He told me he now lives in the park. He has no family. He survives on the few coins he gets shining shoes.

The gangsters finally turned up and I was delighted to hear Steel is going to special tuition with Inam to use his brain and skills for something more than gangstering. Bulldog was disappointed I would miss his wedding, but I had a gift for his bride from Hellen and me.

I took Majid back to the Yellow House where Hellen cooked him a big meal. It was hard to take him back to that park. He has huge eyes and is like a little mouse, his growth stunted by malnutrition. I left, imagining him hiding alone in the dark while every kind of human predator prowled.

On the way to Kabul and the airport, Mohammad slowed. Sometimes, even with a lifetime of photojournalist experiences, my reflexes aren't quick enough to decipher what I'm seeing in time to get a lens up to it. In front of us was an oil tanker with several holes in it, petrol spurted out of them like water from a hose. The smallest spark and the whole thing would explode in a ball of fire. Mohammad decided to risk it and sped past. As we rounded the next corner I heard an explosion and saw a dark cloud rising behind us.

In a few hundred metres there was an Afghan military post, but the soldiers didn't respond to the blaze. This has been the worst year ever for Afghan army casualties, from the looks on these men's faces I could tell t hey didn't want to be added to that list. I thought of getting Mohammad to pull over so I could tell them they had to do something but his eyes were fixed on the road ahead – he wanted to get as much distance between us and the Taliban as possible. He plays this game of Russian roulette every day on this road between Jalalabad and Kabul – he's the veteran and I'm just the passenger. I've managed not to get killed this year, but Afghanistan had given me a fiery send off.

Human Sunshine

Today was the happiest day I can remember. As part of the events around the award of the Sydney Peace Prize, I was driven out to Cabramatta High School where two silk lions, the kind you see at Chinese New Year celebrations, danced towards me with drums beating to welcome me. Me!

The silk lions led me to a crooked pathway lined on either side by students in national costume. I shook their hands and said a few words to them all. It's a multicultural school and I had been to most of the countries these students were from – mainly conflict zones like Iraq, Cambodia, Afghanistan, Syria, and Bosnia – so could talk to them about their history. In the school's garden, hundreds of ceramic model Yellow Houses had been planted on wooden pegs among

the flowers. They all shared the same yellow glaze, but every one was unique, representing the forty-three languages and sixty cultural groups at the school – some were grass huts on stilts, others were clearly Islamic or Oriental. My mother taught ceramics, so I knew how much work it would have been to model, fire and glaze them. I felt wonderfully ambushed. I was surprised to see such a perfect realisation of our dream: the Yellow House around the world. I was then led towards the assembly hall by a parade of students carrying portraits of previous winners, from Hanan Ashrawi to Desmond Tutu, Xanana Gusmão and Noam

Chomsky. Once inside, one of my jobs would be to present a prize to the winner of the competition to paint my portrait. On the way in, the art teacher confided that 'the Jesus thing has been a real problem'. I didn't know what he was talking about until suddenly I was surrounded by hundreds or portraits of what looked like the Messiah – my long hair and beard had become my dominant features.

Aunty Mae, a seventy-three-year-old Aboriginal Elder, gave the welcome to country and the assembly began with a beautiful rendition of the Australian National Anthem. I had never heard our anthem sung with such emotion.

Then it was like the protest era had never ended as the student band played Bob Dylan's 'Blowing in the Wind'.

An image of His Holiness the Dalai Lama was projected behind me as I stepped up to the mike and told the students they filled my heart with hope. There were seven hundred kids in the hall and outside were another sixteen hundred from fourteen local schools. Among them stood nine angel puppets I'd made for today. My puppets seemed to be smiling back at me as I told the assembled students my story, taking them all back to the Rockdale of my childhood, living in a street of migrant kids who were all refugees of World War II.

I felt connected to every pair of eyes looking up at me. I wasn't a visitor from outside, I was someone who had seen what they'd seen, been where they had escaped from, someone who is glad that they've been lucky enough to reach the safety of our lucky country.

After the speech, I was introduced to two girls who could have been twins, both wearing white head scarfs and beaming. They told me they were sisters, two of ten siblings who had fled rural Syria after one of their brothers had been killed in a suicide bombing at a mosque. It was hard to believe the recent trials they have endured. I thought of Shazia, Gul Minah, Steel, Zabi and the ghostbusters and I wished I could wave a magic wand and have them transported from Afghanistan to a school like this. Behind us were a hundred kids with doves, waiting for us to begin the release. The girls and I picked up a dove, their delicate hands over mine. I could feel the heart of the bird beating in fear and anticipation. Then we opened our hands and it soared skywards, joining all the others flying in spirals above the school, around and around, a white vortex in the blue.

It was the greatest day of my life. I don't think anything will ever match the way this filled me with hope for a better future. And as we left, the young multicultural band sang John Lennon's 'Imagine'.

BIG NIGHT

When I walked on stage to deliver my Sydney Peace Prize speech I could hear Hellen singing and see my angel puppets dancing 'The Defeat of the Demons of War' to a packed Sydney Town Hall audience. The Peace Prize organisers looked very worried – all previous winners have delivered a well-rehearsed script. I'd refused to prepare them a written speech. I was thinking, *This is what I love doing, why should I be nervous?*

At the front of the hall, next to Pam and Naomi, I'd arranged for some empty seats to be set aside for those who could not be here: Mum and Dad, Nana and Grandfather, my friend Martin Sharp . . . I looked down and imagined them smiling and waving to me and tears ran down my face. I wiped them away, and saw Bruce Shillingsworth putting his didg to his

mouth, filling his cheeks with air and letting his ancient Aboriginal song reach out past the audience to the city streets beyond, vibrating the windows of passing cars and putting a tremor through the stores, confusing the computers stacked in the glass boxes of the office towers which overshadow his Aboriginal past.

My puppets were positioned on stands behind the rostrum and a big screen displayed images to complement my stories. Waqar was working the projector. I often relate a story to take his mind off danger in Pakistan and Afghanistan, so he knows them all.

I started with my story of a kid in Rockdale, raising money for the Red Cross by staging puppet shows on the back lawn. I talked about my disillusionment with the art world after the Sydney Yellow House, how I wrote to Mother Teresa and how I have tried to follow her advice to use the talents God has given me for the benefit of humanity. The stories rolled out: drawing Immacule in the blood and mud of Kibeho camp as her soul flickered out, promising what had been done to her wouldn't be forgotten; that triumph-of-the-human-spirit day in Pretoria when Nelson Mandela gave his Rainbow Nation speech and I drew Elizabeth and Jacob embracing, lips pressed together, in their *Long-Awaited Kiss of Freedom*.

I have seen the darkness end in countries where no-one ever thought the sun of peace would shine again – from Northern Ireland to Cambodia, Bosnia and East Timor. I know we must eventually evolve beyond rogue apes to creatures who can resolve problems creatively.

Finally, I took the fragment of the Buddha from my pocket. I talked about this Eye of God and told how I had carried it here from the Kabul River. Waqar flashed up an image of me with the old Sufi at our Jalalabad Yellow House. The Sufi was murdered for telling us to seek what cannot be found – the way of the mystic.

But I am here to tell the tale.

Hands - Deprung Tibet 25th Oct 98

At all monastery approaches and exits visitors and Pilgrims have to pass an unpleasant gauntlet of beggars and hucksters.

This morning on my way to Deprung among the maimed, honless mothers with babies at their breasts and snotty nosed children, all chanting the familiar "money, money, money" demand with gesturing palms open, there was an elegant old monk — a red silk cravat beneath his coarse robe - dark glasses and a stack of hand printed scriptures on his lap. He chanted and clapped with a beauty which enclosed the hills and beggars in enchantment — more inclusive in its spiritual effect than entering the decorated and guilded Deprung Monastry — a few hundred metres above.

As his hands moved through the up and down motion of clapping - opening and closing - a momentary distortion occurred in my vision - for a part of a second I retained multiple hand images —

as in time motion photography In this fractured moment the thought came to me

"His hands are many as he reaches out with their clapping to all the beggars - his congregation - as if to change their chants from "Money, Money, Money" into something bright and shiney which flies away each time his many hands are opened."

George Gittoes Deprung Tibet 28 Oct 98 -

Hands
Eternity

At all monasteries, approaching visitors and pilgrims have to pass a gauntlet of beggars and hustlers. This morning, on my way to Drepung, among the maimed were homeless mothers with babies at their breasts and snotty-nosed children, chanting the familiar 'money, money, money' with gesturing palms.

There was an elegant old monk with a red silk cravat below his coarse robe, dark glasses and a stack of hand-printed scriptures on his lap. He chanted and clapped with a beauty that enclosed the hills and beggars in an enchantment more inclusive in its spiritual effect than entering the decorated and gilded monastery a few hundred metres above.

As his hands moved through the up and down motion of clapping – opening and closing – a momentary distortion occurred in my vision. For a part of a second I retained multiple hand images, as in time motion photography. In this fractured moment the thought came to me: His hands are many. He reaches out, clapping, to all the beggars – his congregation – as if to change their chants from 'money, money, money' into something bright and shiny . . . which flies away each time his many hands are clapped.

Front endpaper
Game of Chance
1996
oil on canvas
177 x 215 cm

Inside front endpaper
Old Dog
1998
pencil on paper

Page 2
Blood Mystic Self Portrait
2016
oil on canvas
168 x 190 cm

Page 4
**Bringing Peacocks back to the
Yellow House**
2015, ink on paper
396 x 167 cm

Page 7
**Puppet Theatre
(salvaged detail)**
1971
Gouache on wood
45cm x 33cm

Page 14
The Ladder to Paradise
1994
ink and watercolour on paper

Page 20-21
Mojo Rising
2009
oil on canvas
200 x 260 cm

Page 23
Fear Kibeho – Rubber Bands
1995–2013
Synthage, ink on paper
68.5 x 56 cm

Page 27
The Preacher II
1995
oil on canvas
168 x 250 cm
National Gallery of Australia

Page 31
Orangeman
1997
oil on canvas
177 x 217 cm

Page 33
Ireland
heavy oil on canvas
81.3 cm x 116.8 cm

Page 36
Speedway
1962
poster paint on paper

Page 43
Mirrow and Awliya
1994
oil on canvas
168 x 253 cm
Pro Hart Collection

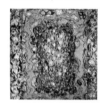

Page 47
Journey's End
1970
watercolour on paper
40 x 28 cm

Page 48
I Love the Rolling Stones
1962
poster paint on paper
42 x 31 cm

Page 50
Power
131 x 134

Page 51
Night Vision
1993–94
oil on canvas
259 x 173 cm

Page 53
Night Vision
1993
pencil on paper
42 x 66 cm

Page 54
The Gallery
1967

Page 56
Monkey Moonlight
2014
oil on canvas
61 x 61 cm

Page 59
Bare Knuckle
undated
pencil on paper
44 x 62 cm

Page 61
Angry Soldier
2009
oil on canvas
158 x 200 cm

Page 62
Untitled Abstract
1968
oil on canvas
152 x 113 cm

Page 63
Untitled Abstract
1968
oil on circular canvas
152 cm diameter

Page 64
Metamorphosis in Gotham
2009
oil on canvas
200 x 200 cm

Page 65
The Hotel Kennedy Suite
1971

Page 81
Untitled
1969
oil on canvas
112 x 81.5 cm

Page 86
Marie
1997

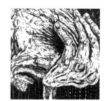

Page 88
Kent State etchings
1971–72
450 x 300 mm

Page 90
Vietnam
1971–72
oil on canvas
101.5 x 71 cm

Page 104
Wahabist Icon
2016
oil on canvas
61 x 91 cm

Page 107
Kagame
2000-13
Synthage, ink on paper
65.5 x 56 cm

Page 112
Kibeho
1997
oil on canvas
305 x 172 cm

Page 113
Mad
1996
oil on canvas
167 x 305 cm

Page 116-17
The Discarded
1995–2013
synthage, ink on papr

Page 124-25
**The Blindfolded Leading
the Blindfolded**
2007–08
oil on canvas
198.5 x 578 cm

Page 128
Salvage II
1989–90
oil on canvas
170 x 250 cm

Page 130–31
Salvage I
oil on canvas
170 x 250 cm
The Philippines

Page 146
Burning Fire and Children
1995
oil on canvas
168 x 176 cm

Page 154
**Self Portrait Drawing
in Somalia**
oil on canvas
168 x 228 cm

Page 157
Charon
2009–10
oil on linen
200 x 260 cm

Page 158
Belly Up
2013
oil on canvas
200 x 300 cm

Page 167
**The Long Awaited Kiss
of Freedom**
1994
oil on canvas
45 x 67 cm

Page 170
Last Nail (triptych)
1980
oil on canvas
198 x 213 cm

Page 173
The Great Coat
1994
oil on canvas
152 x 183 cm

Page 180
Staying Alive
1998
oil on canvas
168 x 259 cm

Page 179
Stari Most
1996
pencil on paper
44 x 62 cm

Page 183
**Game As - Portrait of
Julian Assange**
2015
oil on canvas
153 x 210 cm

Page 184
Empire State suite
1991
etching
20 x 22.5 cm

Page 187
The Artist
2000
oil on canvas
173 x 210 cm

Page 189
Ancient Prayer
1992
oil on canvas
168 x 212 cm

Page 192–93
Living Dead
2007
oil on canvas
200 x 300 cm

Page 199
Knight, Death and the Devil (also referred to as American Soldier)
2006-08
oil on canvas 291 x 198 cm

Page 200
Dora Maria Tellez
1986
oil on canvas
171 x 81 cm

Page 204
Miriam Guevara: Guardian of the Dead
1986
compressed charcoal on paper
176.5 x 113.5 cm

Page 207
The Captured Gun
1986
compressed charcoal on paper
198.5 x 108 cm

Page 209
The Legless Bike
1993
oil on canvas
168 x 396 cm

Page 210–11
Tony Mullingully
1997. From the 'Tony Mullingully' series, 1983-97
oil on canvas
305 x 172 cm

Page 216
Portrait of Bobby Nganjmirra
1987
oil on canvas
169.5 x 197 cm
Wollongong City Gallery

Page 220–21
Rainbow Way series
35 mm transparencies photographed under water at Bundeena, New South Wales, 1975

Page 229
Lot
1993
pencil on paper
62 x 44 cm

Page 230–31
Minefield Bar
1993-94
oil on canvas
158 x 259 cm

Page 234–35
The Beast
2015–16
oil on canvas
196 x 273 cm

Page 238
Mohad Jabary – 9 Year Old Survivor Hebron Massacre
1994
pencil on paper
44 x 62 cm

Page 242
Toxic – Sniper Alley Bosnia
1996
oil on canvas
86 x 101 cm

Page 245
From the Depths
1971
from 'The Hotel Kennedy Suite'
etching, aquatint
19.5 x 22 cm

Page 248
The Always Dictator – Assyria/Iraq
2003
pencil on paper
105 x 76 cm

Page 251
Domination – Babylon – Iraq
2003
pencil on paper
105 x 76 cm

Page 271
White Earth
1994
oil on canvas
138 x 168 cm

Page 275
Saddam ME ME ME
2003
diary page

Page 281
Compassion
1996
oil on canvas
135 x 170 cm

Page 285
The Yellow Room (Afghanistan)
1999
oil on canvas
172 x 257.5 cm

Page 287
Ecstatic Old Sufi
2015
watercolour on paper
76 x 105 cm

Page 294–95
(Detail) A Place in History
2003-04
oil on canvas

Page 294–95
(Detail) A Place in History
2003-04
oil on canvas

Page 296-97
**Super Power – New York –
Baghdad**
2004
oil on canvas
212 x 292 cm

Page 298
Old Sufi – Emerald song
2014-15
oil on linen
121 x 183 cm

Page 301
Death and the Boy
1993
oil on canvas
168 x 227 cm

Page 320
Relja
1996
pencil on paper
62 x 44 cm

Page 322-23
White Room Sachsenhausen
2000
oil on canvas
170 x 306 cm

Page 336
Blinding Lesson
1993
pencil on paper
200 x 285 cm

Page 349
Chatter Box Bosnia
1996
oil on canvas
167 x 305 cm

Page 354-55
Kibeho – The Other Side
1996
oil on canvas
174 x 259 cm

Page 356
Eye Witness
1995
pencil on paper
62 x 44 cm

Page 358
Genocide
1996
oil on canvas
167 x 260 cm

Page 358
Blue Shetani – Eye Witness
2001
oil on canvas
168 x 257 cm

Page 359
Focus-unfocus
1995
oil on canvas
259 x 168 cm

Page 359
Eye Witness
1997
oil on canvas
305 x 167 cm

Page 365
Taliban Head
2009
oil on canvas
200 x 200 cm

Page 367
Shit
1997
oil on canvas
3005 x 172 cm
Rwanda

Page 368
Smokers Afghanistan
2009
oil on canvas
161 x 200 cm

Page 369
Fear.com
2002
Drawing: pencil, NY newspaper
cutting, on paper
72.5 cm x 57.5 cm

Page 371
**The Perfect Moment and
a Bulletproof Mind**
2002, pencil on paper,
photographs
580 x 730 cm

Page 372
Descendence
2010
Etching on paper
36 x 50cm

Page 374-75
Assumption
2010-11
(triptych) from 'Descendence'
oil on canvas
200 x 660 cm

Page 385
Self Portrait – Coming Apart
2006
oil on canvas
198 x 294 cm

Page 392
Night Vision 2015
2015
oil on canvas
101 x 152 cm

Page 394
Hands – Deprung Tibet
1998
pencil on paper
62 x 44 cm

Inside back endpaper
Old Dog
2016
oil on canvas
196 x 214 cm

Back endpaper
Civilisation
2015
oil on canvas 822cm x 304cm
Courtesy Queen Victoria Gallery
Launceston

399